THE NEAR SIDE

THE NEAR SIDE

DEVOTIONALS WHICH WILL DRAW YOU TO THE "NEAR SIDE" OF GOD

"Draw nigh to God, and He will draw nigh to you." James 4:8 (KJV)

Winfred Huff

XULON PRESS

Xulon Press
2301 Lucien Way #415
Maitland, FL 32751
407.339.4217
www.xulonpress.com

© 2019 by Winfred Huff

All rights reserved solely by the author. The author guarantees all contents are original and do not infringe upon the legal rights of any other person or work. No part of this book may be reproduced in any form without the permission of the author. This book may not be copied or reprinted for commercial gain or profit. The use of short quotations or occasional page copying for personal or group study is permitted. The views expressed in this book are not necessarily those of the publisher.

Scripture quotations taken from the King James Version (KJV) – *public domain.*

Scripture quotations taken from the New King James Version (NKJV). Copyright © 1982 by Thomas Nelson, Inc. Used by permission. All rights reserved.

Scripture quotations taken from the Holy Bible, New International Version (NIV). Copyright © 1973, 1978, 1984, 2011 by Biblica, Inc.™. Used by permission. All rights reserved.

Printed in the United States of America.

ISBN-13: 9781545674413

Contents

Dedication	xi
Introduction	xiii
January 1-31	Fresh Opportunities to Experience God's Presence ... 1
February 1-29	Favorable Openings to Encounter God's Love ... 63
March 1-31	Fertile Fields to Explain God's Trustworthiness ... 121
April 1-30	Frequent Stops to Enjoy God's Faithfulness ... 183
May 1-31	Formal Approaches To Exercise God's Freshness ... 244
June 1-30	Faithful Voyages to Envision God's Truthfulness ... 306
July 1-31	Familiar Paths to Examine God's Salvation ... 366
August 1-31	Favorite Trips to Explore God's Grace ... 428
September 1-30	Fashionable Tours to Expand God's Mercies ... 490

THE NEAR SIDE

October 1-31	Focused Channels to Exhibit God's Miracles	550
November 1-30	Fertile Avenues to Exclaim God's Manifestations	612
December 1-31	Fruitful Thoroughfares to Elevate God's Gifts	672

Endorsement

Winfred, the author, has written a series of daily devotionals which are intended to draw the reader to the "Near Side" of God. He has taken every day events and placed them alongside spiritual truths to make for a compelling reading. His application of truth is plain and simple and calls for a closer walk with the Heavenly Father. His approach is an ideal way to see in daily situations a way in which the Father's plan unfolds. His heart is for each Christian to have a daily quite time; and in doing so, each day can become a tranquil voice heard above the din of noise the world generates.

> David Fisher--Senior Pastor of First Baptist Church
> Haynesville, Georgia

Dedication

I dedicate this devotional book to my dad, Thomas Huff. He was an ordained Southern Baptist minister who served a little country church near Unadilla, Georgia. My dad was not only a dedicated husband, father, and pastor, but also a mentor to me in my ministry. He had a large library of books from which I've drawn much inspiration for my preaching, teaching, and writing. I inherited his library and have kept most of his collection. I wish he were here so that he could read the words of this book which were in part inspired by his walk of faith.

Dad enjoyed writing. He would take a passage of scripture and write his own commentary on it. I have several books, cards, and other scraps of paper where he jotted down his thoughts. Some of those tokens became a conception for my own writings. He loved to read, study and preach the Bible. Many of his sermon outlines he used in preaching are precious mementos of his love for the Lord Jesus. I have many memories of him standing behind the sacred pulpit and proclaiming the unsearchable riches of Christ. He never apologized for his belief in the inspired Word of God. You knew where he stood when he spoke. His daily walk was one of prayer and Bible study. He started each day in intercessory prayer and ended each day with a prayer of thanksgiving. He studied his Bible and made practical applications to what he understood to be the will of God.

Introduction

What Jesus said to His disciples in Mark 6:31 is worthy of our consideration today. "Come ye yourselves apart into a desert place, and rest a while" (Mark 6:31 KJV). Today, each disciple should be actively involved in fulfilling the mandate of the "Great Commission," which is to make disciples of all nations. Twelve men, set apart as apostles, had been sent by their Master to do the work of ministry. They had been given authority over "unclean spirits." Their message was that men and women should repent. They anointed with oil many who were sick, and the infirmed were made whole. The endeavor had to be an energy consuming activity. Further, the news of the death of John the Baptist had an emotional impact on these faithful men. Just before the feeding the 5,000, an enormous challenge, Jesus encouraged these beleaguered men to have some "leisure time." As He summoned these workers to have some quiet time in His presence, so does He gladden our hearts to have some down-time with Him.

THE NEAR SIDE

As busy as some of us get, intentionally or unintentionally, the message comes ringing as a clarion call: "Come apart with the Master and spend time with Him, or come apart at the seams of our faith and bring defeat to our walk." I have been burdened to write a daily devotional for those who need a lift each day with a verse of scripture and a comment on the verse(s). The intent of each day is to encourage all who follow the Master to draw near to God for an inspiring and reassuring word.

May each day draw us all closer to the "Near Side" of God. To Him be all honor and majesty and recognition as we obey the words of scripture: "But grow in grace, and in the knowledge of our Lord and Saviour Jesus Christ. To him be glory both now and forever. Amen" (2 Peter 3:18 KJV).

January 1

"I know thy works: behold I have set before thee an open door, and no man can shut it:" Revelation 3:8 (KJV)

January 1st is like a pencil given by God. We use it as an instrument to not only erase the past regrets but to mark the opportunities for a new year at the other end. There is something refreshing about starting over with dreams and hopes for an expected end. The month of January is named after Janus, the god of beginnings and transitions. The name has its beginnings in Roman mythology, coming from the Latin word for door (janua) since January is the door to the year. I saw a sign that encouraged the reader to make sure that the new year was something more than just another 365 days. It read: "Make it a new year not simply a next year." Our Lord has placed before us an open door that He says no man can shut. Some of those open doors could be:

A wide open entrance of reflection. I would encourage you to take time on this first day of the new year to reflect upon last year, even if the season had some setbacks. Our failures can become God's opportunities if we view them from

THE NEAR SIDE

His perspective. Detours can become destinations. There are times when failure is the backdoor to success. On this first day of the year, what better time to start the introspection than today.

An even wider gate of refreshment. As bitter as the past year may have been, there is the old adage of taking your lemons and making them lemonade. The bitterness of disappointment, mixed with the sweetness of fellowship with the Lord, will bring out the best of life, and the first day of a new year is the best opportunity to tap into the resources God has given us. Through the gift of His Spirit, we can accomplish great things in the coming year.

An even greater gateway to recommitment. We can forget those bitter things that are behind us and look forward to the sweet things in front of us, with the confidence that the new year can be the best one we have faced. Our promissory note of a brand new set of 365 days, if it could take on the form of a song, could be: "All to Jesus I surrender, all to Him I freely give."

Thought to ponder: "Ability is what will take a man to the top, but it takes character to keep him there."

January 2

"Seven times a day do I praise Thee because of Thy righteous judgments." Psalm 119:164 (KJV)

I saw a sign the other day that read: "Better to have a daily devotional than a new year's resolution." I know that resolutions, as well as daily devotionals, are only as good as reading them and following through with their challenges. It's good to resolve to lose weight in the new year. Eating less and more healthy are commendable decisions; but a better commitment would be to spend each day in prayer, storing up the energy needed to face the daily demands. Resolving to manage stress is a good way to underwrite a healthy mind and body; but a more sure way of pleasing the Father is to exercise our daily time, and spend each waking minute in intimate fellowship with Him. Having the determination to get a better job will perhaps give us a pathway to a profit boon; but a prize of enormous value will be to have a "Friend" who will stick closer than a brother.

Think about the things we do everyday--go to work, spend time with our family, eat, or maybe watch some TV.

THE NEAR SIDE

Whether it's helping others or getting rest, we'll find value in all of those things; but we must see value in spending time with the Heavenly Father. He created each of us in His own image with the divine purpose to spend time with us. He waits each morning when we arise to hear His child say, "Good morning, Lord. I look forward to spending the best part of the day with You. Glorify Yourself at my expense." With those vital words spoken, we enter a day filled with glorious opportunities to be in fellowship with the Creator. Without a commitment to do so is like squeezing the spiritual life out of our being. We need a daily refreshment of the presence of the Lord in bringing us into a deeper and more intimate relationship with the Father.

Thought to ponder: "The gospel brings man to God; daily devotionals keep him close to the Father."

January 3

"Heaviness in the heart of man maketh to stoop; but a good word maketh it glad." Proverbs 12:25 (KJV)

A friend of mine has an unusual way of extending a greeting. Instead of the normal, "How are you today?" he would ask, "What's the good word?" After several times of that inquiry, I learned to have a proper response for my brother in Christ. What started out as a light-hearted greeting from a friend soon became a passion on my part to share some charity of good favor. My daily routine of meeting other people has been shaped by this manner of greeting. My heart yearns to be an instrument of encouragement to others, and this is just one way I can accomplish that goal.

Over the years I have come across some good words for the heavy-hearted and the discouraged. One would be that of affirming words of encouragement to share with them as they walked the bumpy roads of life. Some of the people I meet are running on tanks that are almost empty. Words of affirmation will go a long way in filling their reservoirs. Other folks I meet are on the down-and-out. Life for some unforeseen reason has handed them an unfavorable outcome. They have been trampled under the feet of a cold and indifferent world, and need some nurturing care. The feeble and the faint are sure candidates for some choice words of hope and expectancy. I trust that you will have an encouraging and uplifting assurance for anyone who asks you, "What's the good word?" We may never know how far a "good word" will go. It will not only be a blessing to others but a boon of good for our well-being.

Today would be a great day to start building a vocabulary of encouraging words. Study the life of our Lord and you will amass a vast treasure of uplifting terms. Look well to the situations He faced and how He responded. He was always on spot. He had the perfect word. The Bible is a great source-book from which to glean the appropriate words for these distinctive purposes. It was always in God's determination for each one of us to utilize the best counsel for the particular situation. Follow the advice of a loving Father, and you never go wrong.

Thought to ponder: "He who thinks by the inch and talks by the yard deserves to be kicked by the foot."

January 4

"If thou faint in the day of adversity, thy strength is small."
Proverbs 24:10 (KJV)

This verse admits up front that we will encounter difficult times in the course of our life. Jesus said in essence that in this world we will have tribulation. If we have not experienced any opposition lately, then we need to ready ourselves because it's at our front door waiting to catch us off-guard. Solomon realized that calamity was couched as a roaring lion ready to pounce upon the unexpected. Since adversity is as sure as the day is long, then one thing that should be as equally sure is that we do not faint. If we lose heart in the face of hostility we strangle the very life out of our faith. We hamstring our commitment to stand tall when the antagonists confront us. When the unfavorable times make their way into our very experience and we faint, then the truth comes to light that our strength was too small.

A good way to combat the faintness of heart in the time of trouble is to feast regularly upon the Word of God. There is nourishment and strength in the spoken and written Word.

THE NEAR SIDE

It gives us the sustenance we need to resist the enemy's taunts. The Scriptures have all the vitamins we need to energize our faith, and a daily dosage of the important ones are of necessity. Vitamin A is holding onto the promise that the Lord is with us **A**lways. Vitamin B is trusting God to **B**ring us through in the hard times. Vitamin C is relying upon Him to **C**arry us when we cannot walk. Having a daily portion of the Bible before us and in us will provide the strength we need to maintain our steadfastness. The Psalmist, in Psalm 119:105, maintained the assurance that the Word of God was "a lamp unto my feet and a light unto my path," and what was good for the Psalmist will be good for us.

Thought to ponder: "If doubt overtakes you, stop for a faith lift."

January 5

"Be sober, be vigilant; because your adversary the devil, as a roaring lion, walketh about, seeking whom he may devour."
1 Peter 5:8 (KJV)

A sign at a local chiropractor business stated: "Our Aim Is To Keep You Well." The letter "w" in the word "well" had fallen ninety degrees to the right and resembled the letter "h." At first glance the sign could have read: "Our Aim Is To Keep You In Hell." Of course the business had no intention of doing that. Their desire was to make sure that you and your health remained at a peak level of wellness.

We, as Christians, have an arch enemy who would love to do what the misrepresented sign advertised. Satan's primary aim is to keep each one of us in our own "hell." The quicker and the longer he can do that, the less effective we will be as members of the Body of Christ. Satan, in the scriptures, is pictured as a ferocious sounding lion erupting fear in the hearts of men, women, boys, and girls. He is constantly on the lookout for those who have forsaken their first love. Even when the Christian is at the top of his game, he is no match

THE NEAR SIDE

for the enemy in his flesh. The accuser of the brethren has a great desire to devour the testimony of every believer, and if possible, their very life. There will be no respite in the battle over our soul. Night and day the enemy is on the prowl, never taking a break from his diabolical intent.

Therefore, the admonition is for us to be sober-minded and constantly vigilant because of our adversary. That is, we are to be sharply focused on the Lord Jesus and have an ever-watching eye toward Him in the time of attack from the enemy. Thus, we will be able to foil every fiery dart that the antagonist will hurl at us. It's when we are asleep at the wheel that we give our foe an opportunity to surprise us with his onslaught. We are to be on our best guard when it comes to the watchfulness of our souls for the attacker is poised and ready to pounce on us.

Thought to ponder: "Remember, you are your own doctor when it comes to curing cold feet."

January 6

"I will therefore that men pray everywhere, lifting up holy hands, without wrath and doubting." 1 Timothy 2:8 (KJV)

Someone handed me a pencil the other day that had these letters printed on it in the form of two acronyms: "A.S.A.P, A.S.A.P." It did not take long to figure out that one of the acronyms meant, "As Soon As Possible." The other acronym meant something entirely different; and if it had not been written on the pencil, I would not have had any idea why it was there. The other A.S.A.P was, "America Say A Prayer."

In this day and time in which the moral compass in America has shifted away from godliness to godlessness, it's incumbent upon her citizens to find their way back to God, and the first step would be to say a prayer for America as soon as possible (ASAP). We know that judgment is coming and America will not be exempt from the heavy hand of God. We need to find our places of prayer and intercede on the behalf of our nation. The prophet Daniel opened his windows toward Jerusalem three times a day and prayed to the

THE NEAR SIDE

God of heaven. It mattered not to him who heard him or saw him. Daniel's approach to intercession would be a good model for all of us to imitate. A discipline of prayer on a regular basis would bring about a keen awareness of the imminent danger that we all face. Who knows what God would do if just one of His children began a systematic approach to prayer. Commit yourself to seek the face of God through prayer as soon as possible three times every day. "A.S.A.P, A.S.A.P." America Say A Prayer As Soon As Possible.

Thought to ponder: "Prayer is the stop that keeps you going."

January 7

"I was glad when they said unto me, Let us go into the house of the Lord." Psalm 122:1 (KJV)

The Perry Area Historical Society and Museum located in Perry, Georgia, offers a collection of artifacts and memorabilia from Perry's earliest days. Of particular interest to researchers is the Museum's Resource Room which contains many family histories and photos. Each room is filled with pictures, mementos, and memories which take the visitor on a journey to the center of their nostalgic mind. When I have the opportunity to visit this show place of history, I am reminded of the contributions that individuals and businesses in the community have made over the years.

When I walk into our church sanctuary, there are certain objects which have some precious memories attached to them. They are fixtures that we, perhaps, have taken for granted over the years because of our familiarity with them. There is the sacred pulpit from which the precious Word of God is proclaimed. It's the place where our pastors, missionaries, and teachers faithfully declare what "thus saith the

THE NEAR SIDE

Lord." There is also the altar where fervent prayer is made. It's the place where we the people of God meet Him and through repentance and confession of ours sins are cleansed from our unrighteousness. Then comes the Lord's Table. It's the place where we are reminded of the shed blood of the Lord Jesus and His broken body. Each time the bread and the cup are passed, they remind us of the tremendous price that was paid for our salvation.

The next time you enter a place of worship, take time to reflect upon the meaning of the pulpit, the altar, and the Lord's table. It's important that we all remember their distinction and the role each one plays in leading us to genuine worship. We would do well to reflect upon each one's contribution to our reverence and honor of our great and awesome God.

Thought to ponder: "If you don't know where you are going, any road will get you there."

January 8

"He is like a man which built an house and digged deep, and laid the foundation on a rock;" Luke 6:48 (KJV)

It stands 103 stories, 1,454 feet high and weighs approximately 365,000 tons. There are 6,500 windows, 73 elevators, 10 million bricks, 210 columns and 200,000 cubic feet of Indiana Limestone in its structure. The masonry facade is supported by steel spandrel beams attached to cast-iron columns. The beams are linked to posts which support the weight of the floor. These beams also extend from the frame to support the weight of the windows and walls for each story. The foundation of the building extends 55 feet below grade. The Empire State Building is one of the most famous skyscrapers in the world; built in just 18 months during the Great Depression, it was the world's tallest building from 1931 to 1972.

Jesus talked about another structure that we, as Christians, are establishing. As important as it is to build faith, confidence, and hope, there is still a more important facet of life, that of constructing our life upon the Lord Jesus

THE NEAR SIDE

Christ. The edifice is our life and obedience to our Lord's Word which is likened to building our well-being upon a rock. When we dig deep beneath the shallowness of mere profession and lay our foundation upon a solid rock, there is no amount of destructive force which can move us. We can sing with confidence one of the standard hymns of our faith, "On Christ the Solid Rock I stand, all other ground is sinking sand." These are the words we can voice with confidence because our trust is in the "Rock Of Ages." The deeper we dig into the vast treasurers of God, the more stationary our life will be.

The Empire State Building has a foundation that stretches 55 feet below ground. It would be foolish to build such a monumental building upon the sand; likewise, it would more foolish to build our life upon the shifting sands of this decaying world. When the rains descend, and the floods come, and the winds blow upon our house, it will not crumble because it is founded upon the "Rock of the Lord Jesus."

Thought to ponder: "Yesterday's unfinished task is a mortgage on today."

January 9

"And be ye kind one to another, tenderhearted, forgiving one another, even as God for Christ's sake hath forgiven you"
Ephesians 4:32 (KJV)

"Upon the first day of the week let every one of you lay by him in store, as God hath prospered him, that there be no gatherings when I come." 1 Corinthians 16:2 (KJV)

Are you forgiving?
Are you for giving?

No, that's not double talk, though it may sound like it. If I were to ask you that verbally, you may not know what I was asking. These are two valid questions that each one of us must answer. I trust that you can answer in the affirmative to both inquiries. The Bible speaks of "forgiving" and "for giving."

In Ephesians 4:32 Paul gives us three important advancements in our Christian walk: kindness tenderheartedness, and forgiveness. These are what I call the "ess" brothers

THE NEAR SIDE

because they are all related. The word "kind" means to furnish what is needed at the time. Harsh words may be hurled at us, and what is needed are not more harsh words in return, but words of kindness. The term "tenderhearted" signifies our being compassionate. Those who are less fortunate than we deserve our deepest sympathy. The choicest of words is that of "forgiveness." Jesus warned us through these words: "But if ye forgive not men their trespasses, neither will your Father forgive your trespasses."

In 1 Corinthians 16:2 Paul gives us three more important advancements in our Christian journey. These have to do with the Lord's tithe and our offering. He gives first of all the day of our giving which is on Sunday, the first day of the week. It is the Lord's Day and our day in which we are obedient to Him in giving of His tithe. Paul also points us to the decision for giving which is to set something aside. I believe that ten percent of our gross income belongs to the Lord. What we give above and beyond that will be our offering to Him. Last of all Paul then summons us to face the degree in giving and that is as the Lord has seen fit to prosper us. However much the Lord has chosen to give into our stewardship, it is out of that giving that we give in return.

Thought to ponder: "Are you forgiving? Are you for giving?"

January 10

"But I would ye should understand, brethren, that the things which happened unto me have fallen out rather unto the furtherance of the gospel." Philippians 1:12 (KJV)

If the apostle Paul's life could be summed up in a few words, it would be said that his was a "Christ-centered life." His perspective on the Christian walk was one that turned tragedy into triumph. Paul was in a Roman jail with no justifiable cause. His freedom had been taken away. He had very few men or women who would stand with him. Life for the servant of God had taken a sharp bend in the road; yet, his view concerning his situation was one that would take the seeming calamities of life and turn them into triumphant shouts of joy.

A Christ-centered life will also infuse confidence in the lives of other Christians. In verse 14 of this same chapter, Philippians 1, we read, "And many of the brethren in the Lord, waxing confident by my bonds are much more bold to speak the word without fear." The way we live our life in the face of adversity will do one of two things for others. We will heat the wax of

THE NEAR SIDE

confidence by our determination to rise above trouble or we will freeze the oil of gladness by giving in to the pressures of life.

In verse 18 of Philippians 1, we see Paul's encounter with those who wished to add affliction to his bonds. His response is one of rejoicing in the proclamation of the Gospel. This is another truth that speaks of the Christ-centeredness of this stalwart servant. Listen to his answer: "What then? Notwithstanding, every way, whether in pretence, or in truth, Christ is preached; and I therein do rejoice, yea, and will rejoice." It did not matter to Paul how others were preaching Christ. Whether out of false motives or true motives, Paul could say that his joy had reached peak level in knowing that Christ was being preached.

Thought to ponder: "The best way to get rid of our duties is to discharge them."

January 11

"Till I come, give attendance to reading, to exhortation, to doctrine." I Timothy 4:13 (KJV)

If our desire is to be an example to believers, it will include our speech, conduct, love, faith, and purity. (1 Timothy 4:12 KJV) Paul gives to Timothy three ways those qualities can become a reality. It starts with the reading of the scriptures. In 2 Timothy 3:15 we read that Timothy had known the Holy Scriptures from his childhood. That is a good place to start; and a better place to continue is through our youthful years, and into adulthood. There is no better way to start the day than to read a portion of scripture. Perusing a passage from the Bible is more than simply filling our mind with knowledge; it is more about storing the word of God in our heart.

Another quality that will be a pattern to believers is through our teaching of those truths which we have discerned from the Bible. If reading the scriptures could be examination, then proclaiming those truths would be exhortation. It is not advice that we give but rather guidance and council

THE NEAR SIDE

from the scriptures. We are not to be simply reporters of the truth but rather exhorters of the virtues of Christ.

Paul ends this admonition to Timothy by giving him the task of instruction. Examination of the scriptures gives way to exhortation of the passages, which in turn offers instruction in the Word of God. This injunction is more than simple words of speech; it's the way we live out what we believe to be the truth of the Word of God. Someone has well said, "I cannot hear what you say because I see the way you live." In the words of a familiar hymn, "Living for Jesus, a life that is true, striving to please Him in all that I do; yielding allegiance, glad-hearted and free, this is the pathway of blessing for me."

Thought to ponder: "Even if you're on the right track, you'll get run over if you just sit there."

January 12

"But seek ye first the kingdom of God, and His righteousness, and all these things shall be added unto you."

Matthew 6:33 (KJV)

I had a college professor who started her class with these words, "First things first." She wanted to make sure that her students had gotten their homework assignments completed; that minds were clear and ready to engage the session; and that each one took pride in their studies. There were times when I had to hang my head and say to myself that I had not done a very good job of prioritizing. Nonetheless, I learned from her classroom manners that completing homework assignments, having a clear mind, and a readiness to undertake the disciplines of study, made the classroom setting more enjoyable and beneficial.

Jesus talked about one particular priority that should head our list, and that was to seek above all else His kingdom first. He at length gave a distinct promise that if God's cause was made the first aim, all the necessities of life would be provided. Our Lord said that we were not to spend our day worrying about what we would eat, drink, or wear. There was a more pressing matter to examine, and that was to undertake first and foremost the kingdom principles. When that pursuit takes place, the other things that matter in life will be provided. May we seek to spread the gospel and the accomplishment of God's kingdom, and may we seek to personally conform to His standards of right living.

The word for "added" that Jesus used in our scripture has the sense of placing an additional amount upon. Our Lord will give more than enough to meet the claims of life. Out of the abundance of His riches, He draws out and confers to each one of us the riches of His grace. Let us place as the number one priority in life that of seeking first the kingdom of God above all else. When we live in a righteous manner, the promise is that the Father will give us everything we need.

Thought to ponder: "The future is as bright as the promises of God."

January 13

"Now the days of David drew nigh that he should die; and he charged Solomon his son, saying, I go the way of all the earth; be thou strong therefore, and shew thyself a man."
I Kings 2:1,2 (KJV)

King David knew he was going where everyone on earth must go someday. He understood there was but a step between him and death, and as quickly as the blink of an eye, death could come quickly. Coming to grips with this reality, David charged his son, Solomon, to be strong and show himself to be a man. The term "Man Up" is used to motivate individuals towards achieving their goals and overcoming whatever obstacles or challenges they may face. Ladies, this charge is to you as well. I will refine the statement to include, "Woman Up." What challenges do we face as the aging process takes the driver's seat?

As we all grow older, there are the encounters common to all. There are times when we cannot perform as we once did. At a juncture when senior citizens long for stability, they are often called on to face drastic, and sometimes unwelcomed, changes. Some of those deviations include: retirement from a job, the loss of a partner, inability that comes with age, and many times loneliness. There are the obstacles of facing the realities of life. The older generation realizes that their physical powers wane and they may have to cope with illness, pain, or loss of mobility. They also become increasingly aware that their life on earth is nearly over and many are afraid of dying. There are the financial matters that bring concern, since half of the elderly are trying to make ends meet on less than half the average wage. It's not a time of life to be sentimentalized, but to be faced with such realism as that shown in Ecclesiastes 12. There Solomon outlines the aging process and the ultimate realities to be faced in aging. So, what kind of response must we have? One is to give control of the situation to the Lord, be strong, and rise to the moment in His power and strength. In other words, "Man Up! Woman Up!"

Thought to ponder: "The most powerful testimony is a godly life."

January 14

"And be not drunk with wine, wherein is excess; but be filled with the Spirit." Ephesians 5:18 (KJV)

Heading in a local newspaper read: "Dentists get their 'fill' at a local conference." Doctors from around the country had gathered in response to sharing their stories, while others had stayed away. You know the old-adage: "It is like pulling teeth." The invitation appeared to fit the bill as the crowds were lower than expected. That seems to be typical when it comes to getting people to show up and participate in the fellowship of kindred minds. Even though attendance waned from previous years, the atmosphere at the gathering was reported to be a "full-filling" affair.

That article led me to ponder where Christians get their "fill." That is, the filling that empowers them to do the work of the ministry. A mandate that has been given us is to make disciples of all nations. The Bible teaches us that there is only one place from which the "full-filling" comes, and that is through the empowerment of the Holy Spirit of God. When Paul spoke of being filled with the Spirit, he was not suggesting

THE NEAR SIDE

something that we do, but rather commending us to a privilege to experience. The tense of the verb "be filled," is in the present tense, continuous. Paul says in essence that we are not to be drunk with wine, which leads to reckless actions, but keep on being filled with the Holy Spirit. From Sunday to Sunday and each day in between, twenty four hours a day, and seven days a week let the Holy Spirit empower us and lead us.

To be filled with the Spirit means to be emptied of self. It is being "crucified with Christ;" "dead indeed unto sin;" "dead with Him," and "dying, behold we live." You will never be able to fill a glass full of liquid if the glass is already full; but you can fill to the brim a glass that is empty. Likewise, you can never be filled (to make replete) with the Holy Spirit until you have emptied yourself. If we think that emptying is something new in the Christian walk, hear what the apostle had to say about the Lord: "And being found in fashion as a man, He humbled Himself, and became obedient unto death, even the death on the cross." (Philippians 2:8 KJV)

Thought to ponder: "The empty-ness syndrome comes when all of self has left home."

January 15

"Yea doubtless, and I count all things but loss for the excellency of the knowledge of Christ Jesus my Lord for whom I have suffered the loss of all things, and do count them but dung, that I may win Christ." Philippians 3:8 (KJV)

My wife and I attended a retreat some years ago at the Georgia Baptist Conference Center in Toccoa, Georgia. It's nestled in the north Georgia mountains near Lake Louise. I have been to other secluded events that have been enjoyable and fulfilling but this area is special for its beauty. Even though many of those spiritual withdrawals seemingly have been glossed over with the years of forgetfulness, there was one where I listened intently as a layman poured out his heart with this impassioned prayer: "Lord, help me to walk more nearly, love You more dearly, see You more clearly, and to know You more sincerely." I have not forgotten those supplications that worked their way out of a hungry heart for fellowship with the Lord. Many times I have lifted those petitions up to Christ, expressing to Him the depths of my heart.

THE NEAR SIDE

Our prayers should never become just something else to do that adds to the baggage we have attached to our relationship with the Heavenly Father. May there be no more Pharisaical prayers that reach no higher than the ceiling, but let those words be those of the Publican who saw himself in need of a fresh touch from heaven. Those heart-felt petitions should always reflect our desire to walk nearer to the Lord every day of our life, to love Him more than anything or anyone else, to be able to see Him in a more definitive light, and to know Him in a deeper and richer measure. Let these supplications come from a true determination to know Christ above everything else. They will add to the richness of beauty in our daily walk with our Lord.

Thought to ponder: "Know Christ—Know Peace; No Christ—No Peace."

January 16

"And when he came to himself, he said, How many hired servants of my father's have bread enough and to spare, and I perish with hunger?" Luke 15:17 (KJV)

"And he arose, and came to his father. But when he was yet a great way off, his father saw him, and had compassion, and ran, and fell on his neck, and kissed him." Luke 15:20 (KJV)

The two-step is a step found in various dances, including many folk dances. It seems to take its name from the 19th century dance related to the Polka. A two-step consists of two steps in approximately the same direction onto the same foot, separated by a closing step with the other foot. Those words "two-step" have a spiritual dimension to them when it comes to the story line that Luke unfolded in chapter fifteen of his Gospel.

One of the most familiar and beloved parables our Lord gave was the story of the prodigal son. He was the younger of the two boys, who came to his father and asked for the portion of goods that would fall to him. He took all of his

THE NEAR SIDE

possessions to the "far country" and there wasted all of his substance. When he joined himself to a local citizen, he was sent into the fields to feed swine. Wasted days and wasted nights could have been his theme song.

In verse seventeen we find the first of "two-steps" taken by the weary and wayfaring son. He "came to himself." One translation has it stated that "when he came to his senses." A part of the two steps the son took was to finally realize that he had it better back home than he realized. Someone has well said that a trip of a thousand miles begins with the first step. This was the positive direction taken, and it would surely fill an empty tank of "nothing" that this young man had.

In verse twenty we read of the second of "two-steps" taken by the tired and beaten boy. He "came to his father." It is one thing to come to oneself, but to stay there would simply drown the good intentions of a desperate soul. The father was waiting and willing to receive his son. All that was needed was for the young prodigal to make his way home, and thus he did.

Thought to ponder: "Don't just entertain new ideas--put them to work."

January 17

"That I (Nehemiah) gave my brother Hanani, and Hananiah the ruler of the palace, charge over Jerusalem; for he was a faithful man, and feared God above many."

Nehemiah 7:2 (KJV)

The old adage, "Do as I say, not as I do" is not worth the paper it is written on. It might have worked on you when you were six years old, but it will not work on a group of Christian believers who are maturing in the faith. They might not let you know explicitly, but they will be unhappy, eventually leave, and this will cut short your influence among the brethren. It may not have immediate repercussions, but eventually any hypocrisy on your part will catch up with you. So, leadership is not merely saying, "Let's go," but actually going.

Nehemiah had the opportunity to appoint a leader by the name of Hananiah. He had some qualities about him that pointed to leadership. At this juncture in Israel's history, the one thing most needed was for men and women to pick up the reins of administration and lead. Some of these propensities that Hananiah possessed were readily recognized by Nehemiah; and this led him to appoint this Hananiah to an all-important position. Some of those noble features were his experience, his faithfulness, and his reverence for God.

Hananiah had the experience. He had been promoted from a lower position of importance to being commander of the fortress and having part of the charge over Jerusalem. The word "charge" signifies an appointment. Nehemiah did not choose just anybody for this all important position, but someone who had the experience. Someone has well said that experience is the knowledge or mastery of an event or subject gained through involvement in exposure to it.

Hananiah was also faithful. One of the things that I want people to say about me is that I am a faithful man; faithful to my Lord, to my wife and family, and faithful to the church. It is said of Hananiah that he was a faithful man.

Hananiah was also known for his reverence. The actual words are: "and feared God above many." That is to say, he reverenced God more than most people did. A deep humble reverence for God shows our love and respect for Him, and those aspirations will raise us up as leaders of the future.

Thought to ponder: "What this country needs are more leaders who know what this country needs."

January 18

"Beloved, I wish above all things that thou mayest prosper and be in health, even as thy soul prospereth." 3 John:2 (KJV)

The aged apostle expressed in his prayer for the "well-beloved Gaius" a wish that it may go as well with him as it did with his soul; and that in his worldly prosperity, his comfort, and his bodily health, he would be as prosperous as he was in his religion. A shorter version of that statement would be that John prayed for Gaius that he would be as prosperous financially and physically as he was spiritually.

For some, that would be a welcomed prayer; but for others it would be less than a beneficial request from a praying Christian. If my soul is not prospering in the Lord, then I cannot expect to flourish in other ways. For if heavenly blessings came to me in the same measure that my outgo of blessings be to the Lord, my well-being would not thrive. I would be an unhealthy, weakly, and sickly child of the King. What a contradiction of terms that is. The very opposite of what should be said of us.

THE NEAR SIDE

May we settle our feet on the unchanging God. May we sink our teeth deeply into the Word of God. May we have our eyes fixed upon the reward of God. May our walk always be in the strait and narrow way. Those steps in the right direction will add dimension to our life. There will be a fullness of joy in our participation of holiness that will overshadow any misstep we may have. God's desire is that we take an interest in the things of the kingdom because our participation in these events will add to the abundance of life.

Thought to ponder: "It's a great idea to take an interest in heaven--that's where we will spend eternity."

January 19

"As far as the east is from the west, so far hath He removed our transgressions from us." Psalm 103:12 (KJV)

Eratosthenes of Cyrene was a Greek mathematician, geographer, poet, astronomer, and music theorist. He was a man of learning, becoming the chief librarian at the Library of Alexandria. He invented the discipline of geography, including terminology used today. He is best known for being the first person to calculate the circumference of the Earth. His calculation was remarkably accurate. We know today that earth's circumference is 24,901 miles. If we could drive our vehicle 62 miles an hour, 24 hours a day, across the lands and oceans, it would take almost 17 days to make our trip around the world.

With my finite mind that is quite a distance. I can fathom driving a hundred miles or even a thousand miles, but to travel over twenty four thousand miles is hard to imagine. Our Lord has promised to remove our transgressions from us much farther than the distance around the earth. His promise is "as far as the east is from the west." This is

THE NEAR SIDE

described by the largest measures which the earth can afford: "So far hath He removed our transgressions from us." That is, He has put them entirely away. They are so removed that they can not affect us anymore. We are safe from all condemnation for our sins, as if they had not been committed at all.

Thought to ponder: "God did not promise an easy voyage but a safe arrival."

January 20

"In My Father's house are many mansions: if it were not so, I would have told you. I go to prepare a place for you."
John 14:2 (KJV)

Antilla Mumbai is the world's most expensive home costing $1 Billion making it the world's first billion dollar house. A custom-built 27-story towering mansion, Antilla in Mumbai is the home of the world's 5th richest man called Mukesh Ambani, head of Indian petro-chemical Reliance Industries, which is India's most valuable firm by market capitalization. Some of the features of this mansion are: parking space for 168 cars; 3 helipads on top; hanging gardens within the structure; a two-story Health centre; a floor for Home theatre with a sitting capacity of 50; and a swimming pool within the structure. Unbelievable. That is the only word fit to describe the fact that the world's tallest, most luxurious, lavish and downright most expensive single-family home on earth belongs to one person.

Jesus spoke about a mansion that He is preparing for us in heaven. It's a permanent residence that is being made ready for

THE NEAR SIDE

each one of His children. Its location is in the Father's House which is far superior to the famous "90210" zip code which had more $10 million-and-up home sales in the past year. This mansion-building project is one of the most certain facts we can count on. Our Lord made it certain when He spoke it. He is at the present arranging all the details and specifications needed for our future dwelling, and the anticipation that each one of us share is that the Lord is coming soon to rapture His children away.

If I had the opportunity to visit Antilla Mumbai, I would certainly go. I would want to experience all the lavish details that this mansion offers. I would stroll the hallways and climb every story of this magnificence edifice, while taking in all the extravagant views, but while touring that mansion, it would only make me home-sick for my mansion in heaven.

Thought to ponder: "For the child of God, heaven is just a heartbeat away."

January 21

"But wilt thou know, O vain man, that faith without works is dead." James 2:20 (KJV)

William Sylvester Harley is not a name you would readily recognize in and of itself. He was born in Milwaukee, Wisconsin in 1880. He received a degree in Mechanical Engineering from the University of Wisconsin in Madison in 1907. Arthur Davidson is another name that you would not consider to be a household name. He too was born in Milwaukee, Wisconsin in 1881. One of Davidson's favorite pastimes was fishing in the Wisconsin wilderness, which inspired him to create a motorcycle that would, "take the hard work out of pedaling a bicycle." He was a story teller, salesman, and United States patriot. By now I think you know what I am referring to. "Harley Davidson" is an American motorcycle manufacturer that was founded in Milwaukee, Wisconsin, during the first decade of the 20th century.

The name Harley by itself doesn't have all the appeal that would cause someone to sit up and take notice. Likewise, the

THE NEAR SIDE

name Davidson doesn't have the draw by itself; but if you put the two together, Harley-Davidson, you have an iconic name that has become an American institution. In the Bible faith in and of itself is not all that God has designed for mankind. We are saved by grace through faith and that not of ourselves, but God has included in His master plan for all of His children the element of "works."

We are taught the importance of faith in Hebrews 11:6a; "But without faith it is impossible to please Him (God)." As equally true is the "works" factor. A faith that does not carry through with good deeds is as our verse states, "Foolish man! Are you willing to learn that faith without works is useless." Faith in and of itself is only part of the plan, but when you place works alongside of it, you have an invincible force that will take on any opposition or foe.

Thought to ponder: "Faith can rewrite your future."

January 22

"How sweet are thy words unto my taste! yea, sweeter than honey to my mouth." Psalm 119:103 (KJV)

When I visited my mother before she passed away, one of the requests she made of me was to read a portion of the Bible to her. When I asked what scripture she wanted me to use, she would say, "It doesn't matter, because I love all the words of the Bible." And she would continue, "I like to hear the nouns, the pronouns, and the verbs." So I would take her Bible, open it to a passage that I knew she would want to hear, and then read several scriptural passages to her. She would close her eyes as if to imagine in her mind what the scriptures were saying to her. If her countenance had been sad, the words seem to bring a peace over her face. If her day had been fitful, the promises I rehearsed in her ears were like bread to a hungry heart and water to a thirsty soul. Though she would say to me that she had been blessed by my reading, I went away more blessed than she.

The benefits of honey don't just stop at satisfying the palate; honey also offers incredible antiseptic, antioxidant

THE NEAR SIDE

and cleansing properties for our body and health, valuable beauty and skin care tips for ladies, and amazing healing properties as a head-to-toe home remedy, from eye infection to athlete foot. Its powerful healing attributes have long been used thousands of years ago and known to promote healing for cuts, cure ailments and diseases, and correct health disorders for generation after generation.

The Psalmist stated that the words of Jehovah were sweet to his taste, sweeter than honey to his mouth. Though the writer didn't have all the scientific advantages of honey at his disposal, he did know for certain that the words of God were gain and profit to him. Though the sweetness of honey would sweeten the mouth for awhile and dissipate, he understood that the sweetness of the scriptures would stay as long as he rehearsed them in his mind.

Thought to ponder: "Contentment occurs when your earning power equals your yearning power."

January 23

"She hath done what she could; she is come aforehand to anoint my body to the burying." Mark 14:8 (KJV)

These are the words of our Lord Jesus as He commented on what Mary, the sister of Martha and Lazarus, had just done to Him. It was an act that many at the gathering asked with indignation, "Why was this waste of the ointment made?" And the reasoning behind their response was that the oil might have been sold for more than three hundred pence (almost the equivalent of a year's salary for the common man). To follow the indignation, we read that they murmured against her. That is, the self-righteous, self-centered individuals began to scold her for the action she had taken. This servant of the Lord did what she could do. Perhaps many at this gathering could have done more or others could only do less, she ignored her harsh critics and did what she could.

"What can I do to have any impact on the kingdom's work?" you may ask. What you attempt to do may not be the equivalent to what a pastor does on Sunday morning as he rises to proclaim the wonderful truths of God's word; or something akin to what a teacher does who expounds the wholesome values of the Bible; or what a singer might do to sing out the wonderful praises of God. In the eyes of the world, there may be much merit and value in those engagements, but with our loving Heavenly Father, whatever we do for Him in the name of Jesus, His Son, and in the power of the Holy Spirit has more eminence and superiority than any observant, spiritual-minded man can have. Mary lays before us the supreme example of doing what she could. May we all discern what God has in mind for us in our ministry of outreach as we exercise faithfully our talent in the fields of service.

Thought to ponder: "Ambition is a get-ahead-ache."

January 24

"Hereby perceive we the love of God because he laid down his life for us; and we ought to lay down our lives for the brethren." 1 John 3:16 (KJV)

There is another John 3:16 in the Bible that was written several years after our Lord's statement of purpose to Nicodemus. To this night-time truth seeker, Jesus said in essence that God so loved the world that He gave the perfect sacrifice, His one and only son. 1 John 3:16 carries the same basic truths as that of the original. That was a message of love and sacrifice, a love that was shown to be genuine on a cruel cross, a love that was known by a willing commitment of Jesus to die for the sins of the world. It was a sacrifice that had been pre-determined before the foundation of the world. It was a sacrifice that was performed since the foundation of the world. Both John 3:16s complement each other because they carry the same message points to a lost and dying world.

The one major difference to these two passages is the additional remark that states, "And we ought to lay down our lives for the brethren." Does John mean that we are to

THE NEAR SIDE

allow ourselves to be crucified on a cross for a brother or sister of the faith? No! It means something far greater. It's dying daily, not once, to our right of privilege and thus giving preference to any member of the body of Christ. We are to do good unto all men, especially those who are of the household of faith. This is how we have come to know love: Jesus has willingly laid down His life for us, and our response is to follow our Leader.

Thought to ponder: "Nothing can compare to the love of God."

January 25

"And whether one member suffers, all the members suffer with it; or one member be honoured, all the members rejoice with it." 1 Corinthians 12:26 (KJV)

During one of our pastor's Sunday evening services, he made two observations from the above scripture that brought about different responses from the congregants. He said that we are to suffer with those who are suffering, and to that statement there were a couple of scattered amens. The second proposition was that we are to rejoice with those who have been honored. To that particular declaration there were many more amens from among the congregation. That led me to believe that most of us are more likely to celebrate with the brethren when they rejoice than we are to feel the pain with them when they suffer.

We need to have a balanced approach to Paul's admonition. In this world of trouble and sorrow, people are going to encounter misery. Some of the anguish may be brought on by unwise choices; other torments may be thrown in the face of determination. The Christian does not get an

THE NEAR SIDE

exemption or a pass in the battle between evil and good. Christians do suffer the consequences of the fall of Adam, but all Christians are dependent one upon another; each is to expect and receive help from the rest. We can condole, sympathize, help, and assist.

To further balance the words of the apostle, we are to rejoice with those who have been honored. The word "rejoice" means that we are to sympathize with gladness and congratulate those who have been esteemed with recognition. That does seem to be an easier approach in fulfilling our call to balance out the suffering with the rejoicing.

Thought to ponder: "Sign tacked on a tree near a convent: "No trespassing; violators will be prosecuted to the fullest extent of the law--Sisters of Mercy.""

January 26

"For this thing I besought the Lord thrice, that it might depart from me." 2 Corinthians 12:8 (KJV)

In the drama presentation "From The Christ Child To the Judgment," there is a scene depicting a mother who had been praying for the healing of her son. She said: "I prayed for healing; I prayed that my son would walk; I prayed and prayed and prayed and nobody was listening; and if God was real, why would He do this to my son?" To those remarks there was another character who responded to this distraught mother with these words: "I do know three things about God: He is real; He is listening; and He cares." What a profound series of remarks that this individual made.

I am convinced that God is real. If you ask me how I know He is real, I can sing along with the musician with these words: "There are some things I may not know. There are some places, Oh Lord, I cannot go; but I am sure of this one thing that God is real for I can feel Him in my soul." To that song I give a resounding AMEN!

THE NEAR SIDE

It's also true that God is listening. The apostle Paul had prayed three times that God would remove a thorn in his flesh; and three times it seemed that God had not heard the plea. Paul could have concluded that God had not heard his supplications, but this is not the case. God simply gave Paul a different answer: "My grace is sufficient for you, for my strength is made perfect in weakness."

It's equally true that God cares. He considers us to be the apple of His eye. He cares more for us than we could ever care for ourselves. He has given the very best that He had so that we could have the very best of life. Even when we have unanswered prayers, know that God does listen. He doesn't always answer our prayers to our immediate satisfaction and instantly deliver us from our trials, but He will always do what is best for us.

Thought to ponder: "Look backward with gratitude and look forward with confidence."

January 27

"The thief cometh not, but to steal, and to kill, and to destroy:"
John 10:10a (KJV)

In a recent comic strip of "Dennis the Menace," the mischievous Dennis says to the bewildered Mr. Wilson: "I don't understand, Mr. Wilson. Who would want to steal your identity." I chuckled when I read those words because inquiring minds, like that of Dennis, want to know. Upon further thought I was reminded of an adversary who wants to do more than steal our identity. He is the arch enemy of every Christian. Jesus likens him to a thief and a robber who has a three-fold purpose: to steal, to kill, and to destroy, and this he attempts to do. His primary attack is toward the heavenly Father and his intermediate work is against those who stand for the precepts of the Christian faith.

Our opponent does not have our best interests in his advance. He wants to steal anything from us that would bring peace of mind, joy unspeakable, or lasting fulfillment. He does this very well by offering an alternative that seems at first desirable but afterwards leaves a bad taste of deceit.

THE NEAR SIDE

Our foe not only had the insatiable desire to steal from us but also to kill our effectiveness. What we determine to do in the power of the Holy Spirit and in the name of the Father, our antagonist tries to block. Our advance toward the good of the "faith" and the benefit of mankind will be met with hostility. Our attacker has an ultimate design vented toward the Father through us, and that is to destroy every viable effort of doing that which is right in the sight of God.

Jesus, on the other hand, has come that we might have the kind of life that He has designed for every child of His. By grace He has given eternal life to everyone who by faith will invite Jesus into his heart. In addition to that gracious offer, Our Lord has made available abundant life, and that offer still stands today.

Thought to ponder: "God's wrath comes by measure; His mercy without measure."

January 28

"But grow in grace, and in the knowledge of our Lord and Saviour Jesus Christ. To him be glory both now and forever. Amen." 2 Peter 3:18 (KJV)

After I retired from the work force of forty-two years, one of the routines of the day was to watch my favorite game show "Family Feud." The show features a competition in which two families must name the most popular responses to a survey question posed to 100 people in order to win cash and prizes. I soon discovered that game shows can become addictive and enlightening. On one particular episode a question was asked and a most unusual answer was given. My initial response was, "I didn't know that" to which someone in the room said, "Well, you know that you can learn something new every day." I took those words to heart in more than one way. Not only did I learn something new from the game-show aspect, but I realized that I could learn something new in the spiritual realm.

There is a weekly exercise that I have adopted for myself. Each day of the week I have appointed a particular regime

THE NEAR SIDE

with the aim of learning more about the Lord and preparing myself for worship. On Mondays my focus is on prayer, and I learn patience as I wait on God's timing. On Tuesdays I devote a larger portion of time to Bible study with the goal of hiding the Word in my heart. On Wednesdays I engage in meditation taking what God has revealed in my prayer time and putting that alongside of the previous day's Bible study to better understand my place in the family of God. On Thursdays I contact one of my Sunday School class members to encourage them. On Fridays my goal is make sure that I am preparing myself mentally and spiritually to participate in Sunday morning and evening services at church. On Saturdays I am making sure that what I have learned Monday thru Friday I am putting into practical application as I obey the dictates of scripture. Then on Sunday I am ready, willing, and able to join other brothers and sisters in Christ to honor the Lord and worship Him in truth and spirit on His day, the Lord's Day.

Thought to ponder: "What people fail to learn from sermons, they later learn from experience."

January 29

"For the word of God is quick, and powerful, and sharper than any two-edged sword, piercing even to the dividing asunder of soul and spirit, and of the joints and marrow, and is a discerner of the thoughts and intents of the heart." Hebrews 4:12 (KJV)

At the start of October 2012, it was reported by founder Mark Zuckerberg that Facebook had passed the monthly active users mark of one billion. Facebook defines active users as a logged-in member who visits the site, or accesses it through a third-party site connected to Facebook, at least once a month. One billion people who spend at least some time on Facebook is mind boggling. To put that into perspective, consider these numbers. The height of a stack of 1,000,000,000 (one billion) one dollar bills measures 358,510 feet or 67.9 miles. This would reach from the earth's surface into the lower portion of the troposphere--one of the major outer layers of earth's atmosphere. The area covered by one billion one dollar bills measures four square miles. This would cover an area equal to the size of 2,555 acres. These numbers stagger the mind.

THE NEAR SIDE

After reading those measurements and considering how large numbers can look, I wondered how many "Grace-Book" users there are in Christendom? By that I mean Bible readers who take advantage of a God-given opportunity to maintain an up-to-date account of kingdom activities. By virtue of Calvary, God has given us an on-line account that we may access freely at any given moment. We who have this open field of privilege can log into our accounts (our Bibles) each day, at any hour, as often as we wish, to hear a fresh word from the Father. This "Grace-Book" takes its name from the gift of eternal life that comes from the Father through the Son by virtue of the Holy Spirit. We who have been saved by grace through faith automatically have an account set up for us with a log-in name of "The Scriptures," a password that is unique to our experience, and a guarantee of full-time access. One billion Facebook users could translate into one billion "Grace-Book" users.

Thought to ponder: "He who wants milk should not set himself in the middle of a pasture, waiting for a cow to back up to him."

January 30

"Then he (Nehemiah) said unto them, Go your way, eat the fat, and drink the sweet, and send portions unto them for whom nothing is prepared: for this day is holy unto our Lord: neither be ye sorry, for the joy of the LORD is your strength." Nehemiah 8:10 (KJV)

One of the ladies in our church recently passed away. She had been a resident at a local nursing home and had spent several years in the facility; but those days and months of her residency had not broken her determined effort to enjoy life to the maximum. When our GROW team visited her, she always had a smile and a positive word to share with us, even though she was usually in bed. There were times when I found myself looking forward to visiting with her because I knew that I would hear an encouraging word.

During the celebration service for her, our pastor said that she was happier now than she had ever been. Though her earthly days of happiness may have been limited by her confinement, her joy in heaven now is without end. Forever and ever. Amen! She knew, as did Nehemiah, that the joy of

THE NEAR SIDE

the Lord was her strength. I am positive that when the days came that she did not feel well, she drew energy in knowing that all things were working together for her good. When she felt alone, she had the grit to keep going because she knew that the Lord had promised to never leave nor forsake her. As her days on earth drew to a close, she knew that to be absent from the body was to be present with the Lord. In all of her situations she understood that the joy of the Lord would always be her strength.

Today you may be facing an uncomfortable situation. Maybe it's an unpleasant circumstance surrounding your world. Things don't look as rosy as they did yesterday, last week, or last month. Even though the darkness of disappointment has engulfed your walk, there is a light that still shines in the obscurity of pain. The glimmer of hope shines brighter because of the joy we have in the Lord. God has given us an opportunity to turn on the sunbeam of His love by trusting His purposes. Regardless of how dark the night can become, the light of Jesus will dispel the fear we have.

Thought to ponder: "Where you go hereafter depends on what you go after here."

January 31

"That ye might walk worthy of the Lord unto all pleasing, being fruitful in every good work, and increasing in the knowledge of God." Colossians 1:10 (KJV)

You can Google most any subject matter on a computer and get some kind of hit. On one occasion I received a message that said there were 1,590,000,000 results in 0.33 seconds. Someone suggested that I Google the following: "The end of the Internet." I did and this was the message I received: "Congratulations! You have finally reached the end of the internet! There's nothing more to see, no more links to visit. You've done it all. This is the very last page..." There are times when we feel, perhaps, that we have maxed out our involvement in kingdom matters. We may think that we have done it all, and that there is nothing else to accomplish. After all, our salvation is secure; our ticket to heaven has been paid for; and our eyes are fixed on the prize. We reason that we are just waiting to hear the trump of God. Could I use the opening words of a song that was sung by the Richard and Karen Carpenter of the "Carpenters"? "We've only just begun to live..." Brothers and sisters, our task of serving the Master is never finished.

Jesus clearly understood the necessity of working the works of the Father. The sun was going down over the beloved city of Jerusalem on that Sabbath day, and Jesus was not going to wait, nor lose the opportunity of doing the merciful will of the Father in restoring a blind man's sight. Jesus also grasped completely the significance of the night coming when no one could work the works of the loving Father. The meaning seems to be that it is the night of death, and of the grave, suggesting our Lord's own death; hereby, that He had but a little time to be in this world, and therefore would make the best use of it. Our life is but short, it is but as the length of a day; a great deal of business is to be done; and death is hastening on which will put a period to all working.

Thought to ponder: "You can tell when you are on the right road--it's all uphill."

February 1

"And a great multitude followed Him, because they saw His miracles which He did on them that were diseased."

John 6:2 (KJV)

On April 27, 1963 the song "I Will Follow Him" was the number one hit on the Billboard Hot 100. It made Little Peggy March, who was fifteen years old at the time, the youngest female artist to have a U.S. chart-topper single. A couple of lines in the song reflect the depth of someone's love for another and a willingness to go wherever and to do whatever:

"I will follow him wherever he may go,
There isn't an ocean too deep,
A mountain so high it can keep, keep me away,
Away from my love."

As I read John 6:2, I am reminded of a time in our Lord's earthly ministry when He had a great multitude of people who followed Him. Many followed because they saw the miracles He did. In Matthew 4:25, we read of our Lord's healing ministry: "And there followed Him great multitudes of people..." After reading these two verses and reflecting on the phrase "because they saw His miracles...," I am led to believe that these particular individuals could not harmonize very well with Little Peggy March's rendition of "I Will Follow Him." They followed not because of the "Miracle Maker" but because of the miracle itself. Their rendition of the March's song would go something like this:

"I will follow Him whenever it's convenient,
For if the ocean is too deep,
And the mountain so high, it will keep me away,
Away from following Him."

Thought to ponder: "The time to get primed for the future is when you are still in your prime."

February 2

"And they straightway left their nets, and followed Him."
Matthew 4:20 (KJV)

"And they immediately left the ship and their father, and followed Him." Matthew 4:22 (KJV)

These two verses give us a great insight into what may be required of us to truthfully and faithfully follow the Lord Jesus in discipleship. It may cost us these valuables:

Our nets: These are the "earthly things" that may blur our vision of who we are and why we are here. The author of the book of Hebrews points us to this great virtue: "Looking unto Jesus the author and finisher of our faith..." Hebrews 12: 2a (KJV) As we take our eyes off our earthly pursuits, we can focus on the One who is worthy to be served.

Our ship: This could the "earthly treasure" that could sink us if we put our trust in it to be our confidence and savior. Jesus said: "For what shall it profit a man, if he shall gain the whole world, and lose his own soul? Or what shall a man give in exchange for his soul?" Mark 8:36, 37 (KJV)

Our father: This is the "earthly tie" that is perhaps the dearest of all ties. We may walk away from our nets, turn our back on our ship, but to forsake mother and father is a price that would be dear to all of us. Jesus said: "He that loveth father or mother more than Me is not worthy of Me..." Matthew 10:37a (KJV)

In the "Online Slang Dictionary" there is a word that we have all used at some point in our Southern lingo. It's the word "terreckly." In Flannery O'Conners' short story "Revelation" he uses the word in this sentence: "It'll quit terreckly." Oftentimes in our response to the Lord's call for discipleship to leave our nets, our ship, and our father, we leisurely say, "I will terreckly." Our actions should be to follow Him "straightway" and "immediately," without reservation.

Thought to ponder: "Where you go hereafter depends on what you go after here."

February 3

"Surely goodness and mercy shall follow me all the days of my life" Psalm 23:6a (KJV)

The Fugitive was a 1993 American mystery thriller film based on the 1960s television series of the same name. After being wrongfully convicted for the murder of his wife, Dr. Richard Kimble escapes from custody and is declared a fugitive. He sets out to prove his innocence and bring those who were responsible to justice while being pursued relentlessly by a team of U.S. Marshals, led by Deputy Samuel Gerard. The movie was a non-stop thriller of the police lieutenant obsessed with the capture of Richard Kimble.

The Psalmist wrote of another relentless pursuit led by the Heavenly Father. His object is His children and His aim is to pursue them all the days of their life with His, "goodness and mercy." Goodness and mercy are like a Hebrew Thesaurus giving us the words: best, beauty, gladness, welfare, favor, kindness and pity. When we realize our Heavenly Father's pursuit, it would be wise for us to slow down and allow these graces to overtake us. After the world has given us its worst, our Father pursues us with His best. When our life is beset with ugliness, our Lord shadows us with His beauty. As the cycles of life brings sadness to our circumstance, our loving Father puts forth His gladness in our path. Whether you call it 24/7 or round-the-clock service, our Lord is surely pursuing us with all the good that He has.

Slowing down for the Father's goodness and mercy to overtake us doesn't come easy for most of us. We oftentimes are guilty of trying to cram 6 days into 1 to make our week more formidable, and the result of such a pursuit only leads to subtraction of God's blessings of grace. We can never outrun God, but He certainly will allow us to get ahead of Him. That's not His perfect plan, but it becomes His permissive will.

Thought to ponder: "He who cannot endure tough times will not see the good times."

February 4

"Know ye not that they which run in a race run all, but one receiveth the prize? So run, that ye may obtain."

1 Corinthians 9:24 (KJV)

Spiridon Louis isn't well known around the world, but he is in Greece. That's because of what happened in 1896 when the Olympic Games were revived in Athens. During the competition that year, the Greeks did quite well--winning the most medals of any nation, but the event that became a source of true Greek pride was the first-ever marathon. Seventeen athletes competed in this race of 40 kilometers (24.8 miles), but it was won by Louis--a common laborer. For his efforts, Louis was honored by king and country, and he became a national hero.

The apostle Paul knew the importance of not only starting well in the race but finishing the same way. He didn't merely talk about running the race; he took it upon himself to get in the race. Paul understood that life gave him the opportunity to excel, and he took full advantage of the earthly options given to him. God had a plan and a purpose for His servant and led him in the way of that adventure. The intention of the runner is to run in such a way that in the end the pursuit would be worth the effort. It is easier to say that I will do something than to actually do it. So well did the apostle run that when he came to the end of his earthly life he could say: "I have fought a good fight, I have finished my course, I have kept the faith..." 2 Timothy 4:7. (KJV)

We have the great privilege to enter the race set before us. It is one filled with wonder and adventure. We may not know what is up ahead, or what awaits us at the next turn. Our pathway may become hard and on the road we may grow weary. However, there is one thing we can be certain of and that is that Someone has already run the race, overcome the obstacles, avoided the pitfalls, and been victorious. He has given us a plain path, a rewarding run, and an everlasting end. He is none other than the Lord Jesus.

Thought to ponder: "Don't pray for an easier life; pray to be a stronger person."

February 5

"Peace be unto you..." John 20:19 (KJV)
"Peace be unto you..." John 20:21 (KJV)
"Peace be unto you..." John 20:26 (KJV)

Three times our Lord said to His disciples, "Peace be unto you." On each occasion the word was used with a different design. Our Lord's intention was to relate to His followers that these aspects of peace could be theirs for the taking.

In verse 19 "peace" was used in respect to the "Provision for Security." Peace had been made with God and the glorious consequences of our Lord's atoning work could be seen. In verse 20 Jesus "shewed unto them his hands and his side." That's what I call "PEACE WITH GOD!" In verse 21 "peace" was used as a way for the "Provision of Service." Jesus said "As My Father hath sent Me, even so send I you." As the peace of God rules in our heart, we are able to rise above the hindrances of our path. That's what I see in the "PEACE OF GOD!" In verse 26 "peace" was used in consideration for the "Provision of Satisfaction." Thomas, the doubter had been absent at the other two "peace" pronouncements. Now he is present and it's as if our Lord says to Thomas, "Satisfy yourself!" In verse 27 Jesus said to this skeptical disciple, "Reach hither thy finger, and behold my hands; and reach hither thy hand and thrust it into my side; and be not faithless but believing." That's what I see as "PEACE IN GOD!"

How many pronouncements of "peace" have we heard from God lately? They are out there waiting for our faith response. God has made them widely available, and we only have ourselves to blame for not residing in His peace. For our security, our service, and our satisfaction, we must have peace with God, the peace of God, and the peace in God. Those provisions have been made in and through the person of Jesus Christ. As we make our way into a world filled with mass confusion, may we take with us these "peace" provisions and share them with a world who seeks after peace!

Thought to ponder: "The greatest homage we can pay to truth is to use it."

February 6

"And be not conformed to this world; but be ye transformed by the renewing of your mind." Romans 12:2 (KJV)

"To be or not to be, that is the question," is the famous opening phrase of a soliloquy in the "Nunnery Scene" of William Shakespeare's play Hamlet. Prince Hamlet bemoans the pains and unfairness of life but acknowledges the alternative might be still worse.

Putting a spiritual twist on Hamlet's confession, two greater questions arise and could be phrased in Shakespearian words: "To be conformed or to be transformed? Those are the greater probes." Those are the questions we must ask about our life. Our entire experience, whether good or bad, will be determined by our response to those two engagements. If we choose to be conformed to the image of this world, we forfeit our daily infusions of grace. To opt for the former, to be transformed, gives us a head wind that will carry us across the finish line of victorious living. The determining vote for which of the two will be cast by me. I can be conformed or I can be transformed!

THE NEAR SIDE

The word "conformed" carries the idea of being fashioned like the world--acting like fallen humanity, speaking in a way characterizing the sinful, and walking in the paths of the hopeless. I can allow myself to be fashioned by a world that is separated from God, and follow its sinful ways, and find myself out of fellowship with the God of creation or I can opt for being transformed by the renewing of my mind. The word "transformed" in the language of the New Testament gives us our English word "metamorphosis." In the butterfly cycle, the butterfly and moth develop through a process called metamorphosis. Our being developed into the image of Christ comes through the renovating of our mind--the meaning of the word "renewing." This action is removing the old things of the world and replacing them with the fresh things of the new life in Christ. I have to ask myself on this day, will I be conformed or transformed? Those are the two most important inquisitions of the hour.

Thought to ponder: "Remember, when you kill time it has no resurrection."

February 7

"Jesus saith unto him, "Thomas, because thou hast seen me, thou hast believed; blessed are they that have not seen, and yet have believed." John 20:29 (KJV)

This verse very well could contain our Lord's last beatitude: "blessed are they that have not seen, and yet have believed." It could be number ten in continuation of the nine "blessed" pronouncements of Matthew 5:3-12. The number ten in scripture is viewed as a complete and perfect number. So, our Lord's declaration to Thomas could bring to a crowning touch the perfect beatitude. The blessing of verse twenty-nine is one of those passages that has our name written all over it. Jesus does not say that Thomas was simply blessed by believing, though that was true. Thomas was blessed because His faith had given way to sight. His doubt had brought him to a crisis of belief, and what he did next revealed what he truly believed about Jesus.

Though we have not seen with our physical eyes the risen Lord; though we have not placed our finger in the nail print of His hands; and though we have not thrust our hand into

THE NEAR SIDE

His "riven side which flowed," we have by faith "not seen and yet have believed." That is one of the ironies of scripture. Our physical eyes have not focused on the Lord Jesus, but in our hearts we have looked by faith into His eyes; and what we see is the compassionate optics of a loving Lord. Without the spectacles of faith, we have no view of the wonders of God, but with the eye of conviction, we see clearly that which God has made known through His Son. In this case not seeing is believing, and that brings about the blessing of John 20:29.

Thought to ponder: "You cannot discover oceans unless you have the courage to leave the shore."

February 8

"and the dead in Christ shall rise first."

1 Thessalonians 4:17b (KJV)

Most of the people I know want to be first, whether it be to eat at a restaurant, to sign up for a free vacation, or to stand in line to purchase the latest gadget. Most of us are driven by the proverbial saying, "the early bird gets the worm." The adage "Whoever arrives first has the best chance of success," or the proverb "Some opportunities are only available to the first competitors," are only means of using whatever power one has to become number one, but what may be true in a world of competition, is not valid in the spiritual realm.

I've noticed in working with the AWANA kids at their game time, that there is a constant battle on the part of the clubbers to see who will be first. The situation oftentimes becomes a shoving match to be at the head of the line. Some win while others have to wait. Others go first while the rest have to wrestle for second or third place. Some get ahead

THE NEAR SIDE

while others have to linger to get their chance, but, as we all know, everyone cannot be the first.

In 1 Thessalonians 4:17 the apostle Paul talked about a group of saints who will be first in line. There will be no jostling for position to see who goes first. There will be no vying for a station at the head of the line. Those activities have no place in God's directed time for the rapture of the church. There is a specific order in which the culmination of an earthly life will take place. From the King James' Version of the Bible, to Young's Literal Translation, and all 23 other translations in between, these words ring out loudly and clearly: "the dead in Christ shall rise first." That is the plain and simple truth of scripture we hold dearly as we await the coming of our Lord.

Thought to ponder: Sign over college classroom clock: "Time will pass; will you?"

February 9

"And it came to pass, when I heard these words, that I sat down and wept, and mourned certain days, and fasted, and prayed before the God of heaven." Nehemiah 1:4 (KJV)

A pastor once prayed that the Lord would move him. Move him, that is, in the sense of removing him from the pastorate he had and placing him in a more suitable/enjoyable position with another church. Well, the Heavenly Father answered the servant's prayer but not in the way he thought. The Lord moved the minister, not from his situation but rather in his situation. The "God, who is full of compassion" (Psalm 86:15), gave to this pastor a rekindled public spirit for the church which he had given up on. His lack of trust and confidence in his circumstances would become the most opportune time for God to give him giant-sized opportunities.

Nehemiah, in our scripture, heard that his brethren were in great affliction and reproach. He also perceived that the walls of Jerusalem were broken down and those left of the captivity were suffering because of circumstances surrounding their captivity. His brother brought word to him that the gates were burned with fire. Upon hearing these heart-rending words, Nehemiah was moved to compassion for his bereft brethren in Jerusalem. He wept; he mourned; he fasted; and he prayed before God. God did not remove Nehemiah from those circumstances of sorrow; rather He delivered him in the circumstances. What will move us to this point?

Thought to ponder: "The worst possible moment for an atheist is when he feels grateful and has no one to thank."

February 10

"And the servants and officers stood there, who had made a fire of coals; for it was cold: and they warmed themselves and Peter stood with them, and warmed himself."

John 18:18 (KJV)

"As soon then as they were come to land, they saw a fire of coals there, and fish laid thereon, and bread." John 21:9 (KJV)

Two different occasions we find Peter around a fire of coals. The first instance was when he was warming himself with the enemies of the Lord. There came a time when the Lord's prediction of Peter's denial would ring true in the ears of His servant. Peter would deny his love for the Lord, and it would be around a fire of coals. As someone has well said, "There's nothing cold as ashes after the fire is gone out." It was at this point in Peter's life that the ashes of his love for the Lord had grown frigid.

The second instance would be after a cold night of fishing with nothing to show for his work. Now around another charcoal fire Jesus would reaffirm His love for Peter and

THE NEAR SIDE

commission him again to the work of an apostle. What a gracious offer the Lord made to His wayfaring servant. From a night of nothing to a gracious act of service, our Lord invited Peter to join Him in a meal of fellowship.

Perhaps we have found ourselves outside the circle of the Lord's warm love. It could be that we have grown cold and indifferent and have tried to warm ourselves within the world's company. We will always fall the way we lean. If we are dependent on anything else but the warmth of our Lord's love, we will find ourselves left out in the cold.

Thought to ponder: "When success turns your head you are facing failure."

February 11

"Be thankful unto Him, and bless His Name."

Psalm 100:4b (KJV)

"Jeopardy" is an American television game show that features a quiz competition in which contestants are given clues in the form of answers, and must phrase their responses in question form. An example would be:

The answer – The quick brown fox jumps over a lazy dog.

The question – What is a sentence that contains every letter of the alphabet?

Let's use the game show Jeopardy in Thanksgiving form:
The answer – Family, Faith, Friends, Freedom, Food.
The question – What are the things I am thankful for?

I am thankful for my family. My wife, two daughters, two sons-in-law, and four grandsons are the light of my life. They are the source of inspiration that keeps me going.

THE NEAR SIDE

I am obliged for the faith that was delivered to me through my mom and dad. They exhibited the kind of rock-solid belief that the Bible admonishes.

I am appreciative of the friends that I have. They are the kind of associates who care as much for you as they do their own physical family.

I am indebted to the men and women in our armed forces who sacrificed their lives so that I could enjoy the freedom that I have in this great country of ours.

Last but not least, I am grateful to the Lord for the food that I and many of you will enjoy in abundance this Thanksgiving.

Now, you fill in the blank for the things you are thankful for this season:
The answer:
The question: What are the things I am thankful for?

Thought to ponder: "He who forgets the language of gratitude can never be on speaking terms with happiness."

February 12

"Get thee behind Me, Satan: for thou savourest not the things that be of God, but the things that be of men."

Mark 8:33b (KJV)

Church signs have for a long time fascinated me. If one wants to get a message out to those who pass by, a word of wisdom promoted on a church marquee will get the job done. I am convinced that the majority of people do read church signs. The other day, I saw an eye-catching proverb that read: "Give the devil an inch and he will become a ruler." How true that saying is.

According to scientists, the smallest unit of distance that we can actually measure is an Angstrom--this is 10 million times smaller than a millimeter. There are even smaller units than this, a femtometer (also known as a Fermi) is 100,000 times smaller, and is about the size of an atomic nucleus. If our Lord spoke the modern language of distance, He could say, "Don't give the arch adversary a Fermi. In doing so, you will become a prisoner of the enemy!"

THE NEAR SIDE

Jesus understood the importance of confronting the accuser of the brethren with a stern word of authority: "Get thee behind me, Satan..." Christ turned His back on the tempter. There must be no dallying or temporizing. It must be quick and decisive. In Matthew 4:10, Jesus utilized the same words with: "Get thee hence, Satan..." What was good for the Teacher to say to the enemy is also good for the disciple to address the adversary! With the devil in front, he is in the wrong place; with the adversary in the back, he is in the right place!

Thought to ponder: "The time to do right is now."

February 13

"For ye have not received the spirit of bondage again to fear; but ye have received the Spirit of adoption, whereby we cry Abba Father." Romans 8:15 (KJV)

Our church media promoted by way of announcements the following invitation to those ladies who had babies present in the worship service: "We have a crying room!" I certainly do understand what they were advertising. The nursery personnel have a room designated away from the sanctuary for babies who can cry till their hearts are content. Moms are encouraged to bring their little ones to this "Crying Room." This not only gives the parent a more reserved time with the Lord in worship but a much quieter time for other worshippers.

I am reminded of another way one could interpret this invitation for a crying room. Maybe our media could tailor another kind of announcement that would offer a room where supplications, intercessions, and prayers would be made. That is, a "Crying Room" individualized as a point of contact for those Christians who would come before the

THE NEAR SIDE

Lord with thanksgiving, and also a time for crying out to the Lord for His anointing for the worship hour. When there is a firestorm of prayer in the congregation, that intensity will fill the pulpit with a fire from heaven. A preacher of the gospel would gladly welcome such an insurgence from heaven. The success or lack thereof can be traced to those crying out to the Lord. Every church should have a "Crying Room" for babies and also for Christians.

Thought to ponder: "Courage is fear that has said its prayers."

February 14

"And walk in love, as Christ also hath loved us, and hath given himself for us an offering and a sacrifice to God for a sweetsmelling savour." Ephesians 5:2 (KJV)

This particular Valentine's Day came on Sunday. During the morning worship hour, as we anticipated the special music, the lady responsible for singing made these remarks before she sang: "Jesus didn't need a special day (Valentine's day) to say He loved us, because we are the objects of His love every moment." What better day could this event take place than on the Lord's Day. Every Sunday we are reminded through our worship services about the love of the Lord Jesus. When our pastor delivers his sermon, he speaks of the attachment that our Lord has to us. During the time for special music we keep in mind the price that was paid for our souls. When the time for prayer comes, we pause to remember the great love of the Lord. As we sit in our Sunday School classes, our teachers affirm the truths of God's great love for us all.

"Jesus loves me this I know, for the Bible tells me so" are the words most of us were taught when we were children. These expressions were instilled in me by my parents. Of all the songs I was taught as a child, this one is at the top of the list. There is no better foundation to build for our children than on the love of the Lord Jesus. As we progressed into our teenage years, we were once again reminded of the love that God has for His child. At this point and time those promises need to be instilled in the young people of our day. Into the middle-age years of our life we embraced tightly the precious truth of the love that the Lord has for us. As many of us enter into the winter of our lives, we still hold precious the promise that God has loved us, is loving us, and will love us until we take our last breath. So, what better time than on a Sunday to join our brothers and sisters in Christ to celebrate the Lord's Day with our songs of praise, adoration, and love for Jesus; and to couple that celebration with words of love and affirmation for the saints.

Thought to ponder: "Love is blind when it sees nothing but good."

February 15

"The steps of a good man are ordered by the Lord..."
Psalm 37:23a (KJV)

When I am hungry and need food, my steps are ordered to the grocery store.

When I need gas in my vehicle, my steps are ordered to the gas station.

When I am in need of medical attention, my steps are ordered to our family doctor.

In a spiritual sense, when I am in need of the Lord's guidance, my steps are ordered to seek Him.

When the Psalmist spoke of "steps," he was speaking of companionship. Our Lord wants to be our constant companion on the paths we trod. When we take certain steps toward the worthy goals of fulfillment, He has promised to be with us always. As we contemplate our next step in search for meaning and purpose, He has pledged in His Word that our reception comes through His acceptance.

When the Psalmist pointed to a "good man," he had in mind those men and women who had their sins forgiven and who were walking in the way of companionship with their Lord. A good man or a good woman would be one who is favored, cheerful, and gracious. That has been the appointed lot of every child of the King. We are favored by the Lord as His children. He loves us with an unconditional love.

The word "ordered" used by the Psalmist signifies that a man's steps are established by the Lord. In other words the companionship (steps) enjoyed by the saint (good man) with his Lord, are established and fixed (ordered) forever. With a walk of confidence we can tread this world's troubled highway with the conviction that we have someone who not only has walked the way, knows the way, but is the way. Our Lord has walked before us to ensure that we can follow Him with certainty throughout our journey.

Thought to ponder: "Those who walk with God reach their destination."

February 16

"And they continued steadfastly in the apostle's doctrine and fellowship..." Acts 2:42a (KJV)

"Brothers Forever," a Christian musical group, recently came to our church. The duo was here for two days in March as a part of "Disciple Now" weekend for our youth group. The group's remarkable sound has managed to place them in front of thousands of people all across the country--from California to New York. We can now add TO HAYNESVILLE!

Long before they arrived with their ministry in music, I took the opportunity by way of a newsletter article to say that I was part of a church fellowship that is Brothers/Sisters forever. When I came to know Christ as my personal Savior, I was brought into a larger fellowship of believers that includes men, women, boys and girls. These are the ones that will be my family throughout eternity. We share a kindred spirit that brings sweet communion into the Family of God.

Our church fellowship celebrated the Lord's presence during those two days. In the Sunday morning and evening services, led by "Brothers Forever," our worship became a time that strengthened our eternal ties as brothers and sisters in Christ. We were reminded of who we were and what we are to be. My prayer was then and is today that we will continually come together as fellow believers and be part of a "pre-homegoing" celebration every Sunday. The group "Brothers Forever" may be absent from our service, but the spirit of brothers and sisters in Christ will always be present.

Thought to ponder: "Always keep your head up, but be careful to keep your nose at a friendly level."

February 17

"for thou hast cast all my sins behind thy back."
Isaiah 38:17 (KJV)

Now let every believer, if he wants to see his sins, stand on tiptoe and look up; will he see them there? No. If he looks down, will he see them there? No. If he looks around, will he see them there? No. If he looks within, will he see them there? No. Where shall he look, then? Where he likes, for he will never see them again, according to the ancient promise, "In those days, and in that time, saith the Lord, the iniquity of Israel shall be sought for, and there shall be none; and the sins of Judah, and they shall not be found, for I will pardon them whom I reserve. " (Jeremiah 50:20)

Can I tell you where our sins are? Christ purged them, and God said, "I will cast all their sins behind my back." Where is that? All things are before God. I do not know where behind God's back can be. It is nowhere, for God is everywhere present, seeing everything. So that is where my sins have gone; I speak with the utmost reverence when I say that they have gone where Jehovah himself can never

THE NEAR SIDE

see them. Look as we may, our sins are nowhere to be found, for they have been purged with the precious blood of Jesus, and they have been all taken away, never to be brought up before us ever.

Thought to ponder: "God's wrath comes by measure; his mercy without measure."

February 18

"Sirs, what must I do to be saved?" Acts 16:30 (KJV)

Can you cry under water? If money doesn't grow on trees then why do banks have branches? What did cured ham actually have? Why is it that people say they "slept like a baby" when babies wake up like every two hours? If a deaf person has to go to court, is it still called a hearing? How come we choose from just two people for President and fifty for Miss America? These are just a few of the nonsensical questions that some people might ask out of sheer curiosity. There is a more serious question that every man, woman, boy, or girl must ask, and then answer.

The question asked in the scripture for today reaches beyond the thirst for the trivial and hits at the very heart of every person's need, and that is the hunger for fulfillment. Paul and Silas had been praying and singing praises unto God at midnight, and the prisoners heard them. I am sure that the jailer also heard what the prisoners heard. Midnight marks the beginning and ending of each day in civil time throughout the world. On this particular occasion, the

THE NEAR SIDE

jailer's day ended with an earthquake and began with personal salvation. The jailer asked the one question that was uppermost on his mind, "What must I do to be saved?" Out of all the questions that could be asked, the most important one is that of the jailer of Acts 16. Now the ball is in our court. We face the most important part of this earthly life, and that is coming to grips of where we will spend eternity.

Thought to ponder: "Guidance means I can count on God. Commitment means God can count on me."

February 19

"I can do all things through Christ who strengtheneth me."
Philippians 4:13 (KJV)

I read a statement the other day to this effect: "God can do without us!" He does not need us to help Him in any way. He is sovereign. He is omnipotent, omniscient, and omnipresent. He owns all. He knows all. He is all. That may be a hard pill to swallow for those who feel as though God should seek their advice. If God can do without us, I wonder what He can do with us? Paul answered that question with the statement "all things." With Christ all things are possible.

I rode by a recycling plant the other day that had this advertisement "The Can Bank." It was a designated place where people could bring their aluminum cans for recycling. I looked inside the container and saw hundreds of cans. Some were large, others were small. There were whole cans and crushed cans. Some cans were decorative while others were plain. I was reminded of another kind of "can bank," one that the Lord Jesus has. Inside are all kinds of "cans" that we are able to do. Though some obstacles we face are large, small, whole, crushed in size, decorated or plain, these "cans" have been given to us with the only requirement being to use them! With this precious promise before us, we "can" march forward in the fullness of His strength to do whatever is required. We truly can do all things through Christ because He infuses His strength into our life.

Thought to ponder: "Every problem is a possibility in disguise."

February 20

"Then we which are alive and remain shall be caught up together in the clouds, to meet the Lord in the air: and so shall we ever be with the Lord." 1 Thessalonians 4:17a (KJV)

One day we are going to be "caught up" in the clouds to meet our Lord in the air. In Christian jargon that means that we are going to be "raptured" away with other saints. Before this rapture takes place, there are some important "ups" to maintain. A daily maintenance of the following will help ensure a successful walk. A failure to persist in our efforts will only lead to a quick demise of our intentions. We need to:

Take up the cross and follow Jesus Christ, and in the spirit of discipleship make Him Lord of all.

Join up with fellow believers to reach a lost and dying world and fulfill the mandate of making disciples of all nations.

Grow up in the Lord in His grace and in the knowledge of Him.

Confess up our sins daily for God is just and faithful to forgive us our sins and to cleanse us from all unrighteousness.

Free up daily time to spend it in fellowship with the Lord in His school of prayer.

Follow up on this daily devotional to ensure that the joy of the Lord will be our strength.

Speak up because the world needs to hear of the love of Christ.

As the daylight of suitability gives way to the fatigue of night, it behooves us to take each second of the day as a workshop of opportunity for the night of life will come when no man or woman can work anymore.

Thought to ponder: "It is important that when we come to die we have nothing to do but die."

February 21

"Christ Jesus came into the world to save sinners"
1 Timothy 1:15b (KJV)

I was walking out of a chain store the other day when I came by two men who were sitting behind a desk that had candy suckers and balloons strewn across it. One of the men asked me as I walked by if I wanted to save a life. Caught off guard my initial response was, "NO!" As I walked away, though, I could not get that question out of my mind. The gentleman was asking me to help support a group of individuals who were encouraging single moms to keep their unborn children rather than abort them.

My thought went beyond that important endeavor to a more serious, "Do you want to save a life for the kingdom's sake?" How could I say no in light of what our scripture states today? Jesus came into this world in which we live to give His life a ransom for many. He stated that He came to seek and to save that which was lost. My search should be no less. Rather than waiting for sinners to come to Him, Jesus pursued sinners where they were. My pursuit should be

THE NEAR SIDE

wherever the prodigals are. Jesus' mission was to give sight to the blind, a path for the lost, and a sense of worth to the down and out. My appointment should be to follow in His steps, trust Him for the results, and be faithfully committed to His mission.

Thought to ponder: "The world has yet to see what God can do through a man or a woman who is fully committed to Him."

February 22

"Let this mind be in you, which was also in Christ Jesus."
Philippians 2:5 (KJV)

I noticed on the side of an exit ramp on the interstate, a transient was holding a sign that all could read: "Need a lift to Florida, am willing to ride in trunk." I thought to myself that this person was willing to do whatever was necessary to make his way to Florida. I don't know if the gentleman made his destination that day, but I certainly do commend him for his willingness to take extreme measures to meet his goal. There was no reluctance on his part even if it meant the trunk of a car.

Jesus was willing to do whatever was necessary to secure the gift of eternal life for each one of us. Our Lord stepped out of the splendor of heaven and became one of us. He humbled Himself by becoming obedient to the point of death--even the death on a cross. He emptied Himself by assuming the form of a slave. He was willing to go the distance by shedding His precious blood. His was a strength of mind, a resolve of steadfastness that brought about the

THE NEAR SIDE

greatest gift that mankind has ever known. Paul, the apostle, wrote in 2 Corinthians 8:9, "For ye know the grace of our Lord Jesus Christ, that, though he was rich, yet for your sakes he became poor, that ye through his poverty might be rich."

May we sing the old Christian standard and live it out in daily life:
"I am resolved to follow the Savior, faithful and true each day. Heed what He sayeth, do what He willeth; He is the living way."

Thought to ponder: "Knowing without doing is like plowing without sowing."

February 23

"So then every one of us shall give an account of himself to God." Romans 14:12 (KJV)

On June 2, 2014, Armando Galarraga, a pitcher for the Detroit Tigers, was one out away from pitching a perfect game; something that is rare in major league baseball. However, on the last out the first base umpire Jim Joyce ruled the runner safe, putting an end to Galarraga's quest for a perfect game. Joyce believed he made the right call until he saw the replay for himself after the game; the replay showed the runner was clearly out and that Galarraga should have gotten credit for a perfect game. Joyce, the umpire, immediately went to the 28-year-old pitcher from Venezuela after the game and apologized for getting the call wrong. That is accountability in all of its purest glory.

One day each and every one of us shall give an account of what we have done with our "3 T's."

The accountability of our <u>time</u>. How we utilized the hours of the day that the Lord gave to us. Someone has suggested that we tithe 10% of our time to the Lord. That means that out of a 24-hour day we give Him 2.4 hours. Intervals of time could be spent in prayer, Bible study and meditation.

The accountability of our <u>talents</u>. How we used our God-given skills. Becoming knowledgeable of the scriptures will help us to become better teachers of the Word. Exercising the wisdom God grants to us will facilitate our readiness to share whenever we are tasked to do so.

The accountability of the Lord's <u>tithe</u>. How we gave to the work of the Lord. We know the truth of the scripture when we read that God loves a cheerful giver--that is a "hilarious" investor.

Thought to ponder: "Talk is cheap, do something."

February 24

"And upon this rock I will build my church; and the gates of hell shall not prevail against it." Matthew 16:18b (KJV)

The headlines for November 16, 1824 were: "New York's Fifth Avenue Opens for Business."

Fifth Avenue is a major thoroughfare in the center of Manhattan in New York City. It is lined with prestigious shops and is consistently ranked among the most expensive shopping streets in the United States. In 2008, Forbes magazine ranked Fifth Avenue as being the most expensive street in the world. The American Planning Association compiled a list of "2012 Great Places in America" and declared Fifth Avenue to be one of the greatest streets to visit in America. This historic street is home to extraordinary museums, businesses and stores, parks, luxury apartments, and historical landmarks that are reminiscent of its history and vision for the future.

On October 9, 1824 another event took place that surpasses the greatness of "Fifth Avenue."

THE NEAR SIDE

In the sprawling community of Haynesville, Georgia, William S. Coalson donated land for what was called a meeting place for worshippers. Later Joseph Tooke would supply lumber to erect a log structure in which to meet. The first church established in Houston County, Georgia, was no doubt the First Baptist Church of Haynesville, and the date was October 9, 1824. What has transpired in the 190 years since then is beyond comparison to "Fifth Avenue." Rather than historical landmarks on Fifth Avenue, there are thousands of souls who are in heaven. Other than vision for the future for Fifth Avenue which includes the material, there is a "Great Commission" vision for the future of the Haynesville Baptist Church. Members of First Baptist are a part of that great legacy which faithful men and women have handed down for 190 years.

Thought to ponder: "Treasure our PAST! Celebrate our PRESENT! Anticipate our FUTURE!"

February 25

"He that goeth forth and weepeth, bearing precious seed, shall doubtless come again with rejoicing, bringing his sheaves with him." Psalm 126:6 (KJV)

The most accurate description that I have read of a "church-wide revival" is: "An increased spiritual interest or renewal in the life of a church congregation."

That little phrase "increased spiritual interest" got me to thinking. What kind of interests should our church have? I have come to the conclusion that there are at least two main considerations that we as a church should posses:

1. An interest in the "lost" of our community.

We are well aware that people without Christ will die and be doomed to an eternal separation from God. That is "hell" within itself. Paul's admonition in Romans 10:9 is in the form of three questions. "How then shall they call on Him in whom they have not believed? How shall they believe in Him of whom they have not heard? How shall they hear without a preacher?" We are all "preachers" in the truest sense of the word; and unless we share the good news of the Gospel, the lost in our community will be less likely to confess Christ as Saviour.

2. An interest in the "saved" of our Church.

This article does not provide enough space to write about the many levels of care and concern that we should have for each other as members in the Body of Christ. One scripture that comes to mind is, John 13:35: "By this shall all men know that ye are My disciples, if ye have love one to another." My prayer for this "increased spiritual interest" (revival) is that we would genuinely fall in love with each other and share the good news of the Gospel with the lost!

Thought to ponder: "Delayed obedience is the brother of disobedience."

February 26

"Wilt thou not revive us again; that thy people may rejoice in thee?" Psalm 85:6 (KJV)

Recently our church went through what many spiritual pundits would label as a "sweeping revival." One would have had to be in the path of this overwhelming renewal to feel and experience the effects of the Holy Spirit's broom. As He swept through the aisles of this church fellowship, the Spirit's "sweeping effect" brought conviction upon many who sat in the pews. This rapid movement swept in such a glorious way that over fifty decisions were made.

An evangelist came to our church, not with a suitcase full of overly preached sermons, but with a fresh wind and fire from heaven. The warmth of the Holy Spirit was greatly ignited by the faith and repentance in the hearts and lives of men, women, boys, and girls. Night after night of the services, the fires of revival burned brighter and brighter. By week's end, the entire congregation was overwhelmed with wonder and amazement.

THE NEAR SIDE

There are three requirements for a physical fire as well as a spiritual fire.

First, there is the need of "oxygen." Oxygen would be the "language" of words in the form of prayer. There was much praying done for our revival, and the language of prayer paid off with some hefty dividends. Lives were changed for time and eternity.

Second, there is the necessity of "heat". Heat came from the "love" that people had for each other; and that devotion was not only seen but felt. Tears are truly a language that God understands, and there were many tears shed over the direction many lives had taken.

Third, there is the order of "fuel." Fuel came from the "largeness" of passionate desires that our church folk had as they sought revival. The claim from each one was that God would send a revival and that the revival would begin in them.

Thought to ponder: "It's not the outlook, but the uplook that counts."

February 27

"Comfort the feebleminded, support the weak, be patient toward all men." 1 Thessalonians 5:14b (KJV)

A church had gathered to pray for a needy family around Thanksgiving. The family needed food and concerned folks from the church got together to pray for them. While the prayer meeting was going on, a young boy came and knocked on the door of the home where members had gathered, entered into the house and told them, "My father said to tell you that he can't come tonight to pray because he is too busy unloading his prayers at the Jones' house. He said to tell you that he is taking a side of beef, a sack of potatoes, a bushel of apples, and some jars of jam. He said he could not be here to pray, but that he has taken his prayers and unloaded them at their house."

Thanksgiving by way of daily thanksliving demands that we pray, yes; but it also demands that we "unload" our prayers at the doorsteps of those who are hungry, lonely, and just plain without. Our hands are God's hands in action. Our feet are His feet as we walk in the way of obedience. Our

THE NEAR SIDE

willingness to give where there is a need comes from the heart of God Himself. He was willing to give the very best that He had in His only begotten Son. This world may never see what God is like unless we are willing to act like Him. The way His heart beats for the downtrodden, is the way that our heart beats. Like Father, like son and daughter.

Thought to ponder: "When God gives, we take. When we receive, we are to give to others."

February 28

"Endeavouring to keep the unity of the Spirit in the bond of peace." Ephesians 4:3 (KJV)

I noticed a check written to a church that had this notation at the bottom: "This check is for my church ties." At first I laughed out loud because this individual had misspelled the word "tithes," though the two words do rhyme. On second thought I remembered the song, "Blest be the tie that binds our hearts in Christian love; the fellowship of kindred minds is like to that above." This individual may have had the right thought in mind that our offerings and tithes could be used to help bind the ties of a church fellowship. After some consideration, I came to the conclusion that maybe when we give our tithes and offerings we could earmark a part of that money to an endeavor to secure the binding of ties for our brothers and sisters in Christ.

Paul, in his letter to the Ephesians, used the word "endeavouring" to point to a prompt or earnest reply to the need of church unity. In the Holman Christian Standard Bible (HCSB) the rendering is, "Diligently keeping the unity of the Spirit with the peace that binds us." We are faced with the moral imperative to do whatever is needed, within the realm of Christian design, to ensure the harmony and agreement within the body of believers. Discord and dissention are to be replaced with amity and sympathy. Maybe, just maybe, our checks to the ministry of the church could be used for our "ties."

Thought to ponder: "Don't be afraid to go out on a limb. That's where the fruit is."

February 29

"For the eyes of the LORD run to and fro throughout the whole earth, to shew himself strong in the behalf of them whose heart is perfect toward him." 2 Chronicles 16:9 (KJV)

This devotional day is written because this year is Leap Year. That means there are 366 days this year and February ends on the 29th instead of the 28th. Leap Years are necessary to keep our calendar in alignment with the rotation of the Earth and the Sun. Without them, we would lose around six hours off our calendar every year. It takes 365 days, 5 hours, 48 minutes, and 46 seconds for the Earth to revolve around the sun. Those extra hours are the reason we have Leap Years. There are at least two important events which take place during the Leap Year: The United States Presidential Election is held, and the Olympics take place. For the child of God, there is another important episode which can take place.

On this extra day of a unique year we have an additional opportunity to be found faithful in the kingdom's work. An additional 24 hours have been placed in our hands, and we

THE NEAR SIDE

must take full advantage of this added time. It will be another four years before this unique occasion will come again. This is one notable day where we can strengthen our efforts to take the great commission of our Lord to an extra level. We have an increased opportunity to take the message of salvation by grace through faith to a world filled with doubt and dismay. Our commitment to share the convictions we have can be put up for display as we go about the Master's business. We would be remiss to let this added day come and go and not find our faith complimented by our good works. With the added time given us, we also have the greater responsibility to be faithful, for we will be held accountable for what we have done with the added time.

Thought to ponder: "Behind every door of opportunity is responsibility."

March 1

"For bodily exercise profiteth little; but godliness is profitable unto all things, having promise of the life that now is, and of that which is to come." 1 Timothy 4:8 (KJV)

A sign on a bulletin board read: "This firm requires no physical-fitness program. Everyone gets enough exercise jumping to conclusions, flying off the handle, running down the boss, flogging dead horses, knifing friends in the back, dodging responsibility, and pushing their luck." I certainly wouldn't want to be part of a working environment that had individuals who got their exercise in that fashion.

In a similar way, I certainly wouldn't want to be a contributor to the spiritual un-fitness of a worshipping environment by running down the leadership, knifing brothers and sisters in the back, dodging my responsibilities, and pushing the spiritual envelope. There are enough of these characters within the church, and we certainly don't need any more added to the roles of our fellowship. These actions are what I would call the unfruitful fruits of the mean spirited. Getting this kind of exercise will only lead to the "grieving of the

THE NEAR SIDE

Holy Spirit." Scripture teaches us that we are not to allow this to happen.

Thought to ponder: "The best way to get rid of your duties is to zealously discharge them."

March 2

"He which testifieth these things saith, Surely I come quickly. Amen. Even so, come, Lord Jesus." Revelation 22:20 (KJV)

Fanny J. Crosby was an American mission worker, poet, lyricist, and composer. A member of the Sixth Avenue Bible Baptist Church in Brooklyn, New York, she wrote many hymns together with her pastor, Robert Lowry. She was one of the most prolific hymnists in history, writing over 8,000 hymns and gospel songs. Near the end of her life she was quoted as saying, "The older I get the fonder of heaven I become."

The apostle John had been banished to the island of Patmos, and while there, had a vision of the coming Lord. He was so moved by the revelation he had received that he put the finishing touches on his vision with a prayer that would end all prayers: "Even so, come, Lord Jesus." A prayer of this passion resonates from a heart that is set on seeing the Lord Jesus face to face. What John longed for and looked for is the same longing and looking we have. One day those desires are going to be fully manifest at the coming of our

THE NEAR SIDE

Lord for He will descend from heaven and we will ascend with Him into heaven.

John could sing in chorus with Fanny J. Crosby, "Blessed assurance, Jesus is mine! Oh what a foretaste of glory diving! Heir of salvation, purchase of God, born of His Spirit, washed in His blood. This is my story, this is my song, praising my Savior all the day long." Oh, what a day that will be when we shall see Him face to face and we will be like Him for we will see Him as He is.

Thought to ponder: "Prayer is the stop that keeps you going."

March 3

"I know thy works, that thou art neither cold nor hot; I would thou wert cold or hot." Revelation 3:15 (KJV)

Someone has suggested that there could be a hymn book found in the pews of a lukewarm church that would contain a list of songs well descriptive of the kind of membership in attendance. The "neither cold nor hot" of the church could proudly sing these songs with a weak sense of commitment. Some could chime in when it seemed convenient or appropriate to their creature comfort while others could join in on the chorus after being aroused from a deep sleep of indifference. Listed below are a number of "all-time" favorites of a "lukewarm" church:

I'm fairly certain that my Redeemer lives.
Sit Up, Sit up for Jesus.
Spirit of the Living God, fall somewhere near me.
There shall be sprinkles of blessings.
Take my life and let me be.
I surrender some.

THE NEAR SIDE

Oh, how I like Jesus.
Pillow of ages, fluffed for me.
Oh, for a couple of tongues to sing.
Amazing Grace, how interesting the sound.
My hope is built on nothing much.
All hail the influence of Jesus' Name.
Above average is Thy faithfulness.
A comfy mattress is our God.

Thought to ponder: "The self-made man always seems to admire his creator."

March 4

"My son, give me thine heart, and let thine eyes observe my ways." Proverbs 23:26 (KJV)

As Christians we are prone to give God the "seconds" of life. These "seconds" take on many different faces but have the same results. We have a tendency to give Him the "seconds" of our time and keep the minutes to ourselves. The least we could give the Lord is 10% of our time. The interlude could become time spent in prayer, meditation, and Bible study. An hour a day with the Father will surely keep the enemy at bay.

We also give our Saviour the "seconds" of our territory by positioning Him second as we take on first place. If God does not occupy all four quarters of our life, He certainly will not be relegated to second place. The first commandment of the Decalogue states unequivocally, "Thou shalt have no other gods before Me."

We have a proclivity to give God the "seconds" or the leftovers. We keep the best for ourselves and give Him the fragments. In reality God is not interested in what we may

THE NEAR SIDE

have leftover but rather what we deem as the best, and giving Him the best that we have will be the best decision we make.

Thought to ponder: "If Jesus is not Lord of all, He is not Lord at all!"

March 5

"And they said one to another, Did not our heart burn within us, while He talked with us by the way, and while He opened to us the scriptures." Luke 24:32 (KJV)

I believe there is validity in saying that Christians need to have a good case of heartburn every now and then. Of course I am not talking about the kind that comes as a result of smoking, obesity, certain medical conditions, overeating, or lifestyle choices. The kind of indigestion I am referring to is spiritual in nature, the same kind that two disciples had while they walked the road to Emmaus. Christ still comes to us in unexpected places. It's not necessarily in the church that we may find Him, but wherever we need Him, and our longing hearts cry out for Him we may expect Him.

I submit to you that if you haven't had a good case of spiritual heartburn lately, today would be a good time to start. In the above scripture, there are two ways to have the kind of indigestion that will be beneficial:

THE NEAR SIDE

1. When we hear the Lord speak. These two disciples admitted that their heart burned within them as the risen Christ spoke to them along the way. Whatever sorrow or disappointment may fill our heart, hearing the Lord Jesus speak will put our heart in high speed motion and will cause our heart to burn.
2. When we understand what He says. The Holy Spirit is our spiritual Guide who reveals to us the things of the Father. He who knows the mind of God will reveal those things to us that will give us heart burn. When we understand the things of the Father, the nourishment derived from the scriptures will give us the heart burn that is daily needed.

Thought to ponder: "The next time you have indigestion, don't reach for the antacid tablet but pull out your Bible and ingest some scriptural verses."

March 6

"But what things were gain to me, those I counted loss for Christ. Yea doubtless, and I count all things but loss for the excellency of the knowledge of Christ Jesus my Lord: for whom I have suffered the loss of all things, and do count them but dung, that I may win Christ." Philippians 3:7,8 (KJV)

In 1972 Walter Cavanagh and a friend bet a dinner to see who could accumulate the most credit cards. Eight years later he won the bet and broke the world record by applying for and getting 1,003 credit cards, weighing 34 pounds and entitling him to $1.25 million in credit. He's still applying for credit cards, and has set a goal of 10,000 cards. I find it quite amusing that someone would resolve to accrue that much when there are so many other worthy endeavors to achieve.

Paul could say that at one point in his life he thought certain privileges and rights were valuable to him, but now considers them worthless because of what Christ had done. He could reason that there are no advantages he may have, whether given or earned, which could compare to the surpassing knowledge

THE NEAR SIDE

of Christ. In putting those earthly gains in the perspective of eternal glory, the apostle could rest assured that losing was really gaining, and giving up was more about receiving.

In respect to our station in life we, too, have the opportunity to put achievements, accolades, and other attainments into perspective. As we look through the lens of eternity, life can be brought into sharp focus. For with the eye of faith we can see that nothing on this earth can compare to what we have in Christ. All things which we may think are gains to us can be counted loss for Him Who is worthy. Knowing Christ in an intimate way far exceeds any knowledge that we may possess. No amount of material possessions generated or given can diminish the worth of Christ. He is everything we will ever need.

Thought to ponder: "Faith is not a pill you take but a muscle you use."

March 7

"But he answered and said, It is written, Man shall not live by bread alone, but by every word that proceedeth out of the mouth of God." Matthew 4:4 (KJV)

A sign at a church located in the downtown area of a city had these words written upon it: "Come As You Are; Join Our Fellowship; And B.Y.O.B." At first glance you may think that the church was inviting people to come to their church and bring their own bottle; but that's not what the church was advertising. They were saying that anyone who chose to come could. The church membership was open to people coming as they were. Visitors were welcomed with opened arms and encouraged to join the time of worship; but the most important part of the message on the sign was that when people came to church they were encouraged to bring their own Bible (B.Y.O.B).

The Bible is considered to be the most important book in the world. Because it is God's inspired word, its value is far beyond that of any earthly wealth. When we read the Bible, we read a message from God Himself. His handprint

THE NEAR SIDE

is found on every word in every chapter. When the Bible speaks, God speaks, and because the Bible is the Word of God, it does more than just pass on information. It makes a promise, a promise of life that is now and that which is to come. Everyone who receives the Bible's message in faith is promised the rich gift of eternal life in the Lord Jesus Christ. The Bible came from God Himself. He chose, motivated, and inspired certain people to write down the words He wanted people to have. Through that Divine inspiration the Bible has been the lifesaver of men and women down through the ages. The Holy Spirit inspired men of old to speak on God's behalf, and you and I have the express privilege of bringing that Bible to church each and every time we attend.

Thought to ponder: "The Bible will keep you from sin or sin will keep you from the Bible."

March 8

"Now this is the confidence we have before Him: whenever we ask anything according to His will, He hears us. And if we know that He hears whatever we ask, we know that we have what we have asked Him for." 1 John 5:14,15 (KJV)

Sometimes when I purchase roses or plants from a nursery catalog, there's a little box on the order form saying, "If we are out of the item you want, may we substitute one of equal or greater value?" I always say no, because I don't think the workers in the warehouse know what's best for my garden, but with the Lord we should always say, "Yes, Lord! You may substitute. You may grant an alternative answer of equal or greater value. I trust You with substitutes."

We can have the confidence of knowing that God knows what is best for us. Though our minds tell us that we know what's superior, the reality is that God has the greater perspective. A pastor friend of mine put it like this, "God has already looked down the road and around the curve. He knows a thought before it becomes a thought, and He knows the beginning from the end. He is the Alpha and Omega, the beginning and the end, and everything in between."

Confidence is a quality that we can posses. It comes by trusting in the loving hand of a patient Father. It doesn't come from churning up enough faith at a given time. Belief in the goodness of God finds its foundation through trusting the Word of God, and the God of the Word. Our life is richer because of the promises of God. They are rock solid and will never change. We trusted them yesterday and we can rely on them tomorrow. The God of the Bible is the God who never changes. He has given His word that he will never forsake us.

Thought to ponder: "When we can't see God's hand, we can trust His heart."

March 9

"These words that I am giving you today are to be in your heart." Deuteronomy 6:6 (KJV)

I have a pastor friend who refers to this passage as "D6" (Deuteronomy 6:6). He said that he wanted churches to become D6 fellowships, parents to become D6 parents, and Christians to become D6 Christians. He said that if we could get this letter-number coded in our minds, we would never have any trouble discerning where God wants His word to reside.

The Word of God is a gift from a loving heavenly Father who wants nothing but the best for His children. He has handed down the most important book that we will ever know. The Bible was written over a span of 1500 years by 40 authors. While using the authors' own writing styles and personalities, God has shown us who He is and what it's like to know Him. The Bible not only inspires us, it explains the complexities of life and what God has in mind for His people. It does not answer all the questions we might have, but enough of them to relieve our anxieties. The Bible is

THE NEAR SIDE

the anchor for our soul and we must secure ourselves to its unchangeableness.

How do we become D6 Christians, fellowships, and parents? When we take the written/spoken Word of God and hide its truths in our heart. The result will be that we will not sin against God. When the Word moves from our head to our heart, we are inspired by the Holy Spirit to put those words into a positive action. A day by day obedience to the teachings of the Bible will bring satisfaction that has no end. Our challenge this day and every day is to take the Word of God and make applications to every facet of our life.

Thought to ponder: "Storms make oaks take deeper roots."

March 10

"For as the lightning cometh out of the east, and shineth even unto the west; so shall also the coming of the Son of man be."
Matthew 24:27 (KJV)

There are several differences in the first coming of our Lord and His second coming. For example:

When He came the first time, there was no room for Him in the inn. When He comes again, the whole world will be His domain. When He came the first time, He came wrapped in swaddling clothes. When He comes again, He'll be dressed in the vestments of victory. He came the first time as King of the Jews. He will come again as King of Kings and Lord of Lords. He came the first time as the Author of salvation. He will come again as the Finisher of our faith. He came the first time with a baby's cry. When He comes again, it will be with the roar of a lion of the tribe of Judah.

His first coming was known only to a few shepherds, a handful of wise men, and a few residents of Bethlehem. When He comes again, it will be as lightning flashing from east to west. He will come in the clouds of glory, and the entire universe will hear the news. When He came at Bethlehem, the angels sang, "Glory to God in the highest" (Luke 2:15). When He comes again, they will sing, "The kingdoms of this world are become the kingdoms of our Lord, and of His Christ; and He shall reign forever and ever" (Revelation 11:15).

Thought to ponder: "One of the greatest things about life is not so much where we stand as what direction we are going."

March 11

"Now then we are ambassadors for Christ, as though God did beseech you by us: we pray you in Christ's stead, be ye reconciled to God." 2 Corinthians 5:20 (KJV)

"Double Duty" Radcliffe (July 7, 1902 - August 11, 2005) was a professional baseball player in the Negro leagues. He is one of only a handful of professional baseball players who lived past their 100th birthday. Playing for more than 30 teams, Radcliffe, according to one biographer, had more than 4,000 hits and 400 home runs, won 500 games and had 4,000 strike-outs. He played as a pitcher and a catcher, became a manager, and in his old age became a popular ambassador for the game. Radcliffe, you could say, did just about everything a baseball player was expected to do and more, but the most important thing about this unusual man was that he was an ambassador for baseball.

Paul speaks of Christians as being ambassadors for Christ. One definition of an ambassador is: "A person who acts as a representative or promoter of a specified activity." We are people of faith, driven by an undying love, and who

THE NEAR SIDE

have been sent by the King of kings to represent Him and promote His agenda of coming into the world to save sinners. We are lights in a dark world and salt to an unsavory society. Our Lord has no hands but our hands; no feet but our feet; no mouth but our mouth. We extend to a lost and dying world the only hope that they have, and that desire comes in the person of Jesus whom we represent. So we are Christ's ambassadors; God is making His appeal through us. We speak for Christ when we plead, "Come back to God!"

Thought to ponder: "Thinking well is wise; planning well is wiser; doing well is the wisest of all."

March 12

"For ye are bought with a price; therefore glorify God in your body, and in your spirit, which are God's."

1 Corinthians 6:20 (KJV)

My wife and I work a couple of days during the week at a local antique mall. There are 200+ booths filled with all kinds of collectibles and antiques. It's a collector's haven. Row after row of items that would tempt any seeker of the unusual. A vendor jokingly said to me, "If you need it and it's not here, it probably hasn't been made."

You may be surprised as to what some people will buy or collect to add to their collections. Old windows and doors that used to be discarded are now treasured items because of Pinterest, which is a visual discovery tool that you can use to find ideas for all your projects and interests. Rusty barbed wire can be found. I am told that there were more than 530 patents for barbed wires. There are over 2000 types of barbed wire including variations of these patents, bootlegged (unlawfully produced), and homemade wires. People have paid up to $150 for a string of four old rusty barbed

THE NEAR SIDE

wires. On and on I could go sharing many of the items most people have thrown away which have become treasures now highly prized.

Paul tells us that we have been bought with a price. A ransom was paid with the precious blood of the Lord Jesus, poured out on Calvary, the old rugged cross. There our Savior paid the price for our redemption. All of our sins past, present, and future were paid for in full. We who were dead in trespasses and sins, without any hope, have now been redeemed by the precious blood of the Lamb. Redeemed, how I love to proclaim it! Redeemed by the blood of the Lamb; Redeemed through His infinite mercy, His child and forever I am.

Thought to ponder: "It doesn't take such a great man to be a Christian; it just takes all there is of him."

March 13

"That which we have seen and heard declare we unto you, that ye also may have fellowship with us: and truly our fellowship is with the Father, and with His Son Jesus Christ."

1 John 1:3 (KJV)

Sports have been a big part of my life. My mother once said that I was born with a sports spoon in my mouth. Starting out as a youngster and progressing through my teenage years into adulthood, I have run the gamut of playing all three big sports. They are baseball, basketball, and football. While I played the games, I had the full support of my mom and dad. They were there to cheer me on when I was victorious, and present when I tasted defeat. My dad had the responsibility of making sure that I got to all the games. On a particular day one of the parents, who had kids playing with me, asked my dad if he were a fan or a follower, and he said to them, "Yes." That meant that he was both a fan and a follower. He was a true blue fan of his son and an even greater follower of his boy.

THE NEAR SIDE

Let's change the subject matter to that with a spiritual twist. In regard to your church membership are you a fan or a follower? I trust that you will answer with a resounding, "YES! I am a fan of the membership that has been entrusted to me, and a follower of the church in its endeavors to fulfill the Great Commission."

I am a fan in the sense of support. I take my church membership seriously, not as a right, but as a privilege. When the fellowship meets together for worship, count me in as a great fan and a super supporter. I want to cheer my brother and sister teammates on and to take my rightful place in the membership to honor the Lord Jesus with my presence and praise. My desire is to be a positive influence on the body of Christ, not a negative sway against the fellowship.

I am a follower in respect to participation. I may be a fan in the sense of support, but I am a greater fan in respect to getting into the game myself. I don't want to be a bystander who watches from the sidelines. "Put me in Coach, I can play centerfield for You." You have equipped me with the armor that allows me to stand against the fiery darts of the enemy. I want to participate in the game of life that has a message of hope to a lost and dying world.

Thought to ponder: "All the roads to success and achievement are uphill."

March 14

"God is faithful, by whom ye were called unto the fellowship of his Son Jesus Christ our Lord." 1 Corinthians 1:9 (KJV)

One way we can view our future is to take a look at life in the past tense. We do so by recognizing the handprint of God on our lives. Those "valley events" that took place during the most inopportune times and caused us to doubt the goodness of God were in reality His ways of drawing us to Himself. We have a tendency to stray from the Father and to lose our way, but the Father is not lax to forget where we are. He will do whatever it takes to bring us back. That's one of those handprints God has placed upon our life. Those mountain-top experiences, when God led us to loftiness, were His ways of saying that the valleys were only detours to the pinnacles of joy. That's another one of those handprints that our loving Lord has pressed upon our circumstances. Looking back on life with those perspectives, we see more clearly that God was intimately involved in all of our situations.

THE NEAR SIDE

Someone has written these words: "When you can't trace the hand of God, trust His heart." That says to me when I cannot see God in those affairs that trouble my mind, I can certainly trust His loving heart. God always has my best interests in mind. Those are good words to remember when the tears of sorrow have wetted the eyes of faith and thrown a dimness over them. God's handprint is there even though we may not see them. The God who created me is the same God who is able to do for me more than I could ever think. We could fill a book of those instances when we saw the handprints of God on our lives. May we, this day, recall them with an assurance that God is always present.

Thought to ponder: "Our God has a big eraser."

March 15

"The Son of Man did not come to be served, but to serve, and to give His life as a ransom for many." Matthew 20:28 (KJV)

The phrase "What would Jesus do?" (often abbreviated to WWJD) became popular in the United States in the 1990s and as a personal motto for adherents of Evangelical Christianity who used the phrase as a reminder of their belief in a moral imperative to act in a manner that would demonstrate the love of Jesus through the actions of the adherents. I believe there is another way to view the WWJD, other than What would Jesus do? That would be, "Why would Jesus die?" (WWJD)

Jesus was born to die. He said, "The Son of Man did not come to be served, but to serve, and to give His life as a ransom for many." He came to give His life, to die, and His death would result in salvation for others. This was the reason He came to earth. His blood was poured out for others. Without the shedding of blood there is no remission of sin. His death was a must for the forgiveness of our transgressions. All we like sheep have gone astray, each to our

THE NEAR SIDE

own way, and God has laid on Him the iniquity of us all. In order for the righteous demands of a Holy God to be met, Jesus had to come to earth as a virgin born child, live a sinless life, be rejected and ultimately crucified on a cross. That death would secure the forgiveness for our sins and pave the way for the righteous demands of a forgiving God to be paid in full. Jesus did it all for us. He died that we might live, and because He lives, we can live also.

Thought to ponder: "Faith hears the inaudible, sees the invisible, believes the incredible, and receives the impossible."

March 16

"If I wash thee not, thou hast no part with Me."
John 13:8 (KJV)

"If I then, your Lord and Master, have washed your feet; ye also ought to wash one another's feet." John 13:14 (KJV)

"If ye know these things, happy are ye if ye do them."
John 13:17 (KJV)

My hometown community of Haynesville, Georgia, has the running joke that if you blink twice while you ride through our quaint little town, you will miss the sights. We have one store, one fire station, two churches, and no blinker light. We are a friendly bunch of folks though, and we will wave at you when we see you rush through our district. We really are not that small, but if you do blink several times you will have made your way into the city limits and out. Though some people may call us tiny in size, others know we are giants in community spirit. As meager as the

THE NEAR SIDE

citizen count is, we still consider ourselves to be important residents of Houston County.

There are small words in the Bible that are really important. Some are so pregnant with truth that if you took time to develop them in study, you would be richly rewarded. One of those remarkable words is "if." In John 13 Jesus used this word three times in what we know to be the washing of the disciple's feet. In verse eight, it is what I call the "if" of fellowship. What Peter could not submit to was that the Master should serve His servant. Our Lord desires intimate fellowship with us and unless we allow Him to wash us through regeneration, we cannot have fellowship with Him. In verse fourteen, it is what I call the "if" of obedience. Our Lord had washed the disciples' feet, and they in return were to be obedient and follow His example. In verse seventeen, it is what I refer to as the "if" of happiness. It is one thing to talk about obeying the Lord, and an entirely different matter when it comes to following through with our commitment. Small towns, great community spirit. Small words, great truths.

Thought to ponder: "If you cannot do great things, do small things in a great way."

March 17

"Wherefore seeing we also are compassed about with so great a cloud of witnesses let us lay aside every weight, and the sin which doth so easily beset us, and let us run with patience the race that is set before us." Hebrews 12:1 (KJV)

There was a time in my life when I was a huge NASCAR racing fan. I can remember Sunday mornings at church waiting for the pastor to finish his sermon so that I could get home and watch the race. Those were the days when Richard Petty was king of the track. Races that saw Dale Earnhardt, the "Intimidator," run by everybody on the oval. Names like "Fireball" Roberts, Freddie Lorenzen, David Pearson, Bill Elliot, and Junior Johnson were revered like giants. Over the years, that passion for racing has waned somewhat. There is not the anticipation of watching every lap of every race, but in February when the season kicks off at Daytona, there is the expectation of a new year of racing. Every race car driver starts at the same position--all even. Daytona has been dubbed as the "Grand Daddy" of all the races. So if I am going to watch one race during the season, I make sure that it is the Daytona 500.

The race that is set before us is our persevering obedience of faith in Christ. The stadium, or race plot, where we run this race is this world; and the prize for which we run is the heavenly glory that will be ours one day. We are to run the race without allowing ourselves to be hindered by any obstructions and without giving out or fainting in the way. We are encouraged by the example of the multitudes who have run the same race before us and who are now looking out upon us from heaven where they dwell. We are to persevere just as they did, not to the bitter end, but to the better end. Our loving heavenly Father has given us a complete ideal for starting, running, and finishing the race. In the next verse of Hebrews 12, we read these words, "Looking unto Jesus the author and finisher of our faith." The Holmon Christian Standard Bible has this reading, "Keeping our eyes on Jesus!" He is the ideal.

Thought to ponder: "The will of God will never take us where the grace of God will not sustain us."

March 18

"Jesus said to them, Verily, verily I say unto you, Before Abraham was, I am." John 8:58 (KJV)

Adrian Rogers was considered by many to be the prince of preachers. Dr. Rogers went home to be with his Lord November 15, 2005. He not only was the pastor of Bellevue Baptist Church in Memphis Tennessee, he was a Southern Baptist minister whose church services aired on television and through radio with the "Love Worth Finding Ministries." He once said in a sermon that God was/is the "I AM" in the midst of "I Need." When we feel that we are in over our head, we can know that all is under Jesus' feet. Every need we have will be met through His overwhelming supply. He is the Great I AM!

I must confess that my life is filled with needs. I have need of sustaining grace. I come short of God's expectation for me. I constantly stand in need of forgiveness. My life is one of constant craving for His presence. There is a hunger and thirst for His righteousness. Every step of the way there is an insatiable desire to be all that I can be for Him. Day and night I long for the Lord's face to shine upon me. In my destitution I cry for His filling. In the good that brightens my path and in the darkness that shadows my steps, I lift up mine eyes unto the hills from whence cometh my strength. Through the lack of my faith, I am reminded that He will never leave me nor forsake me. For every need that I have, the Lord was/is the "I AM" for "I Need!"

Thought to ponder: "People change, fashions change, and conditions change, but God never changes."

March 19

"Now Moses kept the flock of Jethro his father in law, the priest of Midian; and he led the flock to the backside of the desert, and came to the mountain of God, even to Horeb."
Exodus 3:1 (KJV)

I listened to an advertisement concerning the availability of internet connection via satellite. The ad promised that if someone lived in an area where internet was unavailable, they were living in what pundits called a "digital desert." Many counties live on the edge of an internet oasis, but cannot connect. The announcer went on to say that if this were your situation, this particular business had some good news, and that announcement was a satellite connection in any area of the country. So, if you lived in a "digital desert," there was good news!

I think of Moses, the servant of God, who found himself out of the limelight of power and in the darkness of defeat. He was living in his own "digital desert," away from the oasis of Egypt. Fleeing from the face of Pharaoh because of a crime he had committed, Moses had no idea that God would confront him on this day. God had some good news for Moses; He had him right where He wanted him for God would now make the connection with Moses that would dispel the gloom and doom of failure.

To be greatly used by God, we need to have some "back side of the desert" experience. When we are brought to the end of ourselves, it marks the beginning of a new experience with God. An adventure in faith awaits us as we encounter the Creator of this universe. A connection with Jehovah Himself will bring out the best in us. Our desert of defeat will turn into an oasis of involvement, as God uses us to accomplish His purposes. We may be living in our own "digital desert," but we can take heart because God has plans for us that will bring out the best in us.

Thought to ponder: "The only fellow who has all his troubles behind him is a school bus driver."

March 20

"JOHN to the seven churches which are in Asia; Grace be unto you, and peace, from him which is, and which was, and which is to come; and from the seven Spirits which are before his throne." Revelation 1:4 (KJV)

As a youngster growing up in Haynesville, Georgia, my boyhood idol was Mickey Mantle. His nickname was "The Commerce Comet" or "The Mick." He was a Major League Baseball centerfielder and first baseman for the New York Yankees for 18 seasons, from 1951 through 1968. Mantle is regarded by many to be the greatest switch hitter of all time, and one of the greatest players and sluggers in baseball history. He was inducted into the National Baseball Hall of Fame in 1974 and was elected to the Major League Baseball All-Century Team in 1999. As an adorer of "The Mick," I combed my hair the same way he did; I tried to mimic his walk and his talk; and the one thing that I made sure of was to wear his number "7." That number has always fascinated me.

THE NEAR SIDE

As a Christian I have a fondness for the biblical number 7. It is used 735 times (54 times in the book of Revelation alone), and the number 7 is the foundation of God's word. If we include with this count how many times 'sevenfold' (6) and 'seventh' (119) is used, the total jumps to 860 references. Seven is the number of completeness and perfection (both physical and spiritual). It derives much of its meaning from being tied directly to God's creation of all things. In the book of the Revelation there are seven churches, seven angels to the seven churches, seven seals, seven trumpet plagues, seven thunders and the seven last plagues. The first resurrection of the dead takes place at the 7th trumpet, completing salvation for the Church, and I could go on and on speaking about the number 7. Take time today to contemplate this most important number in the Bible.

Thought to ponder: "Keep looking up, this could be day that our LORD comes!"

March 21

"And they were all amazed, and they glorified God, and were filled with fear, saying, We have seen strange things today."
Luke 5:26 (KJV)

I saw a most unusual sight the other day as I was driving home from an antique mall. I noticed a tow truck was pulling a patrol car in for repairs. It seemed to be an awkward event as I surveyed the whole situation. I could envision this patrolman's vehicle pulling the tow truck over and issuing a citation, but it wasn't natural looking for the tire to be on the other rim. I wondered out loud as to how many cars had been pulled over by this patrolman's car; and now it was being pulled down the road, helplessly, by another vehicle. I've seen some strange things before, but not quite like this. It reminded me of the last line of Ernest Lawrence Thayer's poem entitled, "Casey at the Bat." Those words were: "But there is no joy in Mudville - mighty Casey has struck out." On this day, I witnessed a strange occurrence.

The word "strange" in our scripture verse has the idea of something being extraordinary. These were things wonderful,

THE NEAR SIDE

unthought-of of, unexpected, and incredible by carnal reason. These were events that were never seen, nor known before; as that a man, who was so enfeebled by the palsy, that he was obliged to be carried on a bed by four men, and yet, on a sudden chance, by a word spoken, rose up, and carried his bed on his back home. The whole scenario was witnessed by the common people and it moved them to confess, "We have seen strange things today."

I wonder how many remarkable things we have seen during our work in the ministry? As doers of the Word, have we seen events that were explainable only in the light of God's intervention? As ministers of the new covenant, have we seen conditions that were brought about by the movement of the Holy Ghost. With the Great Commission before us, have we seen occasions witnessed only through faith in the ministry of our Lord Jesus? What better time than now to confess that we have seen remarkable things today?

Thought to ponder: "Enthusiasm extinguishes the gloom in the room."

March 22

"And we have known and believed the love that God hath to us. God is love; and he that dwelleth in love dwelleth in God, and God in him." 1 John 4:16 (KJV)

In the list of the top 100 songs of the 1950s, number 88 on the list was a song by the Platters, "Only You." The lyrics of the song speak of the love and admiration that someone has for another. The story line could well be expressed as a, "I love you and I want you in no uncertain terms to know it." I would like to adapt the words of the song to coincide with my confession to the Lord Jesus. He did something for me that I could not do for myself; He paid a debt He did not owe, a debt that I could not pay. These are heartfelt emotions that rise up within me as I consider what He means to me. An anthem that far exceeds any earthly affection that we may have for any person. The most sublime of words which express my love and adoration for what He has done for me and will do through me.

THE NEAR SIDE

"Only You (Lord) can make this world seem right.
Only You can make my darkness bright.
Only You and You alone,
Can bless me like you do;
And fill my heart with love for only You.
Only You can make this change in me.
For it's true, You are my destiny.
When you hold my hand,
I understand the blessings that You bring.
You're my dream come true,
My One and only You."

Thought to ponder: "Love doesn't make the world go 'round.
Love is what makes the ride worthwhile."

March 23

"And this is life eternal, that they may know thee, the only true God, and Jesus Christ, whom thou hast sent."

John 17:3 (KJV)

During one of our AWANA club meetings, we had been watching a video about Jonah and his "Whale Story." One of the characters in the movie mentioned that God sent Jonah on a mission to the Ninevites. Rather than asking, "Who were the Ninevites," one of the youngsters tugged on my pants leg and asked, "Who is God?" I was shocked because I had not heard one of our children ask a question like that. They had quizzed me before on other issues about the Bible, but never a query of who God was. I made certain that the child knew that God so loved the world that He sent His only begotten Son; and that believing the good news of the gospel, people like him could be saved. What I had taken for granted about our AWANA clubbers caused me to reevaluate my thoughts about what our kids really know when it comes to God.

THE NEAR SIDE

There are adults living within a stone's throw of us who do not know who God is in the sense of salvation. Though we live in what is called the "Bible Belt," we must never take the view that people know the God of the Bible. Many may have a head knowledge of the love of God, but unless that enlightenment finds its way into the heart, the receiver has only intellectual understanding. What is needed is for the Word to find a resting place within the life of the believer. When that happens, though we will never know everything about God, we can rest in the fact that God has revealed Himself in the person of His Son, Jesus Christ.

There are three things about God that we can know for sure. First, God is Love. He is the purest embodiment of love. He forever settled the question of His love for us when Jesus died on the cross. Second, God is Light. This is the message we have heard from Him and declare to you; God is light; and in Him there is no darkness at all. Third, God is Life. Jesus said that He was the way, the truth, the life and no one could come to God unless it be through Him. You may ask, "Who is God?" He is our love; He is our light; He is our life.

Thought to ponder: "Beware of a half-truth; you may get hold of the wrong half."

March 24

"And Jesus put forth his hand, and touched him, saying, I will be thou lean. And immediately his leprosy was cleansed."
Matthew 8:3 (KJV)

Around our family clan, my mother was affectionately known as the woman with a green thumb. She had a natural skill for gardening. Mother could take a sickly-looking plant and breathe new life into it. Warren Buffet is an American business magnate, investor, and philanthropist. He was ranked as the world's wealthiest person in 2008 and as the third wealthiest in 2011. It is said that he is a man with a golden thumb. Henry Ford was an American industrialist, the founder of the Ford Motor Company, and sponsor of the development of the assembly line technique of mass production. In the realm of the automobile, he is known as the man with the mechanical thumb. Bill Gates is an American business magnate, philanthropist, investor, computer programmer, and inventor. In the world of the personal computer revolution, he is considered to be

THE NEAR SIDE

a man with a computerized thumb. Our Lord Jesus could very well be dubbed a Saviour who had a "healing hand."

In one of our Sunday services, the pastor called on one of the members of the congregation to lead in an intercessory prayer for the sick. A part of his prayer contained this confession, "What the Lord Jesus touches, He changes." My ears perked up when I heard those stirring words. My heart raced with anticipation in how the Lord was going to answer our prayers for the less fortunate. My mind tried to grasp the possibility of being touched by the Master's hand and being changed for all eternity. What the Lord Jesus touches, He changes. When He touched an open coffin, the dead was raised. As he touched a man's tongue it was loosed and words were spoken clearly. Upon touching blinded eyes, the blind were able to see. When hands were touched, fevers fled. While ears were touched, words never heard before were like a beautiful symphony.

Thought to ponder: "What our Lord touches, He changes; and those He comes in contact with will never be the same."

March 25

"For I know the thoughts that I think toward you, saith the Lord, thoughts of peace, and not of evil, to give you an expected end." Jeremiah 29:11 (KJV)

The "Corpse Flower," aptly named, is among the 10 ugliest flowers in the world. The plant only blooms every four to six years within its 40-year life expectancy. The flower is described as the world's largest; reaching five feet high and four feet wide. For eight hours of the three-day bloom, the flower emits a smell that is described as rotting flesh, attracting a carrion-eating beetle for pollination. It makes you wonder why God would create something that would be so smelly and ugly; and yet God has a purpose for every living thing under the sun. As He has a plan for the Corpse Flower, He has a design for each one of His children.

In Jeremiah's letter to the exiles in Babylon, he had some much needed news for the weary-worn pilgrims from Jerusalem. The prophet seems to say to them that seventy years must pass over them in exile, yet they shouldn't think that Jehovah had forgotten them, for He knew full well what

THE NEAR SIDE

His purpose was toward the captives - a purpose of restoring to them peace and prosperity. There were many dark days during the time of seventy years, but each day would be like a refresher as the captives would remember God's ultimate purpose for them. There would be many discouraging months in which the covenant people would languish in melancholy, but each cycle of dissuasion would be dissipated as the people would remind themselves of the faithfulness of their covenant God. There would be many distasteful years that the prisoners of Babylon would encounter, but each year could bring about a renewed hope that God's plan and purpose for His people would ultimately trump the bitter years of being under the wraps of a destructive enemy.

Thought to ponder: "God has perfect timing; never early, never late. It takes a little patience and it takes a lot of faith, but it's worth the wait."

March 26

"Brethren, I count not myself to have apprehended; but this one thing I do, forgetting those things which are behind, and reaching forth unto those things which are before."

Philippians 3:13 (KJV)

In one of Forrest Gump's famous quotes, he says, "My Mama always said you've got to put the past behind you before you can move on." St. Paul concentrates all his thoughts and his energies on the one great end of life, the one thing needful. He forgets those things which were behind him; that is, not, as some explain, his Jewish privileges and distinctions, but that part of his Christian race already past. Those times could be when he failed to give his very best. It could have been those intervals in life when he let his spiritual health suffer. It may have been those seasons in which he struggled with his "thorn in the flesh." His struggles could have been those durations of physical abuse that led to bearing about in his body the dying of the Lord Jesus. Or it may have been those encounters with the enemies of Christ who tried to stifle his message of salvation by grace. "Those past failures, I put behind me," says the apostle. Like that of an athlete, Paul threw himself forward in the race with all his energies and strained to the very utmost.

We may never encounter and experience all that the apostle did. We probably will never walk in his shoes and be confronted with evil that was cast at him. Our lives, perhaps, will never be placed in such dangerous confrontations. Our walk may never be hindered by those who hate the cross of Christ. Our paths may never be cluttered with the detours from the haters of Christ. If we come face to face with the evil of this world and give in to its threats, we can put the past regrets behind us and move on to a more meaningful encounter with the God of this universe.

Thought to ponder: "Here are five keys to fulfillment: Obey God; dream great dreams; plan great plans; pray great prayers; claim great victories."

March 27

"And when he (Jesus) was come near, he beheld the city (Jerusalem), and wept over it." Matthew 19:41 (KJV)

Alexander the Great lived only about 33 years, from 356 to 323 B.C., but during that time he became one of the most successful military commanders in human history. He conquered a vast region that had been occupied by earlier empires—Egyptian, Assyrian, Babylonian and Persian. It is said of Alexander the Great that he sat down and wept after he had conquered those empires because there were no other worlds for him to conquer.

Jesus Christ lived only about 33 years, but during His lifetime He conquered more than simple empires. Upon His death, He conquered death, hell, and the grave. Before He died, He came to Jerusalem and wept over it. He wept aloud. All the insults and the sufferings of the Passion were powerless to elicit from the Man of Sorrows that expression of intense grief which was called forth by the thought of the ruin of the beloved city of Jerusalem. He was touched with a

THE NEAR SIDE

tender concern for it, His natural passions moved, and tears fell plentifully from His eyes.

The Lord Jesus loves us so much that He was moved to tears for our well-being. He wept over our sinful condition, knowing that His death on the cross would be the only way to bring sinful man back to a holy and righteous God. One of the simplest songs that has the most profound thought is, "Jesus loves me this I know, for the Bible tells me so." Let those deep-seated words sink down into your heart. Jesus, the sinless Son of God, loved me so much that He left His home in glory, to be born of a virgin, to live a sinless life, and to die on a cruel cross for sinful man. What was bitterness of soul for Alexander the Great was the sweetness of victory for Jesus in saving us.

Thought to ponder: "Jesus loves each one of us as if there were only one of us."

March 28

" For the eyes of the Lord are over the righteous, and his ears are open unto their prayers: but the face of the Lord is against them that do evil." 1 Peter 3:12 (KJV)

During our Wednesday evening services, a prayer sheet is handed out that has the names of individuals for whom our church is praying for. The list seems to grow and grow. There are physical, material, and spiritual needs. Each name on the list is called aloud, and then intercessory prayer is made for each one. I sat down the other day and looked over the list of individuals for whom I would be praying, and I noticed that there were several names I didn't know. These were people with which to associate a face with a name. I was tempted to simply call their names out without making any kind of request. The other names that I knew prompted me to spend more time in prayer. I soon realized that all needed prayer, so my supplications included each and every name on the sheet.

Our Lord has a prayer sheet, so to speak, that lists each one of our names. His list, like our church list, grows each

THE NEAR SIDE

day. He knows us by name. He is aware of our every need. There is not an incident that takes place in our life that He doesn't know about. He is aware of our insufficiency and inadequacy. He is never caught off guard when it comes to our deficiency. He is touched with the feelings of our infirmity, and He will always come to our aid at the right time. His presence in heaven is spent making intercession for each one of us. We can rejoice in the truth that our Lord knows all about us, and He spends time praying for us.

Thought to ponder: "Give your troubles to God; He'll be up all night anyway."

March 29

"For I determined not to know anything among you, save Jesus Christ, and him crucified." 1 Corinthians 2:2 (KJV)

The term "bucket list" was made famous by a movie of the same name. Two terminally ill men escape from a cancer ward and head off on a road trip with a wish list of to-dos before they die. The main plot follows two men (portrayed by Jack Nicholson, as Edward Cole and Morgan Freeman, as Carter Chambers) on their road trip with a want-to-do list of things to see and experience before they kick the bucket. It goes to show that some people will go to great lengths to accomplish a goal in life.

As Christians, we should have a "bucket list" of sorts when it comes to achieving some worthy aspirations. We should have a passion to accomplish some specific goals for the sake of the kingdom. With the eminent threat of death facing us each day, our ambition should be tempered by a desire to not simply finish the race but to finish with a flourish. Each endeavor should have a crowning touch of satisfaction in knowing that the ministry of our Lord is enlarged. Our desire should be more than just temporal satisfaction that a job has been done, but a heart for knowing that the Lord Jesus is pleased with our efforts.

Some of those "bucket list" engagements could be aiding in the accomplishment of the "Great Commission" of our Lord to His followers. Making disciples of all nations, baptizing them in the name of the Father, Son, and Holy Ghost, then teaching them to observe all the things the Master taught will be at the top of the list. Also on the schedule would be the salvation of our immediate family. Those parents, siblings, cousins, and other clan members deserve hearing the gospel message from us. That endeavor should be near the top. The list could go on; but one last determination on this "bucket list" of sorts would be the daily growing in grace and favor of our Lord Jesus Christ.

Thought to ponder: "Never live in hope and expectation with your arms folded."

March 30

"But they that wait upon the Lord shall renew their strength; they shall mount up with wings as eagles; they shall run, and not be weary; and they shall walk, and not faint."

Isaiah 40:31 (KJV)

Most runners have to stop when they reach their lactate threshold, but a guy by the name of Dean Karnazes' muscles never tire; he can run for three days and nights without stopping. From club runners to Olympians, every athlete has a limit. Scientifically, this limit is defined as the body's lactate threshold, and when you exercise beyond it, running rapidly becomes unpleasant. We've all experienced that burning feeling, the heart pounding, and the lungs gasping for air--as your muscles begin to fatigue, eventually locking up altogether as your body shuts down. However, there is one man whose physiological performance defies all convention: the afore-mentioned Dean Karnazes is an ultra runner from California, and at times, it seems as if he could run forever.

He has completed some of the toughest endurance events on the planet, from a marathon to the South Pole in temperatures of -25C to the legendary Marathon Des Sables, but in his entire life he has never experienced any form of muscle burn or cramp, even during runs exceeding 100 miles. It means his only limits are in his mind.

Isaiah speaks of those who shall run and not be weary in the way of God's commandments. That shows the great affection that the people of God have for them. They hasten to obey each one of Jehovah's injunctions and have a delight and pleasure to abide by them. Isaiah also adds that there will be a time that the child of God would walk and not faint in the ways of God, as they acknowledge Him as Creator and Sustainer of life. There would be a trusting in Him, continuing to do so, until they received the end of their faith, even the salvation of their souls. One last truth the prophet applies is that they would not sink under their burdens nor give out until they reach the end of their journey.

Thought to ponder: "When we do what we can, God will do what we can't."

March 31

"And Enoch walked with God; and he was not; for God took him." Genesis 5:24 (KJV)

I try to walk at least thirty minutes every day. Research has shown that the benefits of walking and moderate physical activity at that level can help reduce the risk of coronary disease; improve blood pressure and blood sugar levels; improve blood lipid profile; maintain body weight and lower the risk of obesity; and enhance mental well being. It's not always easy to get out of a warm bed on a cold morning and hit the trail, but the benefits far outweigh the effort.

I heard a self-made millionaire make the following statement: "As a professional in my business I sometimes find it difficult to walk with God between Sundays." He went on to say that being in church on a Sunday morning was like walking among sheep--those who went their deliberate way while worshipping with a quiet demeanor. He added that being in the world between Sundays was like working among wolves - their only goal was to rend and devour. He said that

THE NEAR SIDE

he found himself sinking to their methods of madness which only led him into deeper despair.

When you find yourself having a struggle living between Sundays, could I offer some good advice that has been given to me? They are two in number and many more could be added, but these are the top two for me. Number one: make Jesus the first appointment of your day. That will help get you on track to face the demands of the Mondays thru Saturdays. Don't take vacations between those days; make sure that you stick to your assignment book. Number two: be sure that you keep your mind stayed on the Lord. He is the One who will fill your thoughts with things that are honest, just, pure, lovely, and of a good report.

Thought to ponder: "It's alright to be cautious--but even a turtle never gets anywhere until he sticks his head out."

April 1

"These things I command you, that ye love one another."
John 15:17 (KJV)

April Fool's Day is celebrated every year on the first day of April. It has been popular since the 19th Century. It isn't a national holiday in any country, but it is well known in Canada, Europe, Australia, Brazil and the United States. The day is celebrated as a time when people play practical jokes and hoaxes on each other.

On this day, could I suggest that you do something positive for someone rather than playing a prank. A random act of kindness would be an appropriate gesture. The one I am making an annual commitment to will be to write a letter to someone who has made a difference in my life. Keeping in contact with those who have influenced me is a positive way that will also be beneficial to me. Because those people also represent a positive influence in my life and will continue to help me become the person I am striving to be, I owe a debt of gratitude to them. Letting them know they have inspired me will be a way to encourage them to keep on helping others as they have helped me.

From now on every April 1 will become "April Tools Day." God has given us a toolbox that is filled with all kinds of utensils that will enable us to show our love to each other through our words and our deeds. If this day has just begun for you, make sure you perform your random act of kindness. If your day is almost over, rush as quickly as you can to show someone that you genuinely care for them.

Thought to ponder: "No act of kindness, no matter how small, is ever wasted ."

April 2

"Having therefore, brethern, boldness to enter into the holiest by the blood of Jesus, by a new and living way, which he hath consecrated for us, through the veil, that is to say, his flesh."
Hebrews 10:19, 20 (KJV)

I am always getting sales publications in the mail. These are the kind that try to loosen a couple of dollars from my hand. Most of the papers, as attractive as they may be, end up in File 13 since they are mostly a nuisance and have no place among other important papers. Some of the ads are funny, while some are honest, and others are downright ridiculous. Here are a few of them:

"End of The Year Clearance--We Don't Need Them--But You Do!"

"Best Time To Buy Is Now. Don't Wait Another Minute."

"Biggest Sales Event of The Year." (The problem with this ad was that it was only January.)

"Going Out For Business."

"This Sale Is One For The Century."

THE NEAR SIDE

"Really Big Sales Event--You Have To Act Fast."
"Dealer Dicker Day!"
"The December To Remember Event."

When it comes to having a right connection with the heavenly Father, there are no coupons that can be redeemed. There are no rebates given, nor are there any allowances made on how good we are. God doesn't give discounts on being in a right relationship with Him. He doesn't offer to bargain with us from the standpoint of our righteousness. He doesn't trade all of our good deeds for a home in heaven. There are no bargains which we can appropriate for our standing with Him. The only merit we have will be found in the precious blood of the Lord Jesus. God only accepts that payment for our sins, and it is only through the sinless Son of God that we have any standing at all. "What can wash away my sin? Nothing but the blood of Jesus."

Thought to ponder: "Learn from the mistakes of others. You won't live long enough to make them all yourself."

April 3

"Therefore if any man be in Christ, he is a new creature: old things are passed away; behold, all things become new."
2 Corinthians 5:17 (KJV)

A recent visit to a local McDonalds restaurant brought me face to face with a metal bank sitting on the service counter that had these words written: "Your change changes everything." It was a deposit box for money that would help fund the needs of a local charity. I was glad to drop my spare change into the bank, thinking that my left over cash would in fact change someone's life. I do realize that there are many who are less fortunate than I. I'm thankful that there are champions who are willing to go to great extremes to help relieve the suffering of people in anguish. There is a segment in Christendom who have a desire that others may come to know this "new life" in Christ.

Paul speaks of a "change" that takes place in the life of an individual, forever changing their direction. It is a radical innovation. The old things are out and the new things are in. It's a double shift of direction from one that is walking away

THE NEAR SIDE

from God to another turning to God. That sort of innovation will change everything about a person's quality of living. It is the new birth. Paul talked about a "new creature" suggesting that of a new creation. The old things are the ancient things, or all those things which belong to the old Adam. The new creation is the whole sphere of being, and therewith the whole aim and character of life. Paul introduces the "new life" with the word "behold," which expresses his vivid realization of the truth he is about to utter. Our new birth experience is a radical change that will alter everything about us. I like the translation that reads: "Whoever is a believer in Christ is a new creation. The old way of living has disappeared. A new way of living has come into existence." It is the change that changes everything.

Thought to ponder: "It's better to look where you're going than to see where you've been."

April 4

"And His name shall be called Wonderful, Counselor, The mighty God, the everlasting Father, The Prince of Peace."
Isaiah 9:6 (KJV)

One of the privileges I have as a hybridizer of daylilies is to choose an appropriate name for a new introduction of mine. At the current time there are 75,000+ registered and named cultivars, and that means coming up with a unique name is getting tougher by the year. It's exciting to choose a name that hasn't been used. Each daylily has its own unique DNA structure, and each flower is distinctive in its own way. I try to come up with a catchy phrase that best describes how I view the flower. Some of the names I have used in the introduction process are:

White Silver Sands--Jurassic Dark--Sophomore Green--Lollipop Mama--Sea Of Galilee

The Lord Jesus has been given some special names that describe Who He is. Each name is unique within itself because of Who it points to. These designations describe His deity; they provide insights into His ministry; they point us to His splendor; they give us all that we need to know about Him and His relationship with the Father. Some of those names and their meanings are:

Christ--Greek for Messiah (Anointed One).

Son Of God--Jesus was not the son of any mortal man. His father was God, the Father.

The Lord--The confession of the early church was "Jesus is Lord" and could only mean that Jesus is Jehovah.

Savior--The most sublime of all titles, Savior underscores Jesus' role in the divine plan of redemption.

Alpha And Omega--Equivalent to the Old Testament term "the first and the last."

Lamb Of God--In the first Passover, a slain lamb's blood was daubed on Israelites' houses to avert the destroyer. In the New Testament, Jesus is understood as the Passover Lamb supplied by God. Many more are the namesakes of our Lord Jesus, and He is worthy of all and more.

Thought to ponder: "Make long-range plans as if you are going to live forever, and live today as if it were your last day on earth."

April 5

"Jesus Christ the same yesterday, and today, and forever."
Hebrews 13:8 (KJV)

During the invocation of a Sunday morning worship service, one of the deacons assigned to pray included these words in his opening petition: "Lord, the time has changed, but You have not." He was referring to Daylight Savings Time (DST). It is the practice of advancing clocks during summer months by one hour so that light extends into the evening hours. Typically, users of DST adjust clocks forward an hour near the start of spring and adjust them backward in the fall to a normal or regular time.

Many in the congregation were feeling the effects of losing an hour's sleep. Someone was heard to say that they did not like change, and when DST came, it was a struggle for them to maintain their focus. I am thankful that the deacon reminded us that even though DST brings change, our Lord God does not. He is the same at every juncture of the year whether it be winter, spring, summer, or fall. God does not change like the weather; one day cold, the next day

THE NEAR SIDE

hot. He does not have an occasion to be loving in one place and time as opposed to another place and time. He is always the same. It would be contrary to His nature to be otherwise.

The author of the book of Hebrews reminds us that God is a constant. That is one of the most encouraging verses in all of the Bible. It paves the way for me to be consistent in all my pursuits. The unwavering ways of God challenge me to remain faithful in the tough times that our Lord said would surely come. The unchangeableness of God incentivizes me to be constant in my journeys. The absolute trustworthiness of our Lord gives me a gritty determination to remain trustworthy to Him, and because He is faithful to me, I can and must be faithful to Him.

Thought to ponder: "Life is a grindstone. Whether it grinds us down or polishes us depends on us."

April 6

"Call unto me, and I will answer thee, and shew thee great and mighty things which thou knowest not."

Jeremiah 33:3 (KJV)

A local personal injury lawyer has a catchy phrase that advertises his business: "One call, that's all." This particular individual provides legal representation to those who claim to have been injured, physically or psychologically, as a result of the negligence or wrongdoing of another person, company, government agency, or other entity. If you have been injured in any way, you have the assurance that this lawyer has your back. Though his intentions may be more for himself than yours, one thing is certain, and that is: "One, call, that's all!"

Have you ever had an important person give you a card with their unlisted number on it and say, "Call me?" If someone important gives you his private number, that's a great privilege. Almighty God came to Jeremiah and did just that. The scripture verse for today expresses the importance of the Person Who spoke to Jeremiah, and what God was about to do would exceed even the expectations of the prophet himself. Equally true, our loving heavenly Father has made a promise to us that if we will call on Him, He will answer. Like Jeremiah, we have God's personal number. He gave us His card, saying, "There it is. And I want you to call Me." There's not one of us who cannot contact heaven. Never say in a situation, "There's nothing I can do." You can pray, and when you do, start watching for those "great and mighty things" that will begin to happen.

Thought to ponder: "We have to pray with our eyes on God, not on the difficulties."

April 7

"Be kindly affectioned one to another with brotherly love; in honour preferring one another." Romans 12:10 (KJV)

A man was walking down the street and saw a man struggling with a washing machine in his front doorway. The man ran over and said, "Let me help you." After wrestling with the washer for 30 minutes, the helper said, "I don't think we'll ever get this washer in." The homeowner said, "Get it in? I'm trying to move it out!"

We need to make sure that we are helping people rather than hindering them. Some people get bogged down in the daily routines of life and look for someone to not simply give them a handout but a hand-up. Our hands can be buckets of encouragement for the weak and heavy hearted. Our words can be like balloons of joy that lift the spirits of those who are downtrodden. Sometimes life sends a lemon rather than a peach, and that lemon makes life bitter to the taste. Loneliness, disappointment, and frustration are like bars of steel wrapped around the feet, pulling the weak down. There

THE NEAR SIDE

is no exercise better for the heart than reaching down and lifting someone up.

God has given to each one of us the opportunity to be His hands, His feet, and His heart. We have a ministry of help that can be instrumental in nurturing the needy and serving the body of Christ. The means by which we do this is through the empowerment of the Holy Spirit who moves us into the mainstream of ministry. He calls us. He equips us. He helps us. He encourages us. It's all about Him and all for Him.

Thought to ponder: "If you're helping someone and expecting something in return, you're doing business, not kindness."

April 8

"Blessed be the God and Father of our Lord Jesus Christ, who hath blessed us with all spiritual blessings in heavenly places in Christ." Ephesians 1:3 (KJV)

Googolplexian is the world's largest number (biggest) with a name: the number One--followed by a googolplexian of zeros. It goes without saying that that is a rather large number. Not many people could get their mind wrapped around such a vast set of digits. I sure would not want to spend the amount of time it would take to put a dent into such a massive number, but I would like to suggest, though, that we begin to count our blessings. The song states: "Count your blessings, name them one by one; count your blessings, see what God has done! Count your blessings, name them one by one; and it will surprise you what the Lord has done."

We can begin to add up the number of blessings from the Lord on a daily basis. In doing so, it will lead us to such a vast number of advantages, exceeding our imagination. The very air we breathe is a windfall of good. The food we eat is

THE NEAR SIDE

a gift from the hand of a loving Lord. The water provided to us is beneficial to good health. If we want to feel rich, we can count all the blessings that money cannot buy. It is better to lose count while naming those blessings than to lose those blessings while counting our troubles. We have so much to be thankful for, and the very least we could do is to name them one by one.

I received an email the other day that had these words written: "Count your blessings and your problems. If your problems out number your blessings, count again. Chances are the things you take for granted were not added."

Thought to ponder: "Keep calm and count your blessings. Before too long you may have a googolplexian of them."

April 9

"He which testifieth these things saith, Surely I come quickly. Amen. Even so, come, Lord Jesus." Revelation 22:20 (KJV)

When Albert Einstein died, his final words died with him. The nurse at his side did not understand German. For the rest of this earthly life, we'll never know what was on Einstein's mind. On the other hand, the last words of our Lord Jesus can be found in Revelation 22:20, "Surely, I come quickly." Those words have been recorded for us by the apostle John. Down through the years the promise of our Lord's coming would be a treasure of hope for every Christian. John understood to a great extent what the Lord Jesus was saying. He would give a hearty "Amen" to those unforgettable words. They would find a place of permanent rest in John's mind as he lived out his banishment to the Isle of Patmos.

We have no reason to confuse the words of our soon coming Lord, or lose sight of that blessed hope. These final words of Jesus are especially filled with meaning for every Christian. They secure us in the fact that one day Jesus will

THE NEAR SIDE

come and take us to our heavenly home. Our labors on earth will cease and our future will be filled with joy for evermore. The very thought that this could be the day that Jesus returns gives us the confidence to face each waiting minute with expectance. The soon coming, triumphant Lord states unequivocally, "SURELY! I am coming." With those words we can say in chorus with the apostle, "Even so, come, Lord Jesus."

Thought to ponder: "Nothing is more prominently brought forward in the New Testament than the second coming of Jesus Christ."

April 10

"Ye are the light of the world. A city that is set on a hill cannot be hid." Matthew 5:14 (KJV)

The brightest burst of light ever seen peaked at a few hundred billion times the brightness of our Sun and has been witnessed by astronomers. Gamma-Ray Bursts are the most powerful bangs in the cosmos. They occur in far-off galaxies and so are usually faint. The enormous energy released in the explosion was brighter than the light from all of the stars in five million Milky Way Galaxies. The spectacular show was caused by the death of a massive star which collapsed to form a black hole.

Jesus spoke of a greater opportunity that we as Christians have when it comes to the salvation of mankind. He said that we are the light of the world. In other words, what the luminaries (the sun and moon) are in the heavens with respect to corporal light, that we are in the world with regard to spiritual light. We have the privilege of carrying and spreading the light of the Gospel not only in our community but also in our State, our United States, and ultimately to the ends of the earth. We are to faithfully carry the light of the Lord Jesus with us into a darkened environment as we reach out to a lost and dying world.

Jesus does not say that we are like light, but rather we are the light. In this world in which we live, it has been darkened by sin, and the only light that will be seen is that which we allow to shine through us. Jesus Himself said that He is the light of the world and when He is given His rightful place in our life, He will shine Himself through us. There is no greater warrant than to allow the "Light Of The World" to radiate through our life.

Thought to ponder: "Darkness cannot drive out darkness-- only light can do that."

April 11

"How sweet are thy words unto my taste yea, sweeter than honey to my mouth!" Psalms 119:103 (KJV)

The sweetest known substance on earth is Stevia rebaudiana more commonly known as Stevia or simply sweet leaf. It is said that it is 300 times sweeter than sugar. It has no calories and other studies suggest that it might have extra health benefits. The saying that a little goes a long way could very well be said of this sweetener.

Years before Stevia was discovered, the Psalmist spoke of the sweetness of the words of Jehovah. If the Psalmist lived in our century, he could very well say that the doctrines of grace, the truths of the Gospel, were delightful and pleasant to him; like unadulterated milk, desirable by him; like good wine, that goes down sweetly; like good food, that is exceeding palatable; or like honey, and even sweeter. The laws of God were sweeter than honey to David's mouth. They not only had a nourishing nature; they had the refreshing virtue of honey and sweetness that exceeded his taste.

Psalms 34:8 says, "Oh taste and see that the Lord is good." We are challenged to put the matter to the test of experience; there is no other way of really knowing how good God is. As we read the Bible, we are ingesting the very words of God Himself. As we are digesting those precepts, there is a sweetness of taste that lingers in our mouth, a sensation that exceeds even the tastiness of honey itself.

Thought to ponder: "Stick to your job until one of you is finished."

April 12

"Know therefore that the LORD thy God, he is God, the faithful God, which keepeth covenant and mercy with them that love him and keep his commandments to a thousand generations." Deuteronomy 7:9 (KJV)

The movie "Groundhog Day" was a story of Phil Connors (played by Bill Murray) who was an arrogant Pittsburgh TV weatherman who, during an assignment covering the annual Groundhog Day event in Punxsutawney, Pennsylvania, finds himself in a time loop, repeating the same day again and again. After indulging in hedonism (the pursuit of pleasure; sensual self-indulgence), he begins to re-examine his life and priorities. Day after day the same events repeating themselves would drive any sensible person crazy.

When it comes to the faithfulness of God, on the other hand, there is what I call a "spiritual groundhog day" that comes around continuously for every member of the Body of Christ. It is the same events of the Lord's friendly persuasion toward His children. Day following day, the generous supply of all our needs can be experienced. Hour by hour, the

THE NEAR SIDE

trustworthiness of God can be seen is His bountiful provisions. Minute after minute, our Lord draws us ever so closer to Himself. Second by second the joy of the Lord becomes our strength. Every waking minute of every blissful day is in store for those who have put their trust and confidence in the God of this universe. He is steadfast in calling us, and He will perform that which He promised.

Thought to ponder: "Great is the faithfulness of our loving heavenly Father."

April 13

"Sing, O daughter of Zion; shout O Israel; be glad and rejoice with all the heart, O daughter of Jerusalem."

Zephaniah 3:14 (KJV)

When the Bible says, "Let the redeemed of the Lord say so," (Psalm 107:2a) it was not an invitation to consider but rather a command to do so. On the one hand this should not be something that we have to be told to do. On the other hand, because of the goodness of the Lord, we should notify our lips so that they could rejoice aloud in the Lord God.

The prophet Zephaniah issued four triumphant commands to the redeemed of the Lord. He said that they were to sing. Music is the song of the heart. Whether we are trained in music or not, our part is to celebrate with the tongue this melody of praise. It is imperative that we sing unto the Lord. Because of the many benefits and blessings of redemption, we should vocalize our songs.

Not only are we to sing, but we are also commanded to shout to the Lord. Some people are timid when it comes to shouting in a company of believers. There are times to be silent in the presence of the Lord and there are times to make a joyful noise unto the Lord. Every day is the right time to give a shout of praise to our blessed Redeemer.

We are to sing, to shout, to be glad, and to rejoice. Being glad and rejoicing are brought together because one feeds off the other. As we sing and shout to the Lord, it brings out a gladness of heart that issues forth a rejoicing in the Lord. When we rejoice in the Lord, it means that we are glad at heart, and, yes, God does love a cheerful heart. It is our Master's desire to hear the words of praise from His humble servants.

Thought to ponder: "Though I may not be able to 'carry a tune in a bucket,' I can carry a bucket of tunes before the Lord and sing them unto Him."

April 14

"Ye are of God, little children, and have overcome them; because greater is he that is in you, than he that is in the world." 1 John 4:4 (KJV)

On December 8, 1941, the day after the dastardly attack on Pearl Harbor, President Franklin D. Roosevelt delivered his famous "a date which will live in infamy" speech. Within an hour of the public address, Congress passed a formal declaration of war against Japan and officially brought the U.S. into World War II. The United States of America was suddenly and deliberately attacked by naval and air forces of the Empire of Japan. As a part of his speech, President Roosevelt said, "No matter how long it may take us to overcome this premeditated invasion, the American people in their righteous might will win through absolute victory." These words would inspire a nation to rise up together, above the evil acts of the enemy, to secure a triumph of will.

I am thankful that we had a leader at the time who would stand so stanchly against the forces of evil and deliver such

THE NEAR SIDE

a powerful message of response. Our president had the full force of the United States armies at his disposal, so he could count on the victory. As Christians, we have a more sure word of victory over our arch enemy. It comes from the inspired word of God. We are called "dear children" and are assured that we belong to God. Because of our kinship with the Father, we are already victorious over the enemy, and the reason we have the mastery is that we have a power far greater than any human expectation. That force is the Holy Spirit of God. We live in victory because He lives within us.

Thought to ponder: "Victory over the enemy is more than just a group of words, it is a guarantee."

April 15

"Upon the first day of the week let every one of you lay by him in store, as God hath prospered him, that there be no gatherings when I come." 1 Corinthians 16:2 (KJV)

In the United States, "Tax Day" is a colloquial term for the day on which individual tax returns are due to the Federal Government. The term may also refer to the same day for states even though the tax return due date is a different day. Since 1955, for those living in the United States, Tax Day has typically fallen on April 15. The day is not one of those dates you like to see come around, especially if you owe Uncle Sam some money.

Paul wrote to the believers in Corinth and instructed them to make some preparations for their giving. It was not to be done blindly but with eyes wide open, and deliberately. He gave to the believers the day the offering was to be done, and that would be on Sunday, the first day of the week. That would be the most opportune time to give. As believers gather for worship, a part of our homage is in giving our offering and the Lord's tithe. This is one way that all of us can be joined together in worship. Paul also pointed out that "all" were to be involved in giving; the young, old, rich, poor, all were to be linked together in the act of almsgiving. No one was to be exempt. He went on to instruct the believers that they were to give in proportion to how God had blessed them; that is to say, all that His prosperity may permit. The Lord does not look so much on what we give in the amount, but rather what we have left over. We are to give in proportion to what we have been permitted to have. After all, everything belongs to the Father.

Thought to ponder: "Our giving is a silent way of testifying how much we love the Lord."

April 16

"But where sin abounded, grace did much more abound."
Romans 5:20b (KJV)

How many different ways can you say "grace?" No need to get your handy thesaurus out and find a synonym to describe it. It is more than simply substituting for another word. That can be easily done. I am talking about a word preceding grace, describing the way it can be encountered and experienced. Grace can be expressed as the unmerited love and favor of God. It is the love and mercy given to us by God because He desires us to have it, not because of anything we have done to earn it. A good translation of the Romans 5:20 verse is, "But where sin increased, grace abounded all the more."

John Newton was a hymnist and writer. He is best known for his sacred song, "Amazing Grace." It was, according to Newton, a message that forgiveness and redemption are possible regardless of sins committed and that the soul can be delivered from despair through the mercy of God. "Amazing Grace" is one of the most recognizable songs in the

English-speaking world. If you carefully read the lyrics of the song, Newton expresses six qualities of grace. Each one gives us a different way to say "grace."

First, grace is "Amazing." Now you can retrieve your thesaurus and see the plethora of words that will describe amazing: awesome, incredible, marvelous, prodigious, stunning, unbelieving, wonderful, etc.

Second, Newton states that grace is "Teaching." The words are, "Twas grace that taught my heart to fear..." Grace will teach us to have a healthy reverence for God.

Third, grace is "Relieving." Again, the words are, "And grace my fears relieved..." Grace will sustain us in the times we become exposed to dangers.

Fourth, we read that grace is, "Appearing." Newton penned these words, "How precious did that grace appear..." Just when I need grace, the Lord sends it my way just at the right time. He is never too early or too late; He is always on time.

Fifth, grace is "Delivering," The song continues, "Tis grace hath brought me safe thus far..." Grace is a good taxi ride for all of us. God provides the way for His matchless grace to carry us safely along the highway of life.

APRIL 16

Sixth, God's grace is "Leading." And the song vibrates with these words, "And grace will lead me home..." I am thankful that I have a constant companion with me every step of the way as I make my journey to the celestial city of heaven. Grace will be there with me, safely leading me homeward.

Thought to ponder: "Amazing Grace, how sweet the sound that saved a wretch like me."

April 17

"There hath no temptation taken you but such as is common to man; but God is faithful, who will not suffer you to be tempted above that ye are able; but will with the temptation also make a way of escape, that ye may be able to bear it."

1 Corinthians 10:13 (KJV)

"Old Faithful" is a cone geyser located in Wyoming, in Yellowstone National Park. It was named in 1870 during the Washburn-Langford-Doane Expedition and was the first geyser in the park to receive a name. It is one of the most predictable geographical features on Earth, erupting almost every 63 minutes. Eruptions can shoot 3,700 to 8,400 US gallons of boiling water to a height of 106 to 185 feet lasting from 1.5 to 5 minutes. A joke among some geyser gazers, when asked in the summer by a park visitor about when Old Faithful will next erupt, is to ask the visitor about the "Old Faithful Indicator." That indicator states that Old Faithful will come through as it always has.

APRIL 17

The verse today states three truths about the faithfulness of God. Paul said that God has a concern for us. He writes that God is faithful. Those are the most encouraging words anyone could have spoken to them. Of all the physical relationships we have, they have a tendency to fail, but not with our great God who has been, is, and will always be faithful to us. Paul further points out the care God has for us. He says again that God will not allow us to be tested above that we are able. Like a sentinel who stands watch over a valued object, God will not permit anything or anybody to come against His child unless He permits it. Paul ends this thought about the faithfulness of God by adding the cover God has provided for us. Like a roaring fire blazing a way through the wilderness, our loving Father provides a pathway leading out of the wilderness of testing into the street of victory. Truly our great God is faithful 24/7!

Thought to ponder: "Have character, don't be one."

April 18

"Remember Lot's wife." Luke 17:32 (KJV)

The Alamo was once a Spanish mission that was turned into a battleground for Texas independence. Mexican soldiers, lead by Santa Anna, outnumbered, attacked, and defeated the Texans and Tejanos who sought refuge in the mission. The quote, "Remember the Alamo," was the war cry of those soldiers who later attacked and defeated Santa Anna. The words would be a clarion call to rise up and bring victory to Texans.

Jesus said to His disciples that they were to keep before them constantly the words "remember Lot's wife." They were going to face some trying times, and in the midst of their troubles, they were to call to remembrance what happened to Lot's wife. She and her looking back is all that is said of her in the scriptures. The Bible only records her eventual doom. Her heart was in Sodom still. She "looked back-- she delayed--perhaps she desired to take something with her, and God made her a monument of His displeasure.

APRIL 18

Lot's wife had some privileges she took for granted. She married into a godly family and knew the way of salvation. In 2 Peter 2:7 we are told that Lot was rescued by God from Sodom because he was a righteous man. His wife lived under the influence of someone loved by God, but those privileges never made their way into her heart.

Don't just remember her privileges, but remember her sin. She lingered when the angel first spoke to her, and she lingered again. I can, in my mind's eye, almost imagine those two angels. The first angel in one hand has Lot, and in the other hand has his wife, and Lot is running as fast as his feet can carry him. The second angel has Lot's two daughters, and then all of a sudden he is slowed down as Lot's wife starts to linger. Her heart was still in Sodom, and she had to take one last look, and the rest is history.

When we think about the privileges we have and the sins that doth so easily beset us, it is incumbent upon us to keep before us the words of our Lord, "Remember Lot's wife."

Thought to ponder: "If we do not learn from our mistakes, we are doomed to repeat them."

April 19

"Now unto him that is able to do exceeding abundantly above all that we ask or think, according to the power that worketh in us." Ephesians 3:20 (KJV)

I saw an advertisement on the back of a moving van that said, "Anything! Anywhere! Any Time!" The ad insisted that the business could move anything that anybody had, anywhere in the United States, at any time they were needed. That, to me, is a rather strong assertion. There could possibly be someone who could come up with something that would be too large to move. There could also be an area so remote that it would take an act of God to get them there, and I am fairly positive that there would be a time this business could not fulfill their promise. The pronouncement further stated that this was not merely a promise but a guarantee.

Paul tells us that our God is more than able to do for us far above what we may ask or think. This excess is denoted by a double term of abundance: "exceeding abundantly." Try to get your mind wrapped around that glorious thought. It's

APRIL 19

as if the apostle wished to fill our minds with the idea of absolute infinity of the gracious power of God, which is none other than the power "which He wrought in Christ, when He raised Him from the dead." This is Paul's way of celebrating the power of God, a perfection which is essential unto God, and is very large and extensive. The things that are impossible to man are possible with and through God, and we have this unfailing promise from our Father that His word is not merely a promise but a guarantee.

Thought to ponder: "It takes a lot of horse sense to maintain a stable life."

April 20

"For he that will love life, and see good days, let him refrain his tongue from evil, and his lips that they speak no guile."
1 Peter 3:10 (KJV)

Checking out at a local retail store, I swiped my debit card and waited for the cashier to finish the transaction. I had gone through the gauntlet of entering my PIN, no cash back, and "is this amount correct?" I waited, thinking I had done my part and asked the lady behind the counter if I could have my receipt. She had been talking to other employees and probably had canceled the transaction. She looked at me with a puzzled enquiry and said, "You ain't did nuttin' yet."

Being a stickler for grammatical correctness, those words were like the blast of a shotgun ringing in my ear. It was like someone taking a string and running them between my ears. I was taken aback at her response. Now, I am not bashing the lady for the improper use of grammar because I have done the same on many occasions in the past. What her reply showed me was how we as Christians oftentimes use

APRIL 20

the right words but have hearts disengaged. In other words there are situations when we say things which have a hollowness to them.

Sometimes we say, "I love you," and our mouths may be engaged in words, but our hearts are divorced from meaning them. It is easy to say something and not mean it. Our intentions may be good, but, unless we are willing to put action to our words, then all we are doing is talking the talk. Other times we may resemble the idiom, "Speak with a forked tongue." That means we make false promises or speak in a way which is not honest. This can happen when we sing a song out of our hymnbook and not mean the words. A good example may be, "Wherever He leads, I'll go." We are prone to use the right vocabulary and yet miss the commitment to follow through. One of the lines in the song states, "I'll follow my Christ who loves me so; wherever He leads I'll go." Our tongues may sing the words, but our profession doesn't quite make it to our feet so that we may walk the walk.

Thought to ponder: "We are not only a walking miracle, we are a talking miracle as well."

April 21

"Having your conversation honest among the Gentiles; that, whereas they speak against you as evildoers, they may by your good works, which they shall behold, glorify God in the day of visitation." 1 Peter 2:12 (KJV)

A group of scientists has adjusted its imaginary "Doomsday Clock" closer to "midnight," raising awareness of our worlds' vulnerability to catastrophe. Since 1947, the Science and Security Board of the Bulletin of Atomic Scientists at the University of Chicago has published a symbolic clock representing how close we are to a global catastrophe. Pardon the pun, please, but it doesn't take a rocket scientist to see how close we as a church are to the return of the Lord Jesus.

The second coming of Christ is a prevailing theme of the New Testament. It is referenced eight times more often than the Lord's initial coming. It is alluded to more than 300 times in the New Testament. So, there is no excuse for the child of God to be ignorant about the His coming.

APRIL 21

The question should be asked: "What should I do in light of the Lord's coming?" First thing, be ready. 1 Thessalonians 5:2 states, "For yourselves know perfectly that the day of the Lord so cometh as a thief in the night." We do not know the time nor the date of His coming. Matthew 24:36 says, "But of that day and hour knoweth no man, no, not the angels of heaven, but my Father only." Only the Heavenly Father knows when the time has come. Second, be faithful. Don't think that just because the Lord has tarried His coming that we can live as we please. Every day, it's getting closer, going faster than a roller coaster. The Lord is coming, and each waking minute should find us being faithful about the Master's business. Third, and not least, we should be thankful. We should be thankful that the Lord Jesus saved us from the wrath to come, and is preparing a home in heaven for us. Our lives should be lived out of gratefulness that finds its expression in praise and adoration.

Thought to ponder: "You can tell when you're on the right road--it's uphill."

April 22

"By whom also we have access by faith into this grace wherein we stand, and rejoice in hope of the glory of God."
Romans 5:2 (KJV)

Someone suggested the other day that we could treat our Bible as we would an iPhone. This device is called by many as a "smartphone." There can be some very "smart ways" to utilize the sacred scriptures God gave for our use such as using the occasion to capture some of the moments in God's love letter to us to better appreciate Him and His great love rather than letting them lie around the house collecting dust.

A few ways the iPhone could be used smartly would be making payments, avoiding speed traps, tuning your guitar, storing electronic medical records, remotely controlling access to your house, as a cooking guide, and many more usages. As children of God, we should exercise the gift of God's Word in majestic ways. We should never leave home without our Bible. I realize that we cannot carry a Bible with us at every waking moment, but we can hide His word in

April 22

our heart and have it with us at all times. We should depend upon the promises of God to be truthful and trustworthy. This will aid us in getting through the tough times of life. We have access to God's internet of prayer 24 hours a day. We always have a connection to heaven and should avail ourselves of this privilege. Just as an iPhone needs to be charged, so do we in our walk of life. That "charging" comes as we stay close to the Father and allow Him to lead us through the Holy Spirit.

Thought to ponder: "The first step to wisdom is silence; the second is listening."

April 23

"As yet I am as strong this day as I was in the day that Moses sent me; as my strength was then, even so is my strength now, for war, both to go out and to come in." Joshua 14:11 (KJV)

You will see all kinds of people when you work at a local antique mall. There are folks who may be rich or poor, young or old, bargain hunters or big spenders. I cannot help but read the different messages on the tee-shirts that people wear when they frequent the shop. Some carry positive endorsements; others portray things that are downright stupid; while some are conversation starters. I saw one which was worn by a Vietnam veteran with these words, "Worn Out Veteran - Do Not Discard!" Curiously I asked him what the message meant, and he responded, "I have pretty well done everything this world has offered, and now I am just worn-out!" I thanked him for his service and assured him that his life was not totally wasted.

I think about another veteran in the scriptures who had been faithful to the Lord. His name was Caleb. At the age of forty he and Joshua had been sent out by Moses, with

APRIL 23

eight other men, to spy out the country of Canaan, and to bring back a report. Eight of the ten brought back an evil report while two brought back a good report. Caleb and Joshua were bold enough to put their trust and confidence in God to bring them into the land flowing with milk and honey. Fast forward forty years, and Caleb is now eighty years old and he is by no means worn-out. He states that as his strength was then (40 years old), even so now (80 years old) was his strength to do whatever the Lord had given him. When Caleb reached the autumn years of his life, he did not put his life in neutral; he kicked it up a notch to drive the enemy out of his inheritance, Hebron.

Could I offer some things that we are never too old to do: First, we are never too old to stop dreaming. At the age of 65, struggling to make ends meet, Harland Sanders began franchising restaurants touting the secret blend of 11 herbs and spices. By 1965, the Kentucky Fried Chicken chain had grown to 600 franchises and now serves more than 12 million customers daily in 110 countries. Second, we are never too old to make a difference. You can be salt and light in a flavorless and dark society. Jesus did not say that we were like salt and light; He said that we are! If you have a bucket list, get it out and start filling in the blanks. Third, we are never too old to start something new. Fourth, we are never too old to stop caring about the needs of others.

Thought to ponder: "Anyone can steer the ship when the sea is calm."

April 24

"For ye know the grace of our Lord Jesus Christ, that, though he was rich, yet for your sakes he became poor, that ye through his poverty might be rich." 2 Corinthians 8:9 (KJV)

The thought occurred to me that everything I have in my possession, spiritually speaking, is at the expense of the Lord Jesus and what He did for me on the cross. If someone makes a joke about me or laughs at me, the joke or laughter is said to be at my expense. I try not to treat other people like that when I am in their presence or at their absence. I want to be as courteous to them as I would want them to be to me. What we as Christians enjoy in the Lord has come at Jesus' expense. The idiom "at someone's expense" means to be paid for by someone. Jesus truly did pay it all and all to Him we owe.

There are several things that we have in our possession that come as a result of what our Lord has done for us at His expense. Because His heart was broken, our heart has been healed. "Oh what a Savior, O hallelujah! His heart was broken on Calvary." Because of the cross, God has given us a

APRIL 24

new heart. He was despised and rejected, but we have been accepted and are loved. Isaiah 53:3 says, "He is despised and rejected of men." On the cross Jesus cried out, "My God, My God, why hast Thou forsaken Me?" In His shame He was disrobed, but we have been robed in His righteousness. In 2 Corinthians 5:21 we read, "For He hath made Him to be sin for us, who knew no sin; that we might be made the righteousness of God in Him." Because He died, we can live. The words of a classic hymn has these words: "Because He lives, I can face tomorrow; Because He lives, all fear is gone; Because I know He holds the future; and life is worth the living, Just because He lives!" What we have and all that we will ever come into possession of is at the expense of Jesus!

Thought to ponder: "You ask me how I know my Saviour lives; He lives within my heart."

April 25

"But these are written, that ye might believe that Jesus is the Christ, the Son of God; and that believing ye might have life through his name." John 20:31 (KJV)

The hymn, "Almost Persuaded," was suggested to Philip Paul Bliss, an American composer, conductor, writer of hymns and a bass-baritone Gospel singer, after hearing a sermon by Mr. Brundage, who, as he finished his message, said, "He who is almost persuaded is almost saved, and to be almost saved is to be entirely lost." There is something ominous about those words, "Almost Persuaded." They seem to have a good intention driving them, but ultimately the confession becomes empty sounds. They have a deep sense of someone coming so close and yet being so far away. The Christian life is not one of "almost persuaded," but rather of being "fully persuaded."

How can we know that we know that we have eternal life? Not a hope so, but a know so kind of salvation. To have assurance and peace of mind, this question must be addressed and answered. The Word of God presents a clear

APRIL 25

path to eternal life. It starts by understanding that God has given us an important manual for life called the Bible. He is the Author of this book and has given significant, truthful instructions for how we can have joy, hope, and peace in life, and how we can have eternal life.

The scriptures give us the force of believing that Jesus is the Promised One, the Son of God; and by putting our faith in the truth of His Word, we can know that we know that we have eternal life. Rather than asking the Lord for more faith, start by ingesting the Word every day and then digesting it throughout the hours that follow. The Word will then become a burning fire within us, inspiring us to climb to greater heights.

Thought to ponder: "Physical life is short, eternal life is forever."

April 26

"Henceforth there is laid up for me a crown of righteousness, which the Lord, the righteous judge, shall give me at that day; and not to me only, but unto all them also that love his appearing." 2 Timothy 4:8 (KJV)

On this day, April 26, 1931, Lou Gehrig hit a home run but is called out for passing a runner, and his mistake cost him the American League home run crown; he and Babe Ruth tied for the season. What seemed to be a harmless blunder cost Gehrig a crown. He would have to settle with a tie with his teammate. It is said that Gehrig lived for the rest of his life with regret that he had not paid close attention to what he was doing. He said that he was caught up in the moment and things ran awry. A crown would be gone forever.

Paul spoke about the "crown of righteousness" which the Lord had in store for him when he came into His presence. The crown was a garland used to be bestowed on the successful competitor in wrestling, running, and other competitions at the Greek national games. It was something that

APRIL 26

the apostle kept before him in his Christian walk. Every day started out with the stark reminder that he was in the race of his life. The enemy would perch himself at each turn of the journey to hinder his progress. Keeping the crown before him, Paul would double down and with a determined effort keep running the race set before him. When the race was complete and the conflict had been waged, all which was now necessary to complete the whole transaction was merely that the crown be bestowed, and that was what kept the apostle maintaining an unbreakable spirit.

Thought to ponder: "The race does not always go to the swift, but to the ones who keep running."

April 27

"Enlarge the place of thy tent, and let them stretch forth the curtains of thine habitations; spare not, lengthen thy cords, and strengthen thy stakes." Isaiah 54:2 (KJV)

Our faith needs to be stretched in order to be strengthened. God will stretch us to our limits not to disconnect us but to reinforce us. A strength that is small in the day of adversity will falter at the feet of trials. When we expand our muscles, it is a painful experience. "No pain. No gain." That is what bodybuilders teach us. The benefits of developing muscle strength far outweigh the sacrifice. God's plan is not to break us, though that could be one of the results of stretching us. His underlying intention is to invigorate us with His power. Stretched beyond our limits, we have no control over our circumstances; and as a result, we are driven to our knees with total dependence upon God for deliverance.

A "thorn in the flesh" will stretch our faith toward submission to the will of God. Before the Apostle Paul's encounter with his "thorn," there was an attitude of pride.

APRIL 27

He tells his readers about the discomfort that was given him. The apparent purpose of this irritation was beneficiary. Its intent was to keep Paul from conceit on account of his visions and revelations which otherwise may have given him a reason to boast. It sounds like an oxymoron when Paul said that the thorn was beneficial. The godsend was that He was drawn closer to the Lord's side, while hearing these words, "My grace is sufficient for you, for power is perfected in weakness." Paul was stretched beyond his limits with the end result of being strengthened for the task.

Thought to ponder: "Power from the Lord is perfected in our weakness."

April 28

"The Spirit of the Lord is upon me, because he hath anointed me to preach the gospel to the poor; he hath sent me to heal the brokenhearted, to preach deliverance to the captives, and recovering of sight to the blind, to set at liberty them that are bruised." Luke 4:18 (KJV)

A godly minister, whom I look up to as a mentor, once said to me, "As good as some people may think I am, if they look long enough and hard enough they will find something to criticize me about." I certainly do understand what he was saying. People can find wrong in most anything they see. The same could be said about the church where the masses attend. Folks can always find fault in the people who frequent the place of worship. "What is wrong with the church?" is a question many pundits ask. Well, there could be a long list of troubles which could be summed up as "people problems."

"What is right with the church?" should be the greater question. There is so much that the church does that could be labeled as proper and fitting. First, the church has the

APRIL 28

"right message." It is the good news of salvation by grace through faith. In this darkened world in which we live the gospel is the light that shines in the darkness, leading people to a saving knowledge of Jesus Christ. Second, the church has the "right mission." That endeavor is what we call the "Great Commission." The church is going forth bearing the light of the gospel to make disciples of all nations; baptizing them in the name of the Father, Son, and Holy Ghost; and teaching them to observe all that the Lord has instructed. Third, the church has the "right Master." He is none other than the Lord Jesus, who has laid down His life for us and has asked us to do nothing less than to take up our cross and follow Him in the way of holiness. Fourth, the church has the "right ministry." That outreach is to the masses who are hurting. The church should be a hospital for sinners, not a museum for the saints. People who name the Name of Christ and worship within the walls of the meeting place have in their possession the ability to heal the wounds of the tormented and to warm the hearts of the faithful.

Thought to ponder: "Do not mistake activity for achievement."

April 29

"All scripture is given by inspiration of God, and is profitable for doctrine, for reproof, for correction, for instruction in righteousness. That the man of God may be perfect, thoroughly furnished unto all good works."

2 Timothy 3:16, 17 (KJV)

My mother had an appropriate word for most of the situations she faced. Some were light-hearted; others were of the serious kind; while some were down to earth advice. Some of her sayings included: "Better belly bust than good food go to waste."

"Every tub will set on its bottom."

"A watched pot never boils."

"If you jump high in church, make sure you walk straight when you hit the ground."

"When you sleep with the dogs, you will wake up with the fleas."

"If you can't sleep, count your blessings not the sheep."

Mother believed that the Bible said what it meant and meant what it said. She loved the Word of God, and the

APRIL 29

scriptures were not far away from her at any time during her life. If she didn't have a Bible with her, she had its treasures stored away in her heart. Looking at her Bible I noticed that it was marked from the top of its pages to the bottom with notes and remarks. She dated most every sermon she heard and who preached it. She valued the scriptures as if they were a treasure to protect and enjoy.

Just before Mother passed away, her request was for me to read a passage of scripture to her when I visited her. The words were like the salve that would bathe the wounds of her pain. Her countenance would change every time I spoke the name of Jesus. I am not sure what the last words were that entered into Mother's ears before she died; but I am absolutely positive what the first words she heard in heaven were: "Well done good and faithful servant; you have been faithful over a few things, now I will make you ruler over many; enter thou into the joy of the Lord."

Thought to ponder: "The Bible will keep you from sin, or sin will keep you from the Bible."

April 30

"When the ruler of the feast had tasted the water that was made wine, and knew not whence it was: (but the servants which drew the water knew;) the governor of the feast called the bridegroom." John 2:9 (KJV)

There are certain advantages to being "in the know." Insider trading is the trading of a public company's stock or other securities (such as bonds or stock options) by individuals with access to non-public information about the company. That would give parties with inside information a great advantage. To have the inside track on any kind of knowledge would give some people the power to get great gain. Insider information are facts regarding the plans or condition of a publicly traded company that could provide a financial advantage when used to buy or sell shares of the company's stock.

In the Bible there was a group of servants who had the inside view of how water was turned into wine. The unnamed workers at the wedding party in Cana of Galilee had the inside track on the first miracle Jesus performed. Evidently

APRIL 30

no one at the celebration camp had any knowledge of how the miracle drink came to be. The Lord's mother did not know. The ruler of the feast had no inclination. The governor of this party was not in the know. The bride and the groom were oblivious. Only the servants who drew the water knew how and where the miracle came to be.

Obedience will put us on the fast track to being "in the know." Notice how this act of submission came to be. First, there was the filling of the water pots. That was all that was asked of the servants; but they went the extra mile and "filled them up to the brim." Second, there was the drawing out of the water pots. The drawing out of the water is connected with the words, "Whatsoever He (Jesus) saith unto you, do it." Put the water in and draw the water out was probably all that the servants thought they would be involved in. Third, there was the bearing of the wine unto the governor. Once the servants drew out the water turned to wine, they knew then and there where the drink originated--at the hands of the Lord Jesus. If we want to be in the know, o-b-e-d-i-e-n-c-e is the word!

Thought to ponder: "Knowledge is power."

May 1

"And that, knowing the time, that now it is high time to awake out of sleep: for now is our salvation nearer than when we believed." Romans 13:11 (KJV)

The farther America gets away from God, she slowly but surely transitions from being "one nation under God," and tumbles toward being one nation under God's judgment. We as Christians have allowed prayer to be taken out of our schools. We have allowed the killing of babies at a rate of 1.21 million a year. The homosexual agenda has pushed upon Americans their platform of equality, and for the most part we have stood idly by. The church has seen the decline of the moral values of the Bible. There is a lack of interest or concern in the issues pertaining to God. Here in the United States and across the world, the people of God have dealt with increasing restrictions placed upon its religious freedom, and to a great degree we as believers have taken an apathetic stance. We are well on our way to becoming one nation under God's judgment.

The heart cry of the church is that America would see the great evil facing its endeavors. Through confession and

MAY 1

repentance the Christian fellowship must turn back to God; that is the only hope we have. This issue is not something we can put on the back burner hoping that society gets better. The clarion call for each one of us is to wake up, stand up, and take up the cause of revival. Unless there is a turning back to God, there will be the judgment of God turned upon us. It is imperative that we have another "great awakening" in order for God's wrath to be avoided.

Paul tells us that the time is "now" for us to awake out of our lethargy. Today is the day that we must make up our minds that enough is enough. There is no scenario for a tomorrow to begin this quest. Our very being depends upon our standing up for the moral values of the Bible. Our deliverance is assured, but we are not guaranteed a victory without a battle. War has been declared on us by the enemies of the cross, and we have the full armor of God with which to do our battle. As we take our stand, we are assured that we are not alone.

Thought to ponder: "Onward Christian soldiers, marching as to war; with the cross of Jesus going on before."

May 2

"Redeeming the time, because the days are evil."
Ephesians 5:16 (KJV)

The Greenwich Meridian, also known as the Prime Meridian or International Meridian, is the "starting point" for dividing the Earth's surface into time zones. Each time zone is 15 degrees of longitude wide and the local time is one hour earlier that the zone immediately to the east on the map. That means that there are 24 time zones in the world. In Atlanta, Georgia it will be 11:59 p.m., and half-way around the world in Beijing, China it would be 11:59 a.m. With that in mind, consider the following illustration.

I visited a shop recently that had a rather interesting name, "The Right Time Anytime." It was a business that housed hundreds of clocks spread throughout the store. Some were hung from the ceiling while others were fastened to the wall. The sound of the ticks and the tocks was like an orchestra of beats chiming out the notes. The proprietor said to me that in his store it was always the right time. The reason he could say that was because he had a clock for all

24 time zones. Wherever you were in his store it was always the right time.

Paul speaks of the importance of buying up for ourselves the opportunities available today. The idea being that of a merchant who, knowing the value of an article and the good use to which he can put it, buys it up. There were so many opportunities for Christians in the apostle's time as there are today. The privilege of spreading the light and acting according to it is one of the open fields we have. "The days are evil," the apostle states, and the time is now to redeem those occasions. As the old adage states, "Strike while the iron is hot."

Thought to ponder: "Today's opportunity is yesterday's dream and tomorrow's memory."

May 3

"Therefore judge nothing before the time, until the Lord come, who both will bring to light the hidden things of darkness, and will make manifest the counsels of the hearts; and then shall every man have praise of God." 1 Corinthians 4:5 (KJV)

As computers grow even faster, new and better ways to store more data must be developed as well to keep up with the demand. It wasn't all that long ago that a one gigabyte hard drive on a personal computer seemed the stuff of science fiction. On the higher end, even faster supercomputers require not just more data storage but an ability to save and retrieve data faster as well; otherwise they would spend more and more time dedicated to doing nothing but searching for that data. To address the situation, IBM is apparently hard at work assembling the largest data array ever, which will utilize the fastest data storage and retrieval system ever devised, allowing for the storage of 120 petabytes of data (120 million gigabytes) using its newly refined GPFS file system that is capable of indexing files in just forty three minutes.

MAY 3

There is a day coming, that will bring men's secret sins into open day and discover the secrets of their hearts. Nothing in all of creation is hidden from God. We stand naked before Him with whom we have our being. Not one iota of movement escapes His omniscient view. Everything is open and exposed before His eyes, and He is the One to whom we are accountable. God keeps a record of every word that is spoken and every action taken. He has enough space on His "hard drive," to keep up with every engagement for which we are liable. He does not miss any single deed or behavior. He Who does not slumber or sleep has His all-seeing eye focused upon every exercise and exertion of every creature. There will come a day when all of our actions and words will be retrieved, faster than a nanosecond, and brought before us.

Thought to ponder: "As sure as taxes and death is the day of judgment."

May 4

"Are not two sparrows sold for a farthing? and one of them shall not fall on the ground without your Father."
Matthew 10:29 (KJV)

The Hubble Space Telescope has captured the farthest-ever view into the universe, a photo that reveals thousands of galaxies billions of light-years away. The picture, called eXtreme Deep Field, Or XDF, combines 10 years of Hubble telescope views of one patch of the sky. Only the accumulated light gathered over so many observation sessions can reveal such distant objects, some of which are one ten-billionth the brightness that the human eye can see.

The all-seeing God whom we serve has no problem viewing the things which happen to His children no matter how secluded those events seem to be. Those points we oftentimes miss because of our limitations in seeing are nothing in the unlimited eyes of the Father. He not only knows all, He sees all. Nothing escapes His attention. He neither slumbers nor sleeps. He is omniscient and omnipresent. His eye is on the sparrow and He watches over us. When those times of

MAY 4

uncertainty come and we feel all alone as if no one sees our distress, the Lord Jesus has His eye upon us.

One thing is for certain--life can be uncertain. What may be a red-letter day today can become a black day of anguish tomorrow. Waking up to a clear and sunny day can turn quickly into a stormy nightmare. Whether we are basking in the sunshine of God's grace or bowing under the weight of disappointment, we can find ourselves in the throes of the uncomfortable and sometimes it becomes difficult to see any way out of our circumstances. Jesus came that we may have life and have it more abundantly. That does not mean that we will never see trouble. It does say that God knows about our troubles, and He wants us to realize that He is watching over every turning point in our life.

Thought to ponder: "Sometimes in the waves of change, we find our true direction."

May 5

"And this is life eternal, that they might know thee the only true God, and Jesus Christ, whom thou hast sent."

John 17:3 (KJV)

Let's face it, having a USB stick on your person at all times is smart. You never know when you might have to save a quick file or snag something from a friend's computer. If you are going to carry one around, why not make it mushroom-shaped and full of gold and diamonds? According to a Yahoo News source, Swiss jewelry maker La Masison Shawish offers its luxury Magic Mushroom flash drive for the high-end technology geek. The drive can hold up to 32GB of data, which is a lot for a flash drive, but still feels a little like a slap in the face given the item's price tag. There are three available for this one-of-a-kind device: $16,500 with Pink Sapphires, $24,400 with Red Rubies, and the most extravagant being $36,900 that has Green Emeralds.

Jesus gave to the world something of more infinite value than a flash drive that costs $36,900. It is the free gift of eternal life. That bestowal comes to each one of us in the

MAY 5

form of a life-changing offer. It is by grace through faith that the Lord makes this chance of a lifetime available. Everlasting life is not something that can be earned or bought; it is all of grace. We who are in need of this gift can receive it by simply believing in the finished work of Jesus on the cross and acknowledging our need thereof. Our Lord did not do this for a chosen few but for the entire world. The message of the Bible is, "Whosoever will, let him/her come." With this offer in front of us, we have one of two choices, "Receive it, or reject it."

Thought to ponder: "The only way to a happy and eternal life is through Jesus."

May 6

"For what shall it profit a man, if he shall gain the whole world, and lose his own soul." Mark 8:36 (KJV)

In 2015 Giancarlo Stanton of the baseball Miami Marlins signed a contract that was for 13 years at a whopping price of $325,000,000. That would average out to be $25,000,000 each year. Break that down further and that would mean for every game Stanton played (or sat on the bench) would net him $154,320.99. There are 365 days in a year and if you take the $25 million per year, Stanton could expect every day of his life for 13 years to receive $68,493.15. The signing eclipsed the earlier deal with Miguel Cabrera of the Detroit Tigers that would bring him $292,000,000 over 10 years.

Jesus asked, "For what doth it profit a man if he shall gain the whole world, and lose his own soul? Or what shall a man give in exchange for his soul?" I am not suggesting that Giancarlo Stanton has forfeited his soul by signing this staggering contract; but I am saying that some have been led astray with the temptation to make money king of all.

MAY 6

The worst bargain we could ever make would be to trade our soul for the material things of this life. The physical part of this earth will one day melt with fervent heat. Choosing the monetary part of life over that of eternal life would be one bad deal. There can be no profit in making choices that put the decaying of earthly matters above and beyond that of the eternal. There is no amount of money that could ever buy or replace the gift of eternal life through the Lord Jesus Christ.

Thought to ponder: "A successful man/woman keeps on looking for work after he/she has found a job."

May 7

"But his delight is in the law of the Lord; and in his law doth he meditate day and night." Psalm 1:2 (KJV)

I read about a lady who for the past 50 years had read the Bible through each year. There are 1,189 chapters and 31,173 verses in the King James Version. That is the equivalent of 1,558,650 verses this dear lady has read in a span of 50 years. I would like to meet this saint of God. I would relish the time to congratulate her for the dogged determination to stay the course; to encourage her to keep up such a grand object; and to ask her how many of those verses she has taken time to meditate on. To have such an obsession to ingest the word, reading is only half of the goal.

Meditating on the scriptures is more than simply reading the words with our lips, perusing them with our eyes, or allowing them to enter into our ears. Meditating in one sense is letting the Word find a resting place in our heart. It is important to let God's word speak to us personally. It is taking time to permit Him to reveal Himself to us in a real and intimate way. It is equally important to ask God

MAY 7

what He wants us to discern in His message to us, and the adjustments that need to be made. Our walk with the Father will be enhanced by our understanding of His Word as we travel the roads of life. God is faithful when He invites us to call upon Him. In so doing, He will answer us and tell us great and wonderful things which we have never known. (Jeremiah 33:3) Today is the day to take God at His Word about His word. After reading, take the time to meditate on the promises made by a loving heavenly Father. This Word will never fade away.

Thought to ponder: "Take time to meditate on the scriptures which will make you wise."

May 8

"O how I love thy law! it is my meditation all the day."
Psalm 119:97 (KJV)

The cast of "Prospectors" who appear on the Weather Channel's reality show make their living carving precious minerals out of the sides of Colorado's largest mountains. The prospect of striking it rich drives these individuals to do whatever is necessary. Those prospectors featured on the show risk life and limb to find their next big payday. They hike the mountains to search for the next load of treasures. They work long hours of the day and sometimes into the night. They dig in the rain and in the snow hoping that the next shovel of dirt will unearth the rare and precious stones that will bring them wealth. It is an adventure of making it big by searching for that which will richly reward them.

There is another kind of treasure that awaits the child of God. If we are willing to expend the energy demanded, we will be wonderfully rewarded for the effort. Treasures far beyond our imaginations will be ours when we recognize where the valuables are. They are not in some far and distant

MAY 8

land; nor are they buried in the sides of mountains. They are found when we open up the Bible. There in front of our eyes are those precious gems waiting for us to dig beneath the mere surface reading of them. There at our fingertips are the vast treasures of God's Word. Jesus gave us an insight into the worth of the things that come from the mouth of God: "Man shall not live by bread alone, but by every word that proceedeth out of the mouth of God." (Matthew 4:4) As important as bread is for the physical satisfaction and nourishment of our body, the Word of God is the lifeline to our spiritual well-being.

Thought to ponder: "God has a storehouse filled with the treasures of wisdom; and that discernment is found in the Bible."

May 9

"In whom we have redemption through his blood, the forgiveness of sins, according to the riches of his grace."
Ephesians 1:7 (KJV)

"Ivory Soap" is a personal care brand created by the Procter & Gamble Company which includes varieties of a white and mildly-scented bar of soap that became famous for its claim of purity and for floating in water. The famous slogan of "99 and 44/100%" has become an American icon. What's in the other 56/100% has been a question pundits have asked. Harley Procter, of Procter & Gamble, sent samples of the soap to college chemistry professors for analysis. One chemist's analysis was in table form with the ingredients listed by percentage. Procter totaled the ingredients which did not fall into the category of pure soap--they equaled 56/100%. He subtracted from 100, and wrote the famous slogan of "99 and 44/100%". So close to 100% yet so far away.

Our heavenly Father has made a most remarkable promise to us. It is a message from the Lord Jesus, the Word

MAY 9

of life, the eternal Word, which we should all gladly receive. If we make it our habit to confess our sins, in God's faithful righteousness He forgives us for those sins and cleanses us from all unrighteousness (International Standard Version). What a grand and glorious assurance that we have. It's easy to say, "I am a sinner," but if confession is to have value, it must state the acts of sin. Confess your many sins, name them one by one and you will be forgiven of those wrongs done. God in His great mercy has seen fit to meet the confession of our sins with a declaration of "Forgiven-Fully!"

Thought to ponder: "God does more than forgive us 99 and 44/100%; He pardons 100%."

May 10

"Moreover, it is required in stewards, that a man be found faithful." 1 Corinthians 4:2 (KJV)

St. Francis of Assisi, hoeing his garden, was asked what he would do if he were suddenly to learn that he was to die at sunset that day. He said: "I would finish hoeing my garden."

Martin Luther responded to a similar question by saying: "Even if I knew that tomorrow the world would go to pieces, I would still plant my little apple tree and pay my debts."

A lady once asked John Wesley that if he were to know that he would die at 12:00 midnight tomorrow, how would he spend the intervening time. His reply was: "Why madam, just as I intend to spend it now. I would preach this evening and again at five tomorrow morning; after that I would ride to the next town to preach in the afternoon and meet the societies in the evening. I would then go to a pastor friend's house, who expects to entertain me, talk and pray with the family as usual, retire to my room at 10:00, commend myself to my heavenly Father, lie down to rest, and wake up in Glory."

MAY 10

The point to these three examples of faithfulness is that they would all do what they had already set out to do, trusting that their daily plans were according to God's will. Whether it's Wesley preaching, Luther planting and settling of debts, or Assisi's cultivating of his garden, these three saints of God had the right perspective to the end of their earthly journey. Can we truly say that we have such confidence in the activities of our day?

Thought to ponder: "With no promise of tomorrow, make today the pathway of faithfulness."

May 11

"And Joses, who by the apostles was surnamed Barnabas, (which is, being interpreted, The son of consolation (encouragement)), a Levite, and of the country of Cyprus."

Acts 4:36 (KJV)

As a high school basketball coach, John Wooden created a "thank you" rule for his players. Every time a player scored, he was required to acknowledge the person on the team who had assisted. Some of the players thought this rule would take too much time away from the game. However, Wooden explained to his team that a simple gesture like a nod, a thumbs-up, or a wink would take them less than a second. Wooden believed that if you didn't show your appreciation to others, they would have no way of knowing their contributions were recognized. Without recognition, people stat to pull back both from performing and from cooperating with others. Encouragement is a key element of teamwork and success.

We are called to be encouragers in the faith, men and women who will take the time to acknowledge that someone

MAY 11

has had a part in our successes. As John Wooden suggested, maybe a simple gesture to a brother and sister in Christ who have played a pivotal role in our pursuit of holiness; or a thumbs-up to someone who has made an impact on our life's work; or a wink of approval directed toward that individual who has helped to shape our Christian life. It only takes a second or two to encourage others as we travel down the long and sometimes arduous road of life. Take the short time today to be a "son or daughter of encouragement." It will not take long but will go a long way to develop teamwork and cooperation in the kingdom enterprise. That individual who is on the edge of making a difference in someone's life in a positive way could be pushed over the edge with a supporting word of accommodation.

Thought to ponder: "Encouragement can be an 'inch-long' word that will cover 'miles' of fellowship."

May 12

"And let the peace of God rule in your hearts, to the which also ye are called in one body; and be ye thankful."

Colossians 3:15 (KJV)

There is a lot in a name! Names we give about important things in our lives should be special and be carefully picked. Many people are careless though about how they name a church. Church should be a special place to us, yet there are some crazy names for many "churches" out there. Traveling around the country, you can see all sorts of church names. They are rather funny, yet disappointing, because it gives a license to the lost world to laugh and mock our Christian faith. Below are a few of those names:

Halfway Baptist Church - What? People saved there are only halfway saved?
Little Hope Baptist Church - Not very encouraging, but it sounds better than No Hope United Methodist Church.

MAY 12

Vatican Baptist Church - Vatican, Louisiana - These also sound confused much like the pictured St. John the Baptist Catholic Church.
Splitwell Baptist Church - How do they know that?
Hell Hole Swamp Baptist Church - South Carolina
Battle Ground Baptist Church - Greensboro, North Carolina - Named after Battleground Avenue but no longer in existence. Maybe too many battles?

Though there are some rather funny and ridiculous church names, there are some that have merit. There is a church near Dublin, Georgia that has the name, "Thankful Baptist Church." That tiny fellowship has what every Christian Church should possess, that of thankfulness. A spirit of thankfulness will promote harmony and peace among the brethren. An ungrateful people is commonly a tumultuous, agitated, restless, and dissatisfied people. Nothing better tends to promote peace and order than our gratitude to God for His mercies, and giving God thanks will go a long way to dispel the dark shadow of suspicion from a darkened world.

Thought to ponder: "What if you woke up today with only the things you thanked God for yesterday."

May 13

"If any of you lack wisdom, let him ask of God, that giveth to all men liberally, and upbraideth not; and it shall be given."
James 1:5 (KJV)

What if the Lord were to make you the same offer He made to Solomon of the Old Testament? In 1 Chronicles 1:7 we read of this incredible proposition, "In that night did God appear unto Solomon, and said unto him, Ask what I shall give thee." We can think of many things the request could include. We could ask for riches, popularity, or long life. These would be valid gifts if that was truly the essence of life. We reason that our way would be brighter and our experience sweeter if only we had these benefits, but God has something of enormous value that is ours for the asking.

The God of Israel once offered to the king of Israel anything he wanted. Young King Solomon requested wisdom, and God bestowed it freely. Here in James 1:5 we are given the same offer, and the results are as sure as the day is long. The "if" in this verse does not mean that we may have need for wisdom, but rather because we have the occasion of this

MAY 13

transforming grace, we are invited to ask God to grant it to us. The rich promise that is made to Christians is that God will give into our experiences this transforming wisdom, and it will be granted in a most liberal way. An additional promise is that we need not fear to come before God to make this request known. God will not criticize us for coming before Him. The end result is that wisdom will be granted. What greater promise could the God of this universe make to us?

Thought to ponder: "Prayer: Lord, give me the tenacity and determination of a weed."

May 14

"Behold, he that keepeth Israel shall neither slumber or sleep."
Psalm 121:4 (KJV)

Randy Gardner is the holder of the scientifically documented record for the longest period a human has intentionally gone without sleep not using stimulants of any kind. In 1964, Gardner, a 17-year old high school student in San Diego, California, stayed awake for 264.4 hours (11 days 24 minutes). This period of sleeplessness broke the previous record of 260 hours and 17 minutes held by disk jockey Tom Rounds of Honolulu.

On his final day, Gardner presided over a press conference where he spoke without slurring or stumbling his words and seemed in general appearance to be in excellent health. "I wanted to prove that bad things did not happen if you went without sleep," said Gardner. "I thought that I could break that record and did not think it would be a negative experience."

The Psalmist spoke of his God who neither slumbered or slept. The writer said that the heavenly Father had never

MAY 14

taken a nap nor ever dozed off because of tiredness. There was no sleep deprivation for the Creator of this world. The sun had not risen to wake Him up nor had the evening shadows brought on fatigue. For all of eternity the matchless God had been actively engaged in the affairs of His dear children; He has been on the watch, 24-7-365. In the wee hours of the morning before the dew had been erased by the sun, God had been fully awake in light of our circumstances. Into the evening hours when night had put an end to the blazing sun, He had been there all the time watching our every move. On toward the midnight shadows when all of life seemed to be so bleak, God had His all-seeing eye engaged in the activities of His children. Indeed, He who watches over us never slumbers or sleeps.

Thought to ponder: "Fear can keep us up all night long, but faith makes one fine pillow."

May 15

"Thine, O LORD, is the greatness, and the power, and the glory, and the victory, and the majesty: for all that is in the heaven and in the earth is thine; thine is the kingdom, O LORD, and thou art exalted as head above all."

2 Chronicles 29:11 (KJV)

Fort Knox is famous for being one of the largest depositories of gold in the world, but how much is in Fort Knox, exactly? Altogether, there is said to be $278.3 billion worth of gold of various standards of purity in the depository. As you might expect, the security around Fort Knox is very tight and there are no sight-seeing visitors allowed in the area. Between Fort Knox and the U.S. Federal Reserve in Manhattan, the United States holds 2.5% of all the gold ever refined, and owns more gold than any other nation. If all of the gold in Fort Knox was melted down into a cube, the cube would be 20.3 feet on each side.

Everything in the heavens and the earth belong to God. This was David's recognition of the divine prominence of God. All of the silver, gold, and riches of jewels are His by

MAY 15

right of being the creator of all things. He bestows all of this liberality upon the blood-bought child through His Son. God is rich in His grace and adopts us into His family, begets us again into His kingdom, and freely bestows the inheritance on us. As His children we are "heirs of God, and joint- heirs with Christ" (Romans 8:17). We are heirs of all things which are His; we share in His love, grace, and mercy; and His wisdom, power, truth, and faithfulness, and indeed, every perfection of His are engaged on our side and in our favor. We are the recipients of this great favor by virtue of our new birth, made possible through the shed blood of Jesus Christ.

Thought to ponder: "There is nothing wrong with men possessing riches. The wrong comes when riches possess men."

May 16

"Jesus Christ the same yesterday, and today, and forever."
Hebrews 13:8 (KJV)

I read an article about a self-made millionaire who said that gold is the ultimate commodity. He stated that banks can collapse and businesses can fold, but gold always has a relative worth. He cited an expert in the market as saying, "Whole currencies are based on gold reserves, so not only is a coin worth its weight in gold, but it also has the added value of its history." The bottom line to this millionaire's view on gold and the security that it affords was that he never felt more secure than when he was the sole owner of $1 million in gold.

Our security as Christians is not based on the fluctuating value of gold but upon the absolute certainty of a never-changing God. Gold does and will continue to quake in response to supply and demand, price manipulation, peer pressure buying, or a long litany of other factors, but our great God is always trustworthy in that He never changes. He is not up one day and down the other; He does not have

MAY 16

His A-Game on today and fall to the end of the line the next day. He is not merely faithful today and unfaithful tomorrow. He is not a fair-weather friend. He is the same, yesterday, today, and will be forever. That is where our security is based. With this promise, we can draw strength and power. We will never feel more secure than when we internalize this great truth--God does not change!

Thought to ponder: "God never changes. In fact, it is impossible for God to change."

May 17

"Epaphras, who is one of you, a servant of Christ, saluteth you, always labouring fervently for you in prayers, that ye may stand perfect and complete in all the will of God."

Colossians 4:12 (KJV)

You will probably agree with me that there are times when prayer is work. Genuine prayer set aside as an activity by itself is a laborious activity. We oftentimes treat prayer as a convenience for the moment and sometimes as a last resort for help. Intercession on the behalf of others brings out the commitment to exercise our words with great effort. A simple prayer of "now I lay me down to sleep" will not suffice for the needs of others who struggle along under the weight of guilt. A labor intensive prayer is what we need.

Paul spoke of an individual by the name of Epaphras who was a true servant of the Messiah, a worthy bond slave in the sense of being one who had genuine concern for the welfare of others. A follower of Jesus who sensed in his own prayer life that the needs of others were more important than his own. He not only sent his usual greetings of "Peace to

MAY 17

you," he became well known within the circle of Jesus' followers as someone who agonized in prayer for his brothers and sisters in Christ. His prayer was not that God would bless them richly with material blessings, but that He would grant them the blessings of a ripe character and of a clear conviction as to everything which is God's will. That kind of intercessory prayer will take the full effort of a servant to make known the desires of the heart, a monumental effort to accomplish that purpose, a force and a function of struggle, and with this initiation of raising one's voice, Epaphras was well recognized as one who wrestled on the behalf of others in his prayers.

Thought to ponder: "Prayer does not change God, but it alters him who prays."

May 18

"Wherefore God also hath highly exalted him (Jesus), and given him a name which is above every name."

Philippians 2:9 (KJV)

In 1995 a 28-year old software developer by the name of Pierre Omidyar was looking for a way to make something cool online. He posted the sale of a broken laser pointer. To his surprise he found that someone actually bought it. Omidyar only intended the laser pointer sale to be a test but surprisingly this laid the foundation for something of greater magnitude. Thinking he might be on to something, Omidyar started working in earnest on the program. While contemplating names for the site, he initially planned to use the name of his computer consulting company, Echo Bay. However, "echobay" was already taken (and still is) so Omidyar shortened the name to "ebay" and bought the web address that we all know and love. Ebay had a net worth of $60 billion as of 2014.

One of the many beloved hymns of our Christian faith is, "O how I love Jesus," and was written by Frederick

MAY 18

Whitefield. The first stanza says, "There is a name I love to hear, I love to sing its worth; It sounds like music in mine ear, the sweetest name on earth. Oh, how I love Jesus, because He first loved me."

Truly there is no other name that I love to hear more than the name of Jesus. At His name every knee one day will bow and every tongue will confess that He is Lord to the glory of the Father. I love to sing the worth of the name of Jesus by ascribing to Him all the honor and glory that rightfully belong to Him. His name is like sweet music in my ears, echoing His great love for me. His is the sweetest name on earth, exceeding those of others who have achieved earthly fame, but the one reason that I adore the name of Jesus more than any other is because He laid down His life for me. His life for mine is the echo of love to me. There is a name above all others, wonderful to hear, bringing hope and cheer. It's the lovely name of Jesus, evermore the same, what a lovely name.

Thought to ponder: "God has elevated Jesus to the place of highest honor and given Him the name above all other names."

May 19

"Not forsaking the assembling of ourselves together, as the manner of some is; but exhorting one another; and so much the more, as ye see the day approaching."

Hebrews 10:25 (KJV)

Our senior pastor recently preached from Acts 3:1-26 on the subject, "Revival On The Way To Church." He gave five principles that need to be embraced in order that the steps of a Christian would be successful. The first of those directives he used in his message was flashed on the computer screen and it read, "Be open to the needs of others around us as we go about our daily business." As soon as he had spoken those words and they appeared on the screen in front of the church, the computer flashed a warning that read, "Please wait a moment." That kind of prompt happens when the computer is not able to keep up with the commands. That was an interesting moment because it said to me that the enemy of our souls would have us to wait a moment or more before we engage in the ministry of encouragement.

MAY 19

According to the adversary, it's ok to be open to the needs of others around us but wait before we speak to their need.

Some of the important choices of life have a time line. If we delay a decision, the opportunity is gone. There can be no take backs when we postpone our intentions. Better to seize the moment now than to wait until tomorrow when the open field of suitability has been closed. Sometimes our doubts keep us from making a choice that involves change. The old saying, "He who hesitates loses" is a valid proverb when we entertain the notion to be an encourager but delay in doing so and the opportunity is missed. We have ample occasions to be on the look-out for people who are hurting and who need a word of encouragement, and the last thing we need to do is to" wait a moment" before we engage. The scriptures make clear the danger of delay as we may discover that we have run out of time. The God who gives us each day as a treasure will require an accounting.

Thought to ponder: "There can be no second chance to a missed opportunity."

May 20

"And if I go to prepare a place for you, I will come again, and receive you unto myself; that where I am, there ye may be also." John 14:3 (KJV)

"Tear down this wall!" was the challenge issued by President Ronald Reagan to Soviet Union Leader Mikhail Gorbachev to destroy the Berlin Wall in a speech at the Brandenburg Gate near the Berlin Wall on June 12, 1987, commemorating the 750th anniversary of Berlin.

"Four score and seven years ago" is the opening line of The Gettysburg Address. It is a speech by U.S. President Abraham Lincoln, one of the best-known in American history. It was delivered by Lincoln during the American Civil War on the afternoon of Thursday, November 19, 1863, at the dedication of the Soldier's National Cemetery in Gettysburg, Pennsylvania.

"I have a dream" is a public speech delivered by American civil rights activist Martin Luther King Jr. on August 28, 1963, in which he called for an end to racism in the United States.

"I will come again," are the stirring words of the Lord Jesus Christ as He addressed a group of troubled disciples.

MAY 20

He was consoling them because they were affected with grief at the idea of His departure. His leaving had opened a new area of concern of which these followers had no answer. "Where was He going? and how could they know the way?" were the prying words expressed by Thomas. Their ears had heard the words, but their heart had refused to accept them; yet our Lord gave to them some comforting words which would carry them through the uncertain times of their life. Their mourning hearts would find peace and sweetness in the very mention that Jesus would come again.

Thought to ponder: "The early believers were not looking for something to happen, they were looking for Someone to come."

May 21

"He which testifieth these things saith, Surely I come quickly. Amen. Even so, come Lord Jesus." Revelation 22:20 (KJV)

During my schooldays as I studied arithmetic, I remembered that the answers were in the back of the book. I knew that if I struggled with solving the operations, the explanation would be on the last page. There were times when I was tempted to look up the solution without trying to solve the equation. I remember struggling to come up with the right answer, and when I came up with what I thought was the correct one, I was encouraged to look at the answers at the end of the book and have some assurance that I was where I needed to be. I have failed many times in working out some of life's problems, but I am cheered by one unfailing certainty--the answer is on the last page of the Bible.

The last recorded words of the Lord are found in Revelation 22:20, "Surely I come quickly." Knowing that all of my earthly problems will not be solved here, I take great courage in knowing that one day the Lord Jesus is coming

MAY 21

again. When He does, those pesky predicaments will be no more of a concern. The old things will be passed away forever and the new things will be for all of eternity. These great assurances come as a result of our Lord's promise that He is coming. At his descent from heaven, with the shout of victory, and His rapture of the saints, we will be carried away to our heavenly home. There will we be forever with the One Who loved us and gave Himself for us. Therefore, when life's problems do not work out the way we choose, the ultimate answer is found in the back of the book.

Thought to ponder: "Since Jesus may come any day, it is well to be ready every day."

May 22

"Charity suffereth long, and is kind; charity envieth not; charity vaunteth not itself, is not puffed up."

1 Corinthians 13:4 (KJV)

A tourist driving through West Texas stopped at a gas station and observed a piece of rope dangling from a sign labeled, "Weather Forecaster." "How can you possibly tell the weather with a piece of rope?" the tourist wanted to know. "It's simple, sonny," was the answer. "When the rope swings back and forth, it's windy; when it gets wet, it's raining; when it's frozen stiff, it's snowing; and when it's gone, it's a tornado!"

Paul said that there was a sure sign that people could see which would be an indicator of our discipleship. In 1 Corinthians 13, the great "love chapter" of the Bible, he states that genuine love is patient, kind, does not envy, does not boast, and is not swollen with pride. The insignia we wear is called the badge of love; the kind of love that says "no" to our wants and "yes" to the needs of others. It is the type of concern known only to those who have come to know

MAY 22

the unconditional love of the Lord Jesus. Men, women, boys, and girls can see this love by the way we interact with them, and more specifically the way we love the brethren. Jesus, Himself, said that all men would know that His disciples would have a love so uncommon that when it was expressed, people would set up and take notice. It is the kind of love not simply in words, but a love that comes through action and demonstration. Even those who are spiritually blind can see the actions of Christians and see something that is unusual.

Thought to ponder: "If we have love, we have everything."

May 23

"The thief cometh not, but for to steal, and to kill, and to destroy. I am come that they might have life, and that they might have it more abundantly." John 10:10 (KJV)

We live life between two thieves: yesterday and tomorrow.

The thief of yesterday will rob us of our joy by taking us back to places we have forsaken. Past failures, shortcomings, and sins will drain us of our spiritual energy if we engage their false messages. Bringing up those things which have been buried by God in the sea of His forgetfulness is a finger in the eye of God. When God forgives us of our sins, He buries them in the deepest part of the sea and erects a "No Fishing" sign. The thief of yesterday will try to trespass upon the sacred street of joy, and if we do not stop his advance, he will establish a stronghold in our life.

The thief of tomorrow will cheat us of the hope that we have for the future if our eye is on the uncertainties of that day. The only thing we can do about tomorrow is to place it in the hand of the One who knows what the day will bring.

MAY 23

Trying to live tomorrow today is like sitting in a rocking chair: it gives us something to do but never gets us anywhere. Jesus said of our arch enemy that his number one desire is to steal our joy, our hope, and our life and destroy our hope. He will use whatever ploy he has in his arsenal to bring us to desperation, but our Lord, on the other hand, said that He had come to bring us life. Through the life that He gives it will breathe a renewal of hope into our spiritual lungs.

Thought to ponder: "Stop beating yourself up, you are a work in progress."

May 24

"These things have I written unto you that believe on the name of the Son of God; that ye may know that ye have eternal life, and that ye may believe on the name of the Son of God." 1 John 5:13 (KJV)

The Bible is the best resource book that we have available. It was inspired by perfection; written by inspiration; made available for introspection; and given for reflection. It tells us from whence we came; where we are; and where we are going. It serves as a road map that will lead us from the "city of destruction" (the world of sin) to the "celestial city" (heaven). There is no better word that we could hear on a daily basis than a bit of wisdom from the Word of God.

The Apostle John gives us a word of encouragement in his first epistle by telling us that he has championed an inspired word that would gladden the hearts of men and women. The words that he penned would strengthen the belief of eternal life, the life which would begin when one comes to Christ, and the life that one will have with Christ

MAY 24

in heaven. Absorbing those words into our heart will become a barrier against the onslaughts of the enemy of doubt. The reason John writes these words is so that they will become a pathway to fully embracing all that we have available in Christ. The privilege to place our faith and trust in One Who loves us is at the very center of John's gladdening word.

Thought to ponder: "Glad is the heart who receives the Word of God."

May 25

"How much better is it to get wisdom than gold! and to get understanding rather to be chosen than silver!"
Proverbs 16:16 (KJV)

The price of gold and silver is up and down. They are not stable commodities. Gold can be up one day and the next twenty-four hours it may lose its value. After years of gains, the price of gold is steadily dropping. Silver is the same; it can rise and it can fall. In contrast to gold and silver and the unstableness of both, wisdom in contrast is constant, durable, and permanent.

There is a joy and satisfaction of spirit, only in getting wisdom and understanding. The returns of wisdom are more preferable to gold, and the compensations of understanding are to be desired above that of silver. When precious metals lose their value and luster, wisdom and understanding maintain a constant that can be depended on when the "ups and downs" of life come calling. What gold and silver cannot buy, wisdom can give. This wisdom can be had simply by asking. It does not have a price tag of cash or check; nor does it have

MAY 25

a bill of credit. It comes when we by faith "ask of God." The promise is that wisdom will be given to all men liberally and God will not chide us for asking.

Thought to ponder: "With all thy getting, get understanding."

May 26

"For whom the Lord loveth He chasteneth, and scourgeth every son whom He receiveth." Hebrews 12:6 (KJV)

Recently I was introduced to a gentlemen who had a rather interesting job title. He worked for the Elementary School system and had the designation, "Assistant Principal for Discipline." His number one priority was to maintain order among the children at school. He seemed to be a mild-mannered man, who spoke softly, and I am sure he carried a big stick. The Principal of the school, where this disciplinarian worked, shared with a group of parents that the children loved and adored him, even to the point of giving him high-fives when he walked into the room.

The author of the book of Hebrews states, "Whom the Lord loves He chastens (disciplines)." The one truth that comes out of that statement is that discipline is a result of love--God's unconditional love for His people. Our Lord brings correction into our life as a way of expressing His love for us. If we go without instruction of any kind, we are considered to be illegitimate children. When the Heavenly

MAY 26

Father sends chastisement to our physical address, may we receive it as an expression of good and not bad, love and not hate. May we learn that God loves us too much to have us pursue a course of sin that would involve our ruin. Just as He forgives us, pardons us, cleanses us, and blesses us, He chastens us because of His unfailing love.

Thought to ponder: "No chastening for the moment seems joyous but afterward it yields the peaceable fruit of righteousness." (My translation of Hebrews 12:11)

May 27

"For the preaching of the cross is to them that perish foolishness; but unto us which are saved it is the power of God."
1 Corinthians 1:18 (KJV)

I was sitting in my car waiting for an opportunity to exit the parking lot of a local restaurant. A truck sped in front of me cutting me off. As I sat there with surprise written on my face, the driver gave me a menacing look as if I had committed the unpardonable sin. At the same time I saw the ire of the driver, I noticed a cross hanging down from the mirror of his truck. Along with the sinister look of this furious driver, the cross gave a glare that seemed to outshine the moment. Anger, hostility, and antagonism could not blot out the cross that seemed to shine much brighter than the darkness of ugliness.

To the world the cross is accounted as being absurd, ridiculous, and an impossible thing, and what no man of common sense will believe. The preaching of salvation for lost sinners by the sufferings and death of the Son of God, if explained and faithfully applied, appears foolishness to those

MAY 27

in the way of destruction. They can see no good coming out of something that appears to be so absurd. What they fail to recognize is the resident authority couched in the Gospel of Christ.

For those of us who are the saved of God, the proclamation of the Gospel of Christ--the death, burial, and resurrection--is the power of God. The word "power" in the language of the New Testament gives us our English word "dynamite." When the Gospel is proclaimed faithfully and demonstrated fully, it becomes an explosive force in the lives of those who have been changed by the grace of God. We live in this power all the days of our life and we may draw upon it at any time.

Thought to ponder: "At the crossroads of life chose the cross that will lead us down the right road."

May 28

"If we confess our sins, he is faithful and just to forgive us our sins, and to cleanse us from all unrighteousness."

1 John 1:9 (KJV)

What better deal could you get than, "Two for the price of one?" Anyone who has a need for a particular item with this guarantee would gladly embrace such a bargain. I saw this advertised the other day in a local retail store. The clerk assured me that I could choose any designated item on a particular rack and then pick up another of equal value, and I would only be charged one price. I could not let this great buy pass me up. After making the purchase, I walked out of the store feeling good about myself because I had two items that only cost me one money.

What if we could double that offer and get, "Four for the price of one?" John tells us in our scripture text that the offer of "four for one price" is available for every Christian; that is, "if we confess our sins." The word "confess" in the language of the New Testament carries the thought of "saying the same thing." When we agree with God about the nature of our sin, we activate four distinct qualities. I tell our children in church that sin is anything we think, say, or do that displeases God. When we confess our sins, four truths come into play. First, we activate the "faithfulness of God." Second, we experience the "righteousness of God." Third, we meet with the "forgiveness of God." Fourth, we come to know the cleansing power of the blood of Jesus. When we agree with God about our sin, we have this awesome bargain of His faithfulness, righteousness, forgiveness, and cleansing! What more could we want?

Thought to ponder: "God is in favor of forgiveness when we meet His criteria."

May 29

"But you, O Lord, are a God merciful and gracious, slow to anger and abounding in steadfast love and faithfulness."
Psalms 86:15 (KJV)

If you have an email account and have logged on recently, you have probably received a message informing you that millions of dollars can be yours just a click away. People who use a ruse like this will promise you something that they will never deliver. The only funds that will exchange hands will be yours, not theirs. Their promise soon turns to broken guarantees; and if you fall prey to their invitation, you will wind up a loser of your cash. The old adage, "If it seems too good to be true, it is too good to be true" takes on a whole new meaning.

The Bible has a message of love to each one of us. It has been dubbed as God's "love letter" to an unloving world. It carries a promise that God has chosen to shower His affection upon us regardless of how we respond to His overtures. He guarantees that His love will never change, never grow cold, or become indifferent. When the Lord extends an

MAY 29

invitation of grace and mercy to you, coupled with a promise of fulfillment, you can appropriate His unconditional love for you. What may seem at the outset too good to be true will be in actuality "good and true." Take God at His word today about His love for you and live your life as a child of the King.

Thought to ponder: "God loves you beyond measure."

May 30

"But if we walk in the light, as he is in the light, we have fellowship one with another, and the blood of Jesus Christ his Son cleanseth us from all sin." 1 John 1:7 (KJV)

A plumbing business had this advertisement on the side of their service van, "We will flush all of your plumbing needs away." Now that's the kind of plumber I would call to come and take care of my plumbing needs. There are many things I can do--other things I can't do--and some things I just don't want to do, and plumbing is one of them. I am thankful that someone who knows what they are doing will come and work on what I can't do or choose not to do. When I have a plumbing problem, I look for someone who will flush all of my plumbing problems away.

There is one particular problem we all have--a crisis we cannot solve on our own. Even if we wanted to, we are not able to take on the enormous weight of our separation from God. It is the problem of sin--that which has touched every human being born of woman. We need someone who is qualified to come and flush our sin problem away. That someone

MAY 30

is none other than the Lord Jesus Christ. John tells us that it is the blood of Jesus that cleanses us from our sins, for without the shedding of blood there is no remission of those sins. Jesus did something for us that we could not do for ourselves: He paid a debt He did not owe, a debt we could not pay, and with His bloody signature He wrote, "Paid in full!"

Thought to ponder: "What can wash away my sin? Nothing but the blood of Jesus."

May 31

"Let everything that hath breath praise the Lord. Praise ye the Lord." Psalms 150:6 (KJV)

*S*itting on the platform during one of our Sunday morning worship services, I noticed that there was a stuffed animal to my left. A soft and furry frog had been placed there for decoration for our upcoming Vacation Bible School. Our choir was singing special music and our Pastor of Worship had brought the voices of the choir to the apex of the song; it was one of those "get happy" tunes. People were standing and clapping their hands as our choir sang out, "Our God Is An Awesome God!" All the while my furry little friend sat there with an annoying self-satisfied smile on his face. His silence was a powerful message to me that spoke volumes about the way people sometimes respond to God's message through song. My little friend was silent because he did not have any life in him; he could not sing aloud of the mightiness of God because of the absence of any breath of life.

With that thought in mind I began to realize that God has breathed into each one of His children the "breath of

MAY 31

life." The Holy Spirit has imparted a new vigor into our very being: the kind of animation that can tender our voices in a way that will honor the Lord through praise and worship. Our heavenly Father has given each one of us a song that we may sing. Whatever that song may be, or however we may choose to sing it, we can lift up high the Name that is above every name, "The Lord Jesus Christ." One day every knee will bow and every tongue will confess that Jesus Christ is Lord to the glory of the Father. What better time than now, here on earth, to tune up our voices that one day will address our Savior. Let everyone of us, who have the breath of life, praise the Lord our God.

Thought to ponder: "Whenever you feel unloved or unwanted, remember to Whom you belong."

June 1

"And why take ye thought for raiment? Consider the lilies of the field, how they grow; they toil not, neither do they spin; and yet I say unto you, that even Solomon in all his glory was not arrayed like one of these." Matthew 6:28, 29 (KJV)

I visited a daylily garden the other day that had thousands of beauties blooming. They were like a carpet of speckled colors spread over a lush landscape. The wind seemed to blow each one gently with a rocking motion as if to cradle them and lull them into a gentle sleep. The owner of the garden was a throw-back to the 1960s when hippies roamed the streets of San Francisco. Seemingly his only desire was to be lost in the beauty of and the moment of beautiful flowers. I overheard him say that he would not exchange what he had for a million bucks. Though there were thousands of daylilies in full bloom that day, they would soon vanish as the season would draw to an end. What would give only a glancing satisfaction would not always be one of permanent beauty.

JUNE 1

I said to a friend who was with me that I would not exchange my relationship with the Lord Jesus for a million bucks and the garden of flowers I sat in. No amount of money or ownership could ever supplant the love that I have for the Lord. The beauty of all the flowers I witnessed that day did not compare with the "Rose Of Sharon." His radiance far exceeded the shapeliness of any flower I saw that day. His gracefulness is more than any group of flowers could ever display. The amount of money that all the flowers of this garden could muster for its owner would fade into oblivion at the worth of the Master. Jesus asked the question, "What would it profit a man if he were to gain the whole world and lose his own soul? or what would a man give in exchange for his soul?" (Mark 8:36,37 KJV) As attractive as the flowers of that day were, my choice is Jesus!

Thought to ponder: "Jesus is precious because we yearn for beauty."

June 2

"Forasmuch as ye know that ye were not redeemed with corruptible things, as silver and gold ... but with the precious blood of Christ, as of a lamb without blemish and without spot." 1 Peter 1:18, 19 (KJV)

On January 24, 1848, James W. Marshall, the operator of a sawmill in Coloma, California, spotted a few shiny flakes of a substance in the mill's water channel. When word of this discovery got out, it set off a mass migration of nearly 300,000 fortune seekers known as the "California Gold Rush." Fortune seekers from far and wide descended upon this small settlement to begin their quest to strike it rich.

The irony of the discovery of Marshal was that it never gave him a profit. The only thing grand about his discovery was that it opened the way for others to seek their fortune.

Our fortune does not come from amassing great amounts of gold or any treasure. It does not come from what we may have stored away in a safe place--whether it be buried or kept in a vault. Our true wealth comes from our personal relationship with the Lord Jesus Christ, the Son of God. It

JUNE 2

is fellowship with the Divine Son Who loved us and gave Himself for us. We are heirs of God and joint-heirs with the Lord Jesus. All that God has and all that Jesus is belongs to His children, and by virtue of our decision to receive Jesus as our personal Savior and Lord, we have been given the right of passage to become a child of the King.

Thought to ponder: "Fairest Lord Jesus, ruler of all nature, O Thou Of God and man the Son, Thee will I cherish, Thee will I honor, Thou, my soul's glory, joy and crown." (Written by German Jesuits)

June 3

"(For he saith, I have heard thee in a time accepted, and in the day of salvation have I succoured thee; behold, now is the accepted time; behold now is the day of salvation."

2 Corinthians 6:2 (KJV)

John Wayne, whom the world affectionately called "The Duke," was overheard to say, "The most important thing about life is tomorrow." Now I have watched almost all of the Duke's movies and followed his life while he was alive. I respected his stand on the issues Americans faced in days gone by. He was one of the most respected actors in the business. People came to him for advice and were better people by being around him. I would dare to take him on in a face-to-face dispute over anything he said, because after all he is a man's man, but I must take exception to the most important thing about life is not tomorrow. The most important thing about life is TODAY!

With "today" we can tell those closest to us that we love them and appreciate them. We cannot do that tomorrow because tomorrow never comes. Whatever the time may be,

JUNE 3

tomorrow is always a day away. If we put off today what we want to do tomorrow, we lose the opportunity to express our love for those who may not be with us tomorrow. Today is that day, not tomorrow, to share our affection with those who mean the most to us.

With "today" we can make sure of our eternal home in heaven. Tomorrow will not accomplish that because that day does not make its round in time. Tomorrow is always a day late and a dollar short. Waiting for another day to secure our eternal abode in the heavens is like waiting for a train that never comes. Paul said to the church in Corinth that today is the day of salvation. It is imperative that we take advantage of that opportunity and express faith and repentance in Christ.

Thought to ponder: "Why do we wait, dear brothers and sisters? Why do you tarry so long? Our Saviour is waiting to give us a place in His sanctified throng."

June 4

"Wherewithal shall a young man cleanse his way? by taking heed thereto according to thy word. With my whole heart have I sought thee: O let me not wander from thy commandments." Psalm 119:9, 10 (KJV)

There is a sign in our quaint little town that invites tourists of all kinds to stop and take a historical tour of the city and learn some history of our community. It is a self-guided tour, an invitation to spend some quality time among the citizens. The sign reads, "Start Here And Follow The Signs." Each stop along the way provides more information about the area visited. Sights along the trail feature an important aspect of our town's historical significance: a house, a business, a church. By the end of the excursion, the sight-seers are more likely to know the rich history of our beloved neighborhood.

The Bible has been given to us to point out the significance of God's love for us and His plan for mankind. We are invited to start here beginning with Genesis and weave our way to the Revelation. There are signs along the way that

JUNE 4

point out the value of our spiritual heritage. Within the pages of this "Love Letter From God," we will find a story, a message, an invitation, and signs pointing us heavenward. As we take the road through the Bible, we will come to know more about who we are and Whose we are.

God's Word is the story of His great love for us, a narrative that begins with a single sin in the Garden of Eden but is interrupted with salvation on the cross in the person of Jesus Christ. The Bible is a message of hope and an offer of a secured future. God has promised, and will not recant, that ours is an eternal and satisfied life. The Word of God is a generous invitation to come to know this great God through an intimate and loving relationship with His dear Son, our Lord Jesus Christ. These precious offers are like road signs along the highway of life pointing us to our eternal home in heaven.

Thought to ponder: "A wise man is like a tack, sharp and pointed in the right direction."

June 5

"And if it seem evil unto you to serve the LORD, choose you this day whom ye will serve; whether the gods which your fathers served that were on the other side of the flood, or the gods of the Amorites, in whose land ye dwell: but as for me and my house, we will serve the LORD." Joshua 24:15 (KJV)

Ever wonder how many decisions you make every day? Some behavioral specialists say that the number is in the thousands. Every day, rational and thinking individuals, like you and me, make decisions of which we are unaware. Our brains are in a constant mode of decision making as we process the many sights, sounds, and smells against the canvass of our hopes, fears, and memories. There are times when we make decisions that affect only the trivial issues of life; while on the other hand, some decisions are life-changing.

The number one decision that will affect our time and eternity is whether we have received or rejected the invitation of eternal life from a loving and longsuffering God. What we do with Jesus here in this life will determine where we spend our "after-life." No matter how many choices we

JUNE 5

make in the issues of this life, there is only one decision that will bring about salvation, and that is inviting Jesus into our life to be Savior and Lord. Life gives us many approaches to different matters, but only one choice is available that will bring about deliverance from sin. A simple prayer will bring about the gift of eternal life and that is, "God be merciful to me, a sinner." Doing nothing will silently reject the gracious offer of eternal life.

Thought to ponder: "We have no promise of tomorrow, so today is the day for salvation."

June 6

"Wait on the Lord: be of good courage, and he shall strengthen thine heart; wait, I say, on the Lord." Psalm 27:14 (KJV)

One of the first things I am asked to do when I visit my family physician is to have my weight checked. The nurse will come to the waiting room, call my name out, and as I make my way back to the examination room, I am stopped at the weight scales and asked to step on. After doing this a number of times in several visits, I decided to ask the nurse why all the fuss about my weight? She said, "We don't want your weight to fluctuate to the extremes. If so, it becomes a red flag to us that there may be a silent danger lurking." That did not sound too good to me, but I realized that the attendants were truly interested in my physical well-being. My question of, "Why the weight check?" was answered with a concern for physical health.

My spiritual doctor, the Lord Jesus, is interested in not my "weight" but my "WAIT." Learning how to wait upon Him is the key to my success or lack thereof. Getting ahead of God or lagging behind is sure evidence that I have not

JUNE 6

learned the lesson of waiting on the Lord. His promises never fail, nor does He. What He said He would do, He will do in His own way. He is always on time, so I must learn to wait for Him. He is never tardy in the affairs of my life, so I must develop the patience to wait in Him even when I cannot explain the "how and why" of my circumstances. God knows the beginning from the end. He has already looked down the road and around the corner. He knows a thought before it becomes a thought. He knows what lies ahead for me. He is forever interested in my "spiritual well-being."

Thought to ponder: "Waiting on the Lord is not inactivity but the activity of keeping an eye open for His activity."

June 7

"For the hope which is laid up for you in heaven, whereof ye heard before in the word of the truth of the gospel."
Colossians 1:5 (KJV)

"Life Begins at Forty" was a 1932 American self-help book by Walter B. Pitkin. As it was written during a rapid increase in life expectancy (at the time of its publication American life expectancy at birth was around 60 and climbing fast, from being only at age 40 fifty years before), it was very popular and influential. The book Pitkin wrote was more of an extended essay and exhortation than a detailed self-help book in the modern sense. The general thrust of the book was that, given the current conditions of the world, one could look forward to many years of fulfilling and happy existence after age 40.

For the individual who receives Jesus as personal Savior and makes Him Lord, life begins the moment faith is expressed in the finished work of Jesus on the cross. It is not like we have to wait for the magic number of 40 to come around that the festive life will begin. Our confession of faith

JUNE 7

in Jesus opens the door to eternal life now. We do not have to die before we begin to enjoy the life of eternity because eternal life does not commence the moment we pass from this life, but rather the very second faith in Christ is exercised. When we are born the first time, we receive biological life; but when we are born into the kingdom of God, eternal life begins at that very moment. Rather than waiting to enjoy the free gift of life when we walk down the streets of gold in heaven, we can begin now to luxuriate ourselves in the grace and mercy sent our way through the Lord Jesus Christ. When we all get to heaven, what a day of rejoicing that will be.

Thought to ponder: "Why wait?"

June 8

"If my people, which are called by my name, shall humble themselves, and pray and seek my face, and turn from their wicked ways; then will I hear from heaven, and will forgive their sin, and will heal their land." II Chronicles 7:14 (KJV)

A lady in our church talked with me about a program she was on that would help her to become healthier, physically and mentally, in just eight weeks. The name of the program is, "8 Weeks To Wellness." It is a regimen that will, if followed whole-heartedly, bring out the best in a person. It requires faithfulness and fortitude to go through 56 days of life-changing habits. The gist of the program is that you must have the want to in order to finish satisfactorily. There are a plethora of testimonies that cite the success of many who have made the effort. If this is something that you might be attracted to, I would encourage you to sign on the dotted line and begin your pursuit of becoming a better you.

I have a suggestion for a spiritual kind of wellness, a healthier you who can face a turbulent world with the calmness of assured victory over the enemy of our souls. The

JUNE 8

pursuit and attainment is a guarantee made by the Heavenly Father, produced by the Lord Jesus, and strengthened by the Holy Spirit. It is a daily routine of spending time on our knees in prayer, praise, and intercession. The endeavor is not merely for 56 days, but every day. The quest becomes a time on our face, prostrate before God, in humility with a propensity to repent of the sins in our life which so easily beset us. Every waking moment of every day is marked with a determination to set our face toward God to seek Him. The promise of the Father is that He will hear from heaven and bring healing to our sicknesses. There can be no better pledge made in the scriptures for a spiritually healthy me than to seek the Father with all of my heart.

Thought to ponder: "A healthy outlook will go a long way for a healthy mind."

June 9

"Behold, the LORD'S hand is not shortened, that it cannot save; neither his ear heavy, that it cannot hear."

Isaiah 59:1 (KJV)

Waiting in a doctor's office for an appointment can seem like an eternity, especially when you are asked to be on time. It does not seem fair when you are asked to be prompt and the doctor ends up being late. There are so many books you can read while waiting, so much television to watch, and so many people to talk to. Five minutes of waiting to see the doctor can seem like hours. However, the bummer is when the receptionist says to you, "Sir, I am sorry, but we have to reschedule your appointment for a later time."

That is not the case when it comes to our fellowship and prayer time with our loving Heavenly Father. The first part of the "Model Prayer" Jesus gave to His disciples had this at the start, "Our Father, Who art in heaven..." (Matthew 6:9 KJV) If our Father is omnipresent (everywhere simultaneously), then for Him to be specifically in heaven when we pray, says that He has taken the time to meet us there

JUNE 9

when we approach Him. There is no waiting in line for the next available appointment with Him. There is no wondering if the Lord will be delayed or no reasoning that He is too busy. God is able to hear every prayer from every one of His children every time they come before Him. There is no waiting for Him to finish another task before He can accommodate us. There is no need for concern that we will have to reschedule for the next available time. Indeed, the Lord's hand is not too short that it cannot save us, and His ear is not too deaf that He cannot hear us.

Thought to ponder: "God will lead you to no waters He cannot part, no brink He cannot cross, no pain He cannot bear."

June 10

"Then was Jesus led up of the Spirit into the wilderness to be tempted of the devil. And when He had fasted forty days and forty nights, he was afterward a hungered. And when the tempter came to him." Matthew 4:1-3 (KJV)

Adrian Rogers, well-known pastor, was preaching a sermon on the temptation of Jesus, and he made this ear-catching remark: "After the Dove came the Devil!" He was speaking of the glorious baptism of Jesus when the Holy Spirit came and lighted on His shoulder in the form of a dove, and there was a voice heard from heaven that said: "This is My beloved Son, in Whom I Am well pleased." (Matthew 3:17 KJV) It was "immediately" that the Spirit drove Jesus into the wilderness. One of the main points Dr. Rogers made in his outline was that after a great victory for the saint, there will come a vicious attack from Satan, our adversary. Just as he accosted the Lord Jesus in the wilderness, he will come at us as well.

Temptation can come to any person. It came to the Lord Jesus, and if the enemy of our souls approached Him with

JUNE 10

the intensity of hell, he will surely come at us with the same fervor. We are not above the Master in the case of temptation.

Temptation can also come at any place. Following the glorious baptism of our Lord, He was driven by the Spirit into the wilderness to be tested of the devil. The same scenario can be painted for the child of God. After a great experience with the Father there will come an assault from the foe.

Temptation can come at any point. When we think we are able to stand on our own two feet without the help of the Father, becomes the time the enemy makes his way into our experience. If we think we can stand on our own, we will find ourselves in the devil's trash can.

Thought to ponder: "There is something in life that never returns--a lost opportunity."

June 11

"My prayer is not for them alone. I pray also for those who will believe in me through their message, that all of them may be one, Father, just as you are in me and I am in you. May they also be in us so that the world may believe that you have sent me." John 17:20, 21 (KJV)

There is a small wooden church, about the size of a song book, that sits on the pulpit in our church sanctuary. Inside the wooden box are the names of all the family members of our fellowship. Each Sunday morning one of the slips of paper with the family's name on it is drawn out and our church has the opportunity to pray for them during the next seven days. These folks are affectionately known as, "The Family Of The Week" and these members are lifted up to the Lord in prayer for the entire week.

I am thankful that somebody cares enough about me to pray for me at least one week out of the year. I am a blessed individual to have a group of believers who will carry my name to the throne of grace and pray for me for a selected period of time. However, there is Someone else who has been

JUNE 11

praying for me, is praying for me, and will continue to pray for me; and that Someone is none other than the Lord Jesus. He ever lives to make intercession for me and you.

One of the ministries that our Lord has in heaven, as He sits at the right hand of God, is to pray for His people. He Who knows all about us, our weaknesses, our strengths, and our fears knows what we have need of before we ever ask Him. He invites us to come boldly before His throne of grace and find help in time of need. As His servants, we know that He has been in prayer for each one of us and will continue to do so until He comes to take us home in heaven. After the seven days of someone praying for me, I have the sure confidence that Jesus has not stopped His praying.

Thought to ponder: "When praying, don't give God advice. God listens to prayer, not advice."

June 12

"He that hath an ear, let him hear what the Spirit saith unto the churches; To him that overcometh will I give to eat of the tree of life, which is in the midst of the paradise of God."
Revelation 2:7 (KJV)

Many people struggle with hearing loss. If you find yourself having to ask others to repeat themselves or to speak louder should you be on the phone or in a conversation, then the loss of hearing has become an experience that is common as you age. About one-third of the people in the U.S. have some sort of hearing loss. For those older than 75, the number reaches a staggering 1 in 2 seniors. You cannot reverse hearing loss; however, you do not have to live in a world of muted, less distinct sounds. You and your hearing specialist can take steps to improve what you hear.

The Holy Spirit of God is our spiritual "Hearing Specialist." He who knows the mind of the Father helps us to clean out the muck of the world from our ears and replace it with the will and the Word of the Father. When our spiritual antennas cannot clarify what the Lord is saying, the

JUNE 12

Holy Spirit comes along side of us and enables us to raise our antennas higher so that we can hear what thus says the Lord. His voice is broadcast in "Theatre Sound Quality" so clear that we cannot mistake His sure voice. When we have trouble hearing Him, He helps us to discern His will.

John the Apostle, while on the Island of Patmos, wrote to a group of churches around Asia Minor and challenged them to hear what the Holy Spirit was saying to them. He reminded the believers in each church that He had something of great significance to say to each one. The health and the welfare of each fellowship depended on how well they could hear the voice of the Spirit. As the Holy Spirit spoke, He wanted each church to hear what He had to say. It is like the commercial on television that could have said, "My guide is the Holy Spirit, and the Holy Spirit says..." and everyone bends an ear to hear what thus says the Spirit of God.

Thought to ponder: "Happy is the hearing man; unhappy the speaking man."

June 13

"Being justified freely by his grace through the redemption that is in Christ Jesus." Romans 3:24 (KJV)

Our church choir sang a song one Sunday morning that instantly caught my attention. The phrase that brought a smile to my face was, "The closer I get to the cross, the more amazed I am about grace." My heart was pierced as the words sank into my heart because my amazement about grace had waned. I found myself mired in the church of Ephesus in Revelation 2:4 where the Lord Jesus chided those within the fellowship that they had left their first love. I instantly bowed my head and confessed this as a sin, and when I opened my eyes I sensed that I could see in a clearer way that my amazement about the grace of God was keener.

I heard someone say, in a joking way, nothing seems to amaze him anymore. If something happened out of the ordinary, he would shake his head and say, "Just a sign of the times, and I am not surprised." I took those words to heart as a challenge for me to stay in constant amazement about the marvelous, matchless, and wonderful grace of Jesus. The

JUNE 13

more I realized what transpired on the cruel cross, the greater became my appreciation of grace.

The closer I draw to the cross of Christ to recognize what Jesus endured for me as an undeserving sinner, the greater grace became to me. Grace is so great that it takes more than just a glimpse of it in our salvation experience to fully appreciate it. Grace to save, grace to stand, grace to secure, and grace to sanctify are just a smattering of truth in this grand scheme of grace. It may take an eternity to fully value this grace that is so freely given to us.

Thought to ponder: "God's fullest revelation of grace is found in His Son, our Lord Jesus Christ."

June 14

"For when we were in the flesh, the motions of sins, which were by the law, did work in our members to bring forth fruit unto death. But now are we delivered from the law, that being dead wherein we were held; that we should serve in newness of spirit, and not in the oldness of the letter."

Romans 7:5, 6 (KJV)

Travelling the highways, streets, and interstates of our country, you will see a number of sites along the way. These are sites that in some case will bring sadness, others gladness, and still some that would convey madness. There are sad sights of wrecked vehicles, glad sights of the beauty of our country's landscape, and mad sights of the unexplainable. I witnessed one of those ridiculous sights as I noticed an old beat-up wrecker, one that looked like it had been resurrected from the junkyard, pulling a rickety trailer with a brand new Mercedes-Benz on the back. The luxury car still had all the stickers intact on the windows. I mused out loud as I thought of a $500 wrecker pulling a $250 trailer with a $50,000 automobile on it. What a strange sight to have seen on that day.

JUNE 14

As the child of God navigates the highway of life, an even more sad and unfathomable sight is to see the old flesh out in front of the new nature, leading the way. The lust of the flesh, the lust of the eyes, and the pride of life have full sway when the old leads the new. Rather than having the old nature crucified and put into its place and allowing the new life to be in the driver's seat, the old flesh became the $500 wrecker pulling the $50,000 new car behind it. How it must sadden the heart of God to see such a sight for His children. When we were in the flesh, the sinful passions were in full operation through every part of us, bearing the fruit of death; but when we were released from the law of sin that worked in us, we became free to serve in a new way, and it is the "new way" that should be leading the way! Not the old taking the lead.

Thought to ponder: "When God imparts the new nature, the old must be put to death."

June 15

"And Joses, who by the apostles was surnamed Barnabas, (which being interpreted, The son of consolation,) a Levite, and of the country of Cyprus, having land, sold it and brought the money, and laid it at the apostle's feet."

Acts 4:36, 37 (KJV)

I have come to realize that I can be a "CEO" within the fellowship of my church. It is an opportunity available for every man, woman, boy, and girl to become the same within the local church body. I am among brothers and sisters in Christ who have a clear stage to become an important part of ministry. This is not an appointment made by a group of church executives, but rather a choice I make. I can become a CEO or I can opt not to be one. Now the title I am talking about is not a "Chief Executive Officer" but rather a "Christian Encouraging Others."

Barnabas was known as the "Son of Encouragement." In Acts 11:23, we read these words about the ministry he embraced: "Who when he came, and had seen the grace of God, was glad, and exhorted them all, that with purpose

JUNE 15

of heart they would cleave unto the Lord." Barnabas had the gift of encouragement and ministered it whenever and wherever he had the opportunity. The church in Jerusalem had so much confidence in his ministry that they sent him to Antioch to settle and secure the faith of the believers there, and he did that through the service of encouragement.

Of the many things that my heart beats for, the ministry of encouragement is one of the main objectives in my Christian walk. People of all shapes and sizes, backgrounds, and personalities need a word of support in a world that is so desperately wicked and uncaring. When the fruits of disappointment lay heavy on the brokenhearted and downtrodden, the Bible says that a word of counsel, or reproof, rightly spoken, is especially beautiful, as fine fruit becomes still more beautiful in silver baskets (Proverbs 25:11). I want to paint that beautiful picture in my life as I go about my daily routine with a word of encouragement on the tip of my tongue.

Thought to ponder: "It is said that the darkest hour of night comes just before the dawn."

June 16

"So shall I have wherewith to answer him that reproacheth me; for I trust in thy word." Psalms 119:42 (KJV)

My sister recently took a trip to visit her son in Oregon. She spent the night with our aunt so that she could be closer to the airport when morning came. Hoping that she had taken care of all the details surrounding her trip, she made her way to the airport to make her connecting flight. Upon arriving at the terminal she realized that she had misplaced her cell phone. She became frantic as she racked her brain trying to think of where she may have lost it. After a few moments of raw panic, she realized that she had left the phone at our aunt's house. Her take on the incident was that she felt lost without her cell phone because of all the contacts, telephone numbers, and other information she had stored on the device.

God has given us some incredible information contained in the Bible, His love letter to us. His Word becomes our spiritual "cell phone" so to speak. Our contact info is contained on the pages of Holy Writ. How we come to know

JUNE 16

God and maintain an intimate love relationship with Him is stored on the hard-drive of His Word and is accessed by our reading it. Taking time out of a busy day to fellowship with the Creator is a part of the valuable opportunity we have. Instructions for the day concerning our walk is waiting our retrieval as we spend time in Bible study. Learning more about Him and His love for us can be seen upon the screen of our desire to know Him in a more intimate way. If we never leave home without a credit card, how much more important is it to not leave home without the Word of God imprinted upon our hearts.

Thought to ponder: "Sin will keep us from the Word or the Word will keep us from sin."

June 17

"A friend loveth at all times, and a brother is born for adversity." Proverbs 17:17 (KJV)

A local undertaker had a friend of his who had been placed in the hospital's ICU and not expected to live. After several days of not knowing whether his friend would survive or not, he decided to pay a call on the gentleman in the unit. Upon his visit to check on his friend, one of the family members saw him and fainted on the spot. When the relative came to, she was asked why she had become so weak at that particular moment. Gathering her senses, she said that she thought the undertaker had come to take her dad away to have him embalmed. I said to my undertaker acquaintance, "You sure do have a strong presence in this hospital; people take notice when they see you."

Christian, wherever we may find ourselves in our daily walk, we need to have such a strong presence that those around us cannot mistake it. We need the kind of positive influence that will help lift heavy burdens from those who slump in despair; the type of control that will ease the

JUNE 17

concern of those bound up with worry; the habit of sympathy for the welfare of each believer that will allay the bother of problems; the humor of life itself that can help those who struggle with significance to take a lighter view of themselves; and the character of goodness bound up with empathy for those who struggle mightily. This is a friend who will walk in when the world walks out.

Thought to ponder: "A true friend will love at all times."

June 18

"The fear of the Lord is the instruction of wisdom; and before honour is humility." Proverbs 15:33 (KJV)

"Getting your ducks in a row" is an American expression which may mean to get things lined up or organized. It could also mean to be organized in such a way as to be prepared for something to happen or to fix something. Imagine you are a teacher preparing your class for a drama to be put on during the annual concert day. The best you can do before the presentation is to ensure that all the arrangements are in place--the costumes, props, the players having rehearsed their parts and appearing on stage in proper order, and so on. In short you have to "Get Your Ducks in a Row" to make the play a success.

A part of the Christian life is that of getting the areas of our life in their proper order. Seeking first the kingdom of God and His righteousness is at the top of our priorities. It is the only way to navigate with success the road of joy and fulfillment. The way will be rocky at times but perseverance and grit will keep us in the right way. Our Lord has promised

JUNE 18

that when "seeking Him" takes place; the other things in life we deem to be important will take their proper position. Seeking the Lord's will in matters of choice will be at the top of the list of preferences. Choosing not to do so will only sidetrack our ambitions and lead us down the road of dishonor and shame.

Solomon said that humility comes before honor. A man or woman who fears God must be humble, and as the fear of God leads to wisdom, it may be said that humility leads to the honor and glory of being wise and reckoned among the wise. It is imperative that we place humility at the top of our choices, for without it, honor will be as elusive as the proverbial butterfly. When humility is given its proper place, honor will light upon our shoulders and lead us in the ways of righteousness.

Thought to ponder: "The first great test of any great man or woman is their humility."

June 19

"Study to shew thyself approved unto God, a workman that needeth not to be ashamed, rightly dividing the work of truth." 2 Timothy 2:15 (KJV)

Normally when I order my drink at a restaurant, I will ask for sweet tea with extra lemon. Recently when I made my request to the cashier for my drink, a gentleman behind me asked me if I would like a straw for my beverage of choice. I said to him, "I cannot remember ever drinking tea through a straw." With a surprised look on his face and a curious tone in his voice, he asked me, "Why?" At that very moment, I did not have an answer to his question. I had not given it much thought. It's not like this was a matter of life or death. Whether I sip the tea from my glass or pull it through a straw is not a matter of grave concern. I have used a straw to drink beverages like cokes, lemonade, and fruit juices, but never sweet tea. To such a question I had no answer other than, I have never tried it.

Do you have a daily quiet time--few quality minutes you spend with the Lord in prayer, meditation, and Bible

JUNE 19

study--time of repose when you steal away into your "closet" and stay there until heaven becomes sweet to your taste? I hope that you can say with surety, "Yes, I do carve out a time during the day to spend with the Lord."

Whether we take the time or make the time for intimacy with our Heavenly Father is a matter of grave concern. If we, as Christians, cannot answer in the affirmative, then the enemy has gained an entrance into our life. It is a strong case of spiritual life or death in how we answer the proposition. The days of our life are marked with indifference when we fail to be alone with the Lord. The paths we take will be scattered with detours if we don't start the daily walk on our knees. Our journey will be clouded with doubts and discouragement if our day hasn't found us "prayed up." Whether we drink our sweet tea through a straw or not will have no bearing on a good day or bad day; but when we fail to start the day in sweet communion and fellowship with the Lord, it will make for a bleak day.

Thought to ponder: "The most important time of the day is not how it ends, but how it starts."

June 20

"Every man according as he purposeth in his heart, so let him give; not grudgingly, or of necessity: for God loveth a cheerful giver." 2 Corinthians 9:7 (KJV)

I was watching a college football game between the Georgia Tech Yellow Jackets and the Duke Blue Devils. The score of the game was tied, and I had come to the conclusion that one play could determine the outcome for one team or the other. There was a player for the Blue Devils whose last name was "Cash." He was the kind of player who wreaked havoc while playing on defense. He was a difference maker for his team, and when any game was over, it could be said of him that he left it all on the field. After making a tackle that became the game changer, the announcer stated, "It doesn't matter where you put "Cash," he will always pay dividends!"

In the realm of giving to the Lord's work, whether it be through tithing or giving a love offering, it makes all the difference in the world where we put our cash. Our giving to the work of ministry will pay dividends here in this life and

JUNE 20

in the life to come. As God richly blesses us with health to earn a salary, or to receive a monthly paycheck, we have the privilege and responsibility to give back a portion of that blessing to the Lord. It will serve as a token of our love for Him and for those whom Jesus died. That is the very least we could do as our way of showing appreciation. Tithing at its finest comes when we willingly set aside God's tithe or our offering, as God has prospered us, upon the first day of the week, which is Sunday, so that there will be no lack when it comes to reaching the lost and maintaining the work effort for fellowship.

Thought to ponder: "No one has ever become poor by tithing."

June 21

"Make a joyful noise unto the Lord, all ye lands."
Psalm 100:1 (KJV)

There are over 200 times in the Psalms where the people of God are commanded to make music unto Him. These are commands that are not to be questioned but rather obeyed. It is the request of the Psalmist that we enter the Lord's presence with thanksgiving and shout triumphantly to Him in song. Our Lord God loves the music that comes from the heart of His saints. Just as a loving father desires to hear his child speak well of him, so does our Heavenly Father long to hear His people make a joyful noise unto Him. It is the language of praise that gives us entrance into the celebration of song.

He who knows our hearts, when we speak with our lips, takes great joy in hearing His Divine Name extolled in song above other earthly signatures of honor. Our right and privilege as a child of the King is to bear His Name in songs of praise and adoration. What may appear to be a strain of noise coming from our lips to others, becomes a sweet

JUNE 21

expression of love and adoration in the ear of God. He who waits patiently to hear the voice of His saints in praise takes great pride in a single word of devotion and fondness. Our great God is worthy of all the honor, praise, and glory. Let us truly shout out the praises to the Lord.

Thought to ponder: "A heart in tune with God will sing praises to Him."

June 22

"Be ye therefore ready also; for the Son of man cometh at an hour when ye think not." Luke 12:40 (KJV)

The anticipation is building at the Chicago Botanic Garden. People are eagerly awaiting Spike the "corpse flower" to finally bloom. When it does bloom, it won't smell good. Instead, it will stink like rotting flesh. It has already drawn 22,000+ admirers for its large size, odd shape and terrible stench. The Chicago Botanic Garden has set up a live stream of Spike so fans can watch it bloom without threatening their noses. The corpse flower's smell has been described as a combination of limburger cheese, garlic, rotting fish, and smelly feet. Spike will begin releasing his stink about 12 hours before the deep red flower blooms. The stench will last for another 16 hours or so after it opens. Since the odor is strongest in the early hours of the morning, the Chicago Botanic Garden will be open to visitors until 2 a.m. on bloom day with parking fees waived after 9 p.m.

There is a greater expectation for the child of God, and that is the coming of the Lord Jesus. Each day that passes

JUNE 22

brings us one day closer to that return and should heighten our reflection upon the soon coming event. This beam of hope will cause us to become more aware that this could be the very day. As I write this devotional, I am reminded that the Lord could come before I put the finishing touches on it, but if He does not return before I complete this day's task, it will only broaden my expectation that He has made a promise of His return. What He has promised will be fulfilled, in His time, and on His terms. He has yet to break a promise, and He has given us His pledge that He never will. We must all be ready, because the Lord Jesus will come at an hour when we do not expect Him.

Thought to ponder: "He is coming! We do not know when, but we know that He is."

June 23

"Thy word have I hidden in my heart, that I might not sin against thee." Psalm 119:11 (KJV)

In 1996 there was a book published and earmarked as, "The Official Directory For The NASCAR Winston Cup Series Racing." Underneath this title, on the front cover, was an informative line that read: "Your complete guide to NASCAR Winston Cup Series Racing." This periodical had a picture of Jeff Gordon in his Dupont racing suit, along with his famous #24 Dupont sponsored car. It is the kind of book that no racing fan can ignore. Someone who had racing in his blood could not turn away from it or ignore it. The booklet had any and everything that a die-hard racing fan could ever want. From the locations of every major track, to accommodations for sleeping, to eating at renowned restaurants, this publication had it all. One final line on the cover read, "If it's not in here, then it doesn't belong to NASCAR."

I am reminded of the Bible that could very well read, "The Official Directory For The Child of God." Any and everything we need to know about living the Christian life

JUNE 23

is to be found within the pages of Holy Writ. From how to become a Christian, to persevering as one, and sharing that good news are found within the chapters of 66 books. Genesis 1 tells us where we came from, and Revelation 22 tells us where we are going, and the intervening books, all 39 of the Old Testament and all 27 of the New Testament, tell us how to get to our ultimate destination safely.

If heaven is our home, then the Bible teaches us what we can expect to find there when we arrive at our final rest in the presence of God. Because there are pitfalls along the highway of life, the scriptures not only point them out, but also tell us how we can avoid them. Because we are sinful by nature and live in a sin-filled world, the Bible informs us that there is forgiveness and cleansing when we do fall short. If it's not in the Bible, it doesn't belong there. All that we will ever need to know is found in the Word of The Living God.

Thought to ponder: "As we read the Bible, allow the scriptures read us."

June 24

"Ye are the light of the world. A city that is set on an hill cannot be hid." "Let your light so shine before men, that they may see your good works, and glorify your Father which is in heaven." John 5:14, 16 (KJV)

Driving down Interstate 85 just north of Atlanta, Georgia, I noticed a truck which had this sign tucked underneath the trailer that read, "We drive with our lights on."

I could think of several reasons why the sign would be so prominent. It would be for safety reasons so that everyone else on the interstate could see the driver and the truck. It could also be for personal reasons so that the driver could see well enough to maneuver safely through the traffic, or it could be that the owners of the business simply said that all drivers will drive with their lights on.

Jesus tells us to have our lights on all the time: 24/7. He said, "Ye are the light of the world. A city that is set on a hill cannot be hid." He did not say that we were like light, but that we are the light of the world. The emphasis seems to be

JUNE 24

that we are to live our life in such a way that the light of the Lord Jesus is on 24/7. In a world darkened by sin and people groping in that darkness, our light can shine with such radiance that others would be attracted to that beaming light, see our good works, and be led to give the "True Light of The World" the glory that rightfully belongs to Him. Our light can beam a message of hope to the lost and dying that would attract the misguided and beleaguered to a haven of rest for the soul.

My humble interpretation of the above verse could read, "Always let the light of your good works shine so radiantly that others may clearly see those works of love and be led to bow their heads and humbly give the God of creation the glory that is His."

Thought to ponder: "Motel 8 promises to leave the light on for you. We can do one better so that our motto would be, *'We leave our light on 24/7 for all men.'*"

June 25

"These things have I spoken unto you, that in me ye might have peace. In the world ye shall have tribulation: but be of good cheer; I have overcome the world." John 16:33 (KJV)

If I help my wife bake a cake, she will remind me to make sure that all of the ingredients are in the mix before it is placed in the oven. The contents of a cake may not seem to be that important at first, but if the makeshift cake has been baked without the necessary ingredients, there could be a taste difference. Some of the different parts of a cake are bitter, like flour or salt; while others are sweet, like sugar. If tasted by themselves they may be too sweet or too bitter. When you put all the ingredients together, salt, flour, vanilla, sugar, butter, etc., you will have a cake that will reward your sweet tooth with a smack of satisfaction. Because of my craving for something sweet, I cannot image a cake that does not have any sweetness; and yet at the same time, leaving out the flour or salt would also be a disaster.

Jesus said that He had come to give us peace, and at the same time He introduced into the conversation that we

JUNE 25

would have tribulation in this world. Now peace and tribulation are strange bedfellows. They do not seem to share the same attributes which would make for life a better experience. Yet these two components, peace and tribulation, are a part of a life that will bring our energies into balance. I do enjoy the peaceful and serene times afforded me, but I do not relish the periods of trouble and sorrow. Without the two exercising themselves for my good, my very being would be too bitter or too sweet. An old ancient Chinese proverb states, "All sunshine makes a desert." We need the peaceful seasons in our walk to cheer us on, but we also need some of the bitter interludes to make us appreciate the times of calmness.

Thought to ponder: "A gem cannot be polished without friction."

June 26

"The Lord is far from the wicked; but he heareth the prayer of the righteous." Proverbs 15:29 (KJV)

One of the men in our church made mention of sin being like quicksand during his opening prayer. I was caught off guard by his remarks about the subject. That is not to say that I was not engaged in his prayer because I was intent on having a spiritual time of worship, and his invocation would help pave the way. I must confess, though, that I heard very little of his ending petitions. His prayer was not out of order but rather "ear-catching." His words were, "Lord, help us to avoid the quicksand of sin." I began to water that seed thought with my own thoughts, and held it close to the flashlight of God's Word, and these were the "harvest truths" which came from my heart. Sin is like "quicksand" in at least three ways.

First of all sin is deceitful. The odd thing about quicksand is that it appears solid. One may think that he could scoot across the misleading appearance of hardened soil without any danger and be quickly fooled. So it is with sin

JUNE 26

in our life. We may think that we can dabble in a little sin and not be hurt. It is much like playing carelessly with fire and believing that it cannot harm you. The enemy deceives us into believing that sin is no big matter. Sin is deceitful!

Second of all sin is disabling. Human strength is no match for quicksand. The harder one struggles, the quicker the demise. Sin can sink the strongest of us if we allow it. Our sin will quickly disable us in our relationship with the Father. The Psalmist said in Psalms 66:18, "If I regard iniquity in my heart, the Lord will not hear me." Sin is disabling!

Third of all sin is destructive. Without someone's help, quicksand will suffocate its victim. The only hope that one has is for someone to throw out a "lifeline" to rescue them. Without that good fortune, there is no assurance of rescue. The only hope we have from the quicksand of sin is for a Saviour to come alongside our plight and pull us from the death grip that sin has on us; that One is the Lord Jesus Christ who paid our sin debt. Sin is destructive!

Thought to ponder: "Throw out the lifeline of the gospel! People are drifting away."

June 27

"Rejoice in the Lord always; and again I say, Rejoice."
Philippians 4:4 (KJV)

Watching a football game can be entertaining and informative. Observing the different players jockeying for position is like playing a game of chess, trying to secure the best posture. One of my favorite occasions during the contest is when a running back breaks away from the defense for a large gain in yardage and then watching him as he celebrates his invincibility. One would think that the player has conquered the world by his antics. The next play, though, with the same running back carrying the ball, is thrown for a 10 yard loss; but this time he does not jump up and down to celebrate but rather hangs his head and walks slowly back to the huddle to take part in the next play. It's like the air has been let out of his balloon. I wonder why he did not observe with wild antics his 10-yard loss? It must be, as someone has observed, "It's all in the game! You win a few, you lose a few."

JUNE 27

In the area of victorious Christian living, we should be rejoicing at all times. Not simply leaping with joy when things are going well, but celebrating with unspeakable joy during the rough times of life. The path of the child of God is not broken down into segments of "fairy-tale days" today, and "dark and dismal days" tomorrow, but rather every day finding us on an even keel of rejoicing with exceeding great joy that our great God is in control. That journey of faith comes through an understanding of who God is and whose we are.

Recognizing that God is a faithful creator Who controls our situations will be an impetus to rejoice always. Our awareness that God is concerned for our well-being will give us words to express our joy. Coming to grips that God has a master plan for our life will give us the desire to celebrate the Lord's "good work of grace" in our every position. Seeing the hand of God in our past victories and the promise of future accomplishments will enable us to, "Shout to the Lord, all the earth, let us sing, power and majesty, praise to the King."

Thought to ponder: "When times seem the darkest, rejoicing will brighten even the most obscure times."

June 28

"Wherewithal shall a young man cleanse his way? by taking heed thereto according to thy word." Psalms 119:9 (KJV)

Sitting in the San Antonio, Texas airport waiting to make my connecting flight to Georgia, an announcement was made that there would be a 30-minute delay before our departure. With extra time on my hands, and very little else to do, I began to notice how many travelers had their noses buried in some type of mobile device. 55 people out of 70 were either on their iPad, iPhone, laptop, or some other device. Their eyes were glued to the screen, moving to and fro across the surface as if to find some nugget of information; or their fingers were pointing at some graphic on the screen to touch that would take them to another level of interest. What was so amazing to me was that they were completely enamored with their "one-eyed monster." If those same 55 people would have their minds engaged in the Bible, seeking a word from God their Creator, how much more would they be "spiritually educated."

JUNE 28

The Father wants to speak to each one of His children. He wants to make Himself known to us in order to have a deeper relationship with Him. His desire is to make known to His child His perfect will, thus enabling all to know Him in a deeper and more meaningful way. Oftentimes we find ourselves in the fog of static, not able to discern His sweet voice. We allow the disturbing noise of worry to weaken our closeness to the Lord. We permit the chatter of deceptive words from the enemy to overturn the pursuit of lasting peace and joy. We invite the false promises of contentment to dominate our search for significance. All the while, the Father is seeking to make Himself known. He is the perfect gentleman, though, and will not force Himself into our conversation and pursuits. He waits patiently at our heart's door to come in and have fellowship with us.

Thought to ponder: "A word from the Father is of more value than gold that perishes."

June 29

"And one of them, when he saw that he was healed, turned back, and with a loud voice glorified God." Luke 17:15 (KJV)

There are a number of questions in the Bible which deserve an honest answer. The Philippian jailer of Acts 16:30 asked the one question that all of us must ask if we are to be saved, "Sirs, what must I do to be saved?" In Genesis 4:9, Cain made this inquisition, "Am I my brother's keeper?" In Job 14:14 Job made this inquiry, "If a man die, shall he live again?" And Pilate asked this question of all time in Matthew 27:22, "What shall I do then with Jesus which is called Christ?"

Jesus asked two of the most pressing questions in Luke 17:17. Those queries are: "Were there not ten cleansed? but where are the nine?" One had returned with gratitude in his heart for what the Lord had done for him. The other nine had no heart to turn around and give God the glory for their healing. These questions Jesus asked are a two-pronged challenge to us.

First of all, I am reminded of what Jesus did for me. In His own words He asked, "Were there not ten cleansed?" I

JUNE 29

am among those ten who have been washed in the blood of Jesus. There was a time in my life when I was plagued with the "leprosy" of sin. Then one day the Holy Spirit shone the light of God's love into my life. He convicted me of my sin and pointed me to the One Who could cleanse me from this blight. I want to be the "one" who returned to glorify God with a loud voice.

Not only am I reminded of what the Lord has accomplished in my life, I am reprimanded for not expressing my love for Him. I can never fully repay the Lord for what He has completed in my life. The debt is too great to pay. Even if I had all the money in the world, it would be a paltry sum to put up on my behalf. After all, it's not my money that the Lord is looking for me to put up, but rather my mouth to put out the honor and glory He rightly deserves. I have the obligation and the privilege to express my deep love to God for sending His only begotten Son to die in my place.

Thought to ponder: "What Jesus did for you, He will do for others. Tell them about it."

June 30

"And whosoever shall compel thee to go a mile, go with him twain." Matthew 5:41 (KJV)

I enjoy walking as an exercise for two basic reasons: physical and mental activity. I usually walk a mile almost every day to keep my blood pressure down, my heart rate up, and my diabetic concerns on an even level. I also walk as a means of escape. I listen to music as I make my way around the winding paths, and in doing so, I think through some pressing decisions of the day, week, or month. Someone asked me about the distance I walk and I responded, "At least one mile a day because, as they say, a mile a day keeps the doctor at bay." They asked if I had considered walking two miles rather than one to which I replied, "It's enough to walk one mile much less two," and their retort was, "If you are not willing to go an extra mile, you never know what the results could be."

I was immediately reminded of Jesus' admonition to His disciples when He said, "And whosoever shall compel thee to go a mile, go with him twain." The expression "extra

JUNE 30

mile" refers to acts of service for others that go beyond what is required or expected. If anybody forces you to go a mile with him, do more--go two miles with him. If there is to be a marked difference between the Christian and the non-Christian, it will be seen in a willingness to do more than is required of us. When a request is made, whether it be to give of ourselves or our resources, may we go the extra mile and give more. If we are to be light in this darkened world, then giving of our time, our abilities, and our monies will certainly give light to those who have chosen a path of selfishness.

Thought to ponder: "Go the extra mile, it's not a crowded road."

July 1

"Now therefore be not grieved, nor angry with yourselves, that ye sold me hither: for God did send me before you to preserve life." Genesis 45:5 (KJV)

One area of our life we struggle to gain the victory over is forgiveness. It's not an easy landscape on which to settle down on and live triumphantly. The bumps and pot holes of misguided fears have been strategically devised by the enemy of our souls to bring our spiritual journey to an abrupt end, or the devilish schemes of the adversary are proposed to sidetrack us so that we are detoured to a life of sub-par living. One of the hardships we face in forgiving others lies in our inability to look beyond the evil against us and to see the good that God has for us. A clear and definitive picture of how we are to face those who have wronged us can be seen in the life of Joseph. He was treated unfairly in many areas of his life, and yet he was able to discern God's activity in the midst of hardship. Joseph is a good example of how we can face the tough times of misfortune.

JULY 1

God can and does bring good out of the evil that comes our way. What man may devise as evil against us, God will take and design as good for us. Even when the act of mischief is so large that it buries us under its ton of weight, God uses that kind of adversity to bring about an expected end. God's clear vision of our future is ever before Him. He does not overlook any event in our life. Joseph's words to his beleaguered brothers are not only informational but transformational as well: "And now don't be worried or angry with yourselves for selling me here, because God sent me ahead of you to preserve life." Joseph's discernment of God's flurry of action in the midst of misery came not merely as a result of what he had heard about God, but what God had personally revealed to him.

Thought to ponder: "A bend in the road is not the end of the road--unless you fail to make the turn."

July 2

"Whoso stoppeth his ears at the cry of the poor, he also shall cry himself, but shall not be heard." Proverbs 21:13 (KJV)

Ever think about the invisible things in life? What we are able to see with our eyes is very limited compared to what remains invisible to us. Here is a short list of the things which are totally invisible to our eyes, but they are surely there because we use them or witness their power every day. There are different types of signals coursing through the air: TV, Citizen Band radio, telegraph, magnetic, infrared. There are other kinds of indications unseen: Sonar, Radar, and the invisible oxygen and carbon dioxide in the air. There are sound waves, X-ray beams, gamma rays, and the list could go on.

There are some voices which can be clearly heard. There are many people with needs who can be definitely seen; they are not like the unseen and unheard things of nature. They are those areas of need which are clear as day. Those who have been crushed by the pressures of life and can only see one avenue of escape, the lifting up of their voices in need,

JULY 2

are the ones to whom Solomon spoke of in the above text. They are those who are poor, inadequate, and inferior. Jesus said, "For the poor always ye have with you." (John 12:8 KJV) It's not like we have to go and search for those under a cloud of distress because many of them are only an earshot away. They could be living next door to us, down the street, or across the railroad tracks. Their cries for help are the signals which we should pick up on.

There is a twofold retribution threatened on the unmerciful. Those who refuse to listen to the cry of the needy will face these dire circumstances. He also shall cry himself, but shall not be heard. He himself shall fall into distress, and shall appeal to his neighbors for help, but his cry will be in vain. His howl for deliverance will be like the invisible signals--not heard, not seen!

Thought to ponder: "The mute button is for noise, not for the cries for help."

July 3

"These things have I spoken unto you, that my joy might remain in you, and that your joy might be full."

John 15:11 (KJV)

One of the first songs I remember learning to sing that involved acting the words out with motions was the children's song, "I've got the joy, joy, joy, joy, down in my heart…down in my heart to stay." I was taught to raise my hands in the air and wave them back and forth to show that real joy was in my life. Then I was instructed to bring my hands down and put them over my heart to show that the joy was there to stay. Over the years, when I hear these words, I am reminded of what my Sunday School teacher instilled in me as a child at any early age. Just to recollect the words brings a sense of cheerfulness.

Jesus spoke of the kind of joy that only He can give. It was His joy and He wanted to give it to His children. It's different from the enjoyment we receive at the birth of a child or a grandchild. It's more unique than the happiness of a marriage between one woman and one man. It's more

JULY 3

gratifying than the celebration of a graduation, or retirement, or any kind of event that would bring an occasion of delight. Jesus spoke of a two-fold kind of joy which He brings to the believer.

The first part of this "Jesus Only Joy" is that of an everlasting one. Jesus' desire was that His joy, would remain in each one of us. It would not be a quality of life which Jesus would recall or remove from our reach. It would be timeless, and it would be endless. Perpetual and eternal joy is ours for the receiving. If our Lord had a desire for His child, it would be to take His joy and give it away freely and fully. It's not a matter of asking but of receiving.

The second part of this "Jesus Only Joy" is that of an overflowing one. His words are, "that your joy might be full." The word "full" in the language of the New Testament gives us our English word "plethora." That means the joy our Savior gives us is one of abundance. It speaks of completeness, boundlessness, immeasurability, and fully furnished, and the conduit through which this joy comes is, "These things have I spoken unto you."

Thought to ponder: "As we feast upon the words of Jesus, the joy of the Lord becomes our strength."

July 4

"Greater love hath no man than this, that a man lay down his life for his friends." John 15:13 (KJV)

President Harry Truman is quoted as saying, "Our debt to the heroic men and valiant women in the service of our country can never be repaid. They have earned our undying gratitude. America will never forget their sacrifices." This fourth of July, we might find ourselves barbecuing, congregating with loved ones, and enjoying our precious free time. However, July Fourth is also a time to step back, take stock, and appreciate the deep freedoms we enjoy every day. Freedom is not free and we should not treat it so lightly or take it for granted. Many have laid down their lives for the luxuries we as Americans enjoy every day. Precious blood has been shed to guarantee our right to pursue life, liberty, and happiness.

On this day we celebrate the freedoms we have as Americans. As a nation we have been so blessed by those men and women who gave their lives in the line of duty. Someone was willing to respond to the call of duty to help ensure that

JULY 4

my freedoms were upheld. I have a debt of appreciation to the fallen that I probably can never repay. Jesus said, "Greater love hath no man than this, that a man lay down his life for his friends." The greater part of those who sacrificed never knew me by name. I may never know their name; but this one thing I do: I will remember for the rest of my earthly pilgrimage those fallen soldiers as genuine heroes whom I can hold up as role models. Real heroes do not have a name on the back of a jersey; they have their country's flag on the arm of a uniform. Thank you soldier for my freedom!

Thought to ponder: "Freedom is not free; someone paid for it."

July 5

"For what is a man profited, if he shall gain the whole world, and lose his own soul? or what shall a man give in exchange for his soul?" Matthew 16:26 (KJV)

While visiting our daughter and her family in San Antonio, Texas for Thanksgiving, I read the following:

"It was a hot, 99-degree August day in San Antonio when a 10-month-old baby girl was accidentally locked in a parked car by her aunt. Frantically the mother and aunt ran around the auto in near hysteria, while a neighbor attempted to unlock the car with a clothes hanger. The infant was bawling at the top of its lungs, beginning to turn purple and foam from the mouth, a combination of anxiety and the intense heat inside the car. It had quickly become a life-and-death situation when Fred Arriola, a tow-truck driver, arrived on the scene. He grabbed a hammer from his truck and smashed the back window of the car to free the baby. Was he heralded a hero? Not so. According to an article in the *San Antonio Tribune*, he is quoted as saying, "The lady was mad at me

JULY 5

because I broke the window." I just thought, "What's more important--a baby or a window?"

Jesus asked a similar question, one that had a more pressing issue than the above article. As needful as it was for the baby to be rescued from eminent danger, it is of greater importance that a man or woman be delivered from the hell of suffering eternal separation from God. We all have sinned and come short of God's glory. Not one of us has enough goodness within us to merit the love and favor of God. In this earthly life of which we live, what is of more significance will be determined by the choices we make. Our decision is one of two: receive by faith the gift of eternal life or reject the free offering of heaven's reward. Rejecting the sacrifice of the Lord Jesus will prove that our desire to gain the world's advantages were of more weight than spending eternity in the riches of heaven. By looking beyond all that God has provided us in His Son, we forfeit His forgiveness of our sins. What is more important--eternal punishment or eternal bliss?

Thought to ponder: "The dividends of heaven far outweigh the vanishing accounts of earth."

July 6

"Go ye therefore, and teach all nations, baptizing them in the name of the Father, and of the Son, and of the Holy Ghost."
Matthew 28:19 (KJV)

My home church has a motto that was chosen by our senior pastor to best describe the kind of church he wishes to pastor. Over the years, it has become an iconic statement of faith coming from our church fellowship. The expression is printed on road signs in the community, is emblazoned on tee-shirts, and is written permanently on our web site. It is a good advertisement for people who share a like sentiment. If a member of our church were to hear this expression, they would know that it spoke of our church. The tag phrase of which I speak is: "A Going Church For A Coming Lord!"

The mandate in Matthew 28:19,20 was given to the early church by the Lord Jesus and becomes the impetus for the expression our church shares. As we "Go" and share the good news, our directive becomes clear enough to follow. We are to make disciples of all nations, baptizing them in the name

JULY 6

of the Father, and of the Son, and of the Holy Ghost. As we go forth in faith with the message of a coming Lord, we shine the light of hope to a lost and dying world that the Master is soon coming. The time to respond is now, for the offer of salvation is not guaranteed forever. We don't go because we are commanded to go; we advance because of our commitment to Him, Who loved us, and gave Himself for us. As we have had the "good news" of the gospel shared with us, and we have responded, it is our aim and desire that others might share in these tidings of joy. The motto of our church is a banner we raise to all we meet. Whether they see it on our signs, our tee-shirts, or our website, we shine the light upon the "Light of The World."

Thought to ponder: "The Lord is coming for sure! Are we going to tell others of this news?"

July 7

"And I will profess unto them, I never knew you; depart from me ye that work iniquity." Matthew 7:23 (KJV)

Miss Universe 2015 was the 64th Miss Universe pageant, held on December 20, 2015 at the AXIS Theatre in Las Vegas, Nevada. Paulina Vega of Columbia crowned her successor, Pia Wurtzbach of the Philippines. The show was marred when host Steve Harvey mistakenly announced Ariadna Gutierrez from Columbia as Miss Universe 2015, even though it had been decided by the judges that Pia Wurtzbach from the Philippines had won. The wrong woman was initially crowned, and about three minutes passed before it was removed and given to Wurtzbach.

It was termed the blunder of the ages by pundits. It was an oversight to say the least. There was no ill-intent on the part of anyone to destroy the grandiose moment. Mistakes are a part of life when human oversight happens. I cannot imagine how the newly crowned Miss Universe felt when she had the tiara removed and given to someone else. The rush of adrenaline that raced through her body as she joyously

JULY 7

waved to the crowd was soon erased as the announcement was made. This was truly a devastating time for her.

I am reminded in the scriptures that there will come a time when many will say, "Lord, Lord, have we not prophesied in thy name? and in thy name have cast out devils? and in thy name done many wonderful works?" The day approaches when many will think that they have built their life on a solid rock of goodness when in reality it was the shifting sands of time. Based upon their perceived "good deeds," there will arise a falsehood that will lead them to the disappointment of the ages. The eternity that is to come will not be enough time to grieve for the blighted hope that has come to them. All of the good works they have done, the many times they have spoken of the Lord to others, the numerous moments of a false sense of security will come to an abrupt end when the Master will say, "I never knew you; depart from me ye that work iniquity."

Thought to ponder: "The wrong ladder, stationed on the wrong wall, with all good intentions will only bring us the blunder of all the ages put together."

July 8

"And the angel of the Lord appeared to him in a flame of fire out of the midst of a bush: and he looked and behold, the bushed burned with fire, and the bush was not consumed."
Exodus 3:2 (KJV)

On the cover of a lady's Bible were these words, "My Bible--God's Burning Bush For Me!" Those lines of text proved to me that this lady was familiar with the account in Exodus 3:1-4 of Moses' encounter with God at the burning bush. She understood, by her emphatic statement on the cover of her Bible, that an experience with God can bring about some dramatic changes in life, transformations which will last a life-time. Evidently her meeting with God through His Word made such an impact on her that it brought her Bible to life. A bush that burned, but was not consumed, would be a sight that no one could pass up.

Our Bible can become an appointment with God each time we open it up to ingest it and to digest it. The times we read the Word of God will lead us to a kind of burning bush experience, a time when we come face to face with the

JULY 8

Creator of this world. Just as God spoke to Moses out of the flaming bush and made Himself known to His servant, He can and does speak to us. He articulates His counsel in such a way as to reveal Himself, His purposes, and His ways. While Moses turned aside to see this great sight before Him, the Lord spoke loudly and clearly to him. Each day we have appointments with God that we should fulfill; by doing so, we come to know Him in a greater way. God's desire is to make Himself known to us. Unless we give Him our undivided attention, we cannot have a life-changing moment. As He does speak, and we hear Him intently, His words become as a fire shut up in our bones.

Thought to ponder: "Our hearts are the antenna that picks up the broadcast of God."

July 9

"To appoint unto them that mourn in Zion, to give unto them beauty for ashes, the oil of joy for mourning, the garment of praise for the spirit of heaviness; that they might be called trees of righteousness, the planting of the LORD, that he might be glorified." Isaiah 61:3 (KJV)

I received an email from a friend who instructed me to click on the following link: "25 casseroles you can make with Christmas leftovers." I wondered why my acquaintance would send me a link of this nature. I do not spend much time in the kitchen trying to figure out what to do with meal leftovers. Whatever the reason, though, I am glad he did because it became a seed thought for this particular devotional. The closing lines to the attachment informed me that some of the iconic chefs had contributed to this post. One of the chefs stated, "Taking the leftovers and making something tasty out of them is a passion of mine."

I am reminded in the scriptures that God is the "Master Chef" when it comes to taking the bitter leftovers of our broken lives and making something tasteful out of them.

JULY 9

"For he knoweth our frame: he remembereth that we are dust" (Psalms 103:14). God is also a "Master Blender" when it comes to putting together the good and the bad and causing something attractive to emerge from the mixture. God is a "Master Maker" when it comes to taking the miseries of life and making music out of them. God can and will take the bitterness of failure, the harshness of defeat, the hardness of disappointment, the despair of rejection, the agony of pain, the misery of loneliness, and sprinkle them all together to make something whole out of our brokenness. Out of the ashes of despondency, God will raise us up to become a work of art. He has His "Master Recipe" for each of our lives. He knows the different ingredients needed and the measures required to make something beautiful of our life.

Thought to ponder: "Smiling faces are beautiful faces, and God has given us this face-lift."

July 10

"Brethren, if a man be overtaken in a fault, ye which are spiritual, restore such a one in the spirit of meekness; considering thyself, lest thou also be tempted." Galatians 6:1 (KJV)

I heard a song the other day on the radio that brought back some memories of the 1960s when I was approaching my years as a teenager. The song was sung by Gene Pitney and the title was, "Town Without Pity." The song was recorded in 1961 for the film of the same title. The closing line of the song that caught my attention has these words, "No, it isn't very pretty what a town without pity can do!" Those words reminded me of another situation that has greater import, and it has to do with the church when its members fall into sin and out of fellowship. If I could reword the closing line of the song, it would be, "No, it isn't very pretty what a church without pity can do!"

The church is to be a hospital of sorts--a ward set up by concerned believers who are open to receive the wayward. We, who have been cared for and set free, will have an appetite to reach out to those who are struggling with the

JULY 10

weight of failure. As Christians we have become doctors and physicians who return the favor given them by the "Great Physician," the Lord Jesus. The badge of our ministry will be that of compassion. Our passion is to see others released from the snags of life. The assembly of Christians will be a place where the broken can come to be mended from the miscarriages and missteps of life. The fellowship of believers must be an area of concern where the down and out can receive an "uplift." The body of Christ will become an open door, with open arms, to those who have had to face the heavy hand of rejection. The song that followed "Town Without Pity" put a flourish on my thoughts. It was a hit single recorded in 1966 by Jimmy Ruffin. The words of the record recalled the pain that befalls the brokenhearted. I wondered out loud the same thought in the words of the song, "What Becomes of The Brokenhearted?" As a member of the body of Christ, what becomes of the brokenhearted Christians?

Thought to ponder: "Every day is an opportunity to be an encourager."

July 11

"The thief cometh not, but to steal, and to kill, and to destroy; I am come that they might have life, and that they might have it more abundantly." John 10:10 (KJV)

I saw a message on the marquee of a local church which read, "God loves you; Satan hates you; Don't get the two mixed up."

God loves me! That is for certain. He cares for me so much that He gave His one and only Son to die on the cross for my sins. The Father delights in having me as His son or daughter. I never have to question His affection for me because the Bible tells me that I am deeply loved beyond measure. At one point in my life I was living in darkness, separated from God, bound for hell. God took the initiative to come to where I was, steeped in my sin, and manifest His kindness and tenderness toward me. After all the rejections of Him on my part, He never gave up on me, but came time and time again to knock on the door of my heart and plead with me to open up so that He could come in and fellowship with me and I with Him.

JULY 11

Satan hates me! That is for sure. He dislikes me so much that he has set a watch to destroy me. Every waking hour of every waking day he stands poised to deliver his darts of deception. His dastardly plan to strike at God is done through the child of God. He is as a roaring lion, walking about incessantly seeking to devour me. His path to defeat is strewn with temptations to stray from the straight and narrow path. My broken fellowship with the Father is his invitation to come knocking on my heart's door. The enemy of my soul has a devious plan to bring me to utter shame and defeat. He awaits at every turn in my life to ambush me and destroy my testimony. When I think I am a match for him, I will certainly wake up in his trashcan with defeat smeared all over me.

Thought to ponder: "God loves you; Satan hates you; Don't get the two mixed up."

July 12

"The steps of a good man are ordered by the Lord: and he delighteth in his way." Psalms 37:23 (KJV)

When we find ourselves in some unsure situations, there are some certain truths we can rest upon. For every circumstance we face, God has a plan and purpose. It is what the Bible speaks of as a promise that God's love never ceases, and a certainty that He will never abandon us. So, when we find ourselves in a pinch, we can rest assured that God has a four-fold directive for the issues of our life.

First, we are where we are by His divine appointment. It may not be the ideal place from His perspective, but where we find ourselves is where the Lord has allowed us to be. He knows what is best for us, and the ideal place to experience His best is where He has placed us.

Second, we are protected in the place where we have been appointed to be. We are under His keeping, His watchful eye, and His constant protection. Nothing can happen to us unless it comes through the Father's perfect will. His permissiveness is for our good.

JULY 12

Third, we are under His training where we have been appointed and protected. The Father wants to teach us some lessons that can only be learned in the tough times of life. Where the Shepherd leads, there will be the green pastures, the still waters, and the paths of righteousness. He will instruct us in ways which are beyond our imaginations.

Fourth, we are where we have been appointed, protected, and trained for God's duration. It is His timetable that we must abide by. Not one day too long and not one day too short will be the course for His perfecting us. Some of the fruit in our life is spoiled by harvesting it too early. We are to allow God's timing to take us through the matters of life.

Thought to ponder: "We are strengthened by the things which weaken us."

July 13

"Faithful is he that calleth you, who also will do it."
1 Thessalonians 5:24 (KJV)

I heard a minister once say, "When we step out in faith, God shows out in faithfulness."

God waits in the wings for His servant to take a step of faith so that He can show Himself strong on his behalf. If without faith it is impossible to please God, and it is an impossibility, then with faith it is possible not only to please Him but to experience Him in ways we have never imagined. As we exercise our God-given faith, we activate the Omnipotent, Omniscient, and Omnipresent God, who can and will and does accomplish mighty things through weak vessels, and He waits patiently for us to come to our spiritual senses for it's our place of privilege to be in such a position.

God delights in confounding the self-conceited wise-man of the world. He chooses what seems to be nonsense to the world in order to make those who think they are more wise than others feel ashamed. God selects what appears to be weakness in the world to make the self-proclaimed strong

JULY 13

feel ashamed. His greater delight is not only to call us into the kingdom of His dear Son, but to also fulfill every promise He has made to us. Not one thing pledged for our good will go unfulfilled. Every commitment made has a lifetime warranty. There is no out-of-date stamped on any of heaven's promises. God who cannot lie will do what He says He will do. His calling us to a life of faith is the commencement of a series of blessings which ends magnificently in our glorification.

Thought to ponder: "God never procrastinates when it comes to keeping His promises."

July 14

"Upon the first day of the week let every one of you lay by him in store, as God hath prospered him, that there be no gatherings when I come." 1 Corinthians 16:2 (KJV)

I received a planning book for the new church year that had a rather interesting page inside. Towards the end of the calendar days was a page labeled as, "Holidays/Special Days." The page listed a series of special days for the upcoming calendar year. There were 52 unique days that people all across America could choose to celebrate. From New Year's Day to New Year's Eve, and with days like Valentine's, Easter, Grandparent's, there was a menu of special occasions to choose from. 52 particular days would be an average of one per week. So, for every week of the year, there was an awesome day to look forward to.

As Christians, we have a Sunday every week which has been called the "Lord's Day." Every Sunday we have the privilege as believers in Christ to meet together and lift our voices in praise and adoration to the One Who deserves our very best. We have a debt of gratitude that can never

JULY 14

be fully repaid. The Lord has made every provision for our every need, and He has given us one amazing day out of every week of the year to celebrate His goodness.

The Father, Himself, has designated the "Lord's Day" as one out of seven in which we lay aside the appointments of the week and concentrate on His divine appointments. This day is an opportunity for us to consecrate our all upon the altar of sacrifice to Him Who gave His all. This extraordinary day finds its fullness as we commemorate the time of our Lord's resurrection from the dead. One day out of seven has been designated as His day, the Lord's Day, and it's on this day that we are able to bring the sacrifice of praise into the house of the Lord.

Thought to ponder: "Sunday is a good day to celebrate 'Son Day.'"

July 15

"Like as a father pitieth his children, so the Lord pitieth them that fear him." Psalms 103:13 (KJV)

My dad passed away at what I consider to be an early age. He was 65 years old when he went home to be with the Lord. As a veteran of World War II, he served in the United States Navy and represented his country well. He was a fun-loving husband who not only loved his wife, but also truly loved his family. He was an ordained minister of the gospel and took his ministry seriously as he ministered among his parishioners. When dad took his last earthly breath, I not only lost a friend, a confidant, an encourager, but a mentor. Someone said to me at his funeral that he was the kind of husband and dad and friend that everyone could look up to. Though he is gone, his memories are still in my heart.

I have a heavenly Father who loves me much more than my earthly dad could ever think to do. It's the kind of affection that someone has that leads them to sacrifice the very best they have. God so loved the sinners of this world that

JULY 15

He gave up the one and only Son He had, to take their place and die in their stead. Ours was a guilt of sin we could not be rid of except through the blood of Christ. It took the sinless blood of the Savior to cleanse us from all our sins. Without the shedding of blood there is no remission of sin. The Son willingly left the splendor of heaven, to robe Himself in humankind, to die on a cruel cross, to secure the pardon of our sin. The Father loved us so much that He turned His back on His Son and turned a deaf ear to His cries of, "My God, My God, why hast Thou forsaken Me." There in the midnight hour of love's greatest triumph on the cross, the Father said of those who turn to Him in faith: "I love you this much!" That's the kind of love that my heavenly Father has for me, and it's the friendship of love He has for you.

Thought to ponder: "The cross of Christ proves the Father's love for us."

July 16

"Bear ye one another's burdens, and so fulfill the law of Christ."
Galatians 6:2 (KJV)

I saw one of the most intriguing sights the other day when I noticed that a tow truck was being pulled by another tow truck. Evidently one of the carriers had broken down and needed a lift. That proved to me that even tow trucks need a "pick-me-up" at certain times. These vehicles, tow trucks, are used to move disabled, improperly parked, impounded, or otherwise indisposed motor vehicles. This may involve recovering a vehicle damaged in an accident, returning one to a drivable surface in a mishap or inclement weather, or transporting one via flatbed to a repair shop of another location. I see in a tow truck this encouraging thought: Christians, at times, need a "tow-lift" a "pick-me-up of sorts."

As Christians we are prone to become disabled over some incident in our life that cripples our testimony. We need a spiritual tow truck, a sympathizing brother or sister,

JULY 16

to come alongside of us to pick us up, dust us off, and put us back on track. There are times when we may be improperly parked at some unsavory sight and have need of a concerned believer to shine a flashlight of love in our direction to lead us out of danger. Other times we may become impounded by our sins, and get out of fellowship with the Father and have need of a member of the community of faith to come and give us a hand of encouragement. When we find ourselves damaged by our own doings and have need of a fellow believer to assist us and to put us back on a drivable surface, a "tow truck Christian" can pull us to a location where we can find restoration. Whatever the weather may be, rainy, snowy, windy, or blustery, "tow trucks" can help us make our way through the mazes of life.

Thought to ponder: "Throw out the life line, someone is drifting away."

July 17

"Be careful for nothing; but in every thing..." Philippians 4:6a; (KJV) "In every thing give thanks...
1 Thessalonians 5:18a (KJV)

I have a friend who has a manner of responding to me in conversation with, "and everything." Riddled throughout his speaking, he is constantly ending a sentence with those words. I have come to the place in my conversing with him, that I am more prone to count the number of times he says, "and everything" rather than listen to his dialog with me. As good a colleague as he is, and will always be, there are times when I grow weary of hearing those same words, "and everything."

On the other hand, in a similar way, the Lord is saying to me, "In everything..." That is, "in everything by prayer and supplication with thanksgiving, let your requests be made known unto God." (Philippians 4:6) I am being reminded with these challenging words that in every aspect of my life, the Father is deeply concerned with my welfare and wants

JULY 17

the very best for me; and He invites me to come boldly before the throne of grace to find help in the time of need.

I also call to mind the apostle Paul's admonition with the daring words of 1 Thessalonians 5:18, "In everything give thanks: for this is the will of God in Christ Jesus concerning you." Those promising words remind me that in all the situations and concerns of life, the good and the bad, the up and the down, the joyful and the sorrowful, I am to offer up my gratitude and indebtedness to Him who knows all about me and who desires what is ultimately best for me. It is in the keeping of His hands that I am safe from all harm.

Thought to ponder: "The best protection we can have is that of courage."

July 18

"O how I love thy law! it is my meditation all the day."
Psalms 109:97 (KJV)

A sign at a local service station read, "Are you road ready?" Underneath this question were these additional comments: "We can get you ready with our road-proven amenities." They promised the customer with any feature that provided comfort, convenience, or pleasure. Among the promises were gas, full-service, snacks, and clean restrooms. Their aim was to please the customer in every way; and in so doing, purchasers would return for more "Road-Ready-Services!"

The Christian life has been likened to an adventure of faith, a stepping out, not knowing where the road may take us. With all the uncertainties in life, someone who can offer that kind of service is a welcomed sight to any would-be traveler. We all face roads which will lead us into paths which are sometimes strewn with bumps of uncertainty, and other excursions which are dark and daunting. We were never promised that we could see clearly to the other side, but we

JULY 18

have been assured that the Lord will be with us each step of the way. We can become road-ready by utilizing the map the Father has placed in our hands--the Bible. Within the covers of sacred writ are the instructions to help us along the way. It's through the study of scripture that we can make sense of our continuing journey, and through our attentiveness to this Word, we can pay closer attention to the traps and detours of life.

Thought to ponder: "Rather than road rage as we walk through this life, may we be road-ready."

July 19

"Even so the tongue is a little member, and boasteth great things. Behold, how great a matter a little fire kindleth!"

James 3:5 (KJV)

Art Linkletter hosted a comedy series as a part of his "House Party" edition titled: "Kid's Say The Darndest Things." The premise of the show is that the host would ask a question to a child (around the age of 3 to 8) who would usually respond in a cute way. Sometimes the children would answer in a manner that would border on being close to questionable. Other times their response would bring a gasp of incredulous unbelief. I have laughed at some of the childhood takes on the simple things of life. Children in their innocence have a unique way of responding on the spot to some simple questions.

As Christians we need to learn how to guard our speech. The words we speak with our lips come from the thoughts of our heart. What is on the inside will eventually find its way on the outside. The deep inner secrets of our being will find themselves clothed with the words of intention. If we are not careful, we will contradict the confession of our faith by letting slip our two-sided tongue. Our credibility hinges mainly on the way we use the tongue. The tongue can be a source of good or it can be a destructive instrument that will ruin the listener as well as the speaker.

An unruly tongue is one of the great evils on earth. The affairs of this world are thrown into confusion with the improper use of the tongue. We are taught in the scripture to secure our tongue in such a way that it would promote the virtue and integrity of the life of Jesus. When Jesus was reviled, He did not revile in return with like kind. When He suffered, He did not threaten those around Him but entrusted Himself to the One who judges justly. We could do no better than to follow the example of our Master, the Lord Jesus.

Thought to ponder: "The tongue is an unruly evil, but it can be a well-spring of good."

July 20

"And I say also unto thee, That thou art Peter, and upon this rock I will build my church; and the gates of hell shall not prevail against it." Matthew 16:18 (KJV)

I passed by a vacant church building that had been put up for sale. It had been vacated for several months and the time had come for the transaction to take place. The sign announcing the sale had an eerie look to it: "Church For Sale By Owner." Now I understand what the individual meant when he placed the sign there with those words. The intent was for the public to know that the church facility had been abandoned and needed to change owners, but I could not get beyond the reference that this church was for sale by the owner. It's obvious that a church building can be owned by someone who has the money to buy it, but in the biblical sense, the Church belongs to the Lord Jesus; and He has given us the assurance that His Church will never change owners.

His ownership is evidence that the body of believers will never be for sale. Believers in Christ are so valuable and so

JULY 20

loved that a sale of them has never been and will never be an option. The Bible informs us that Christ loved the church so much that He gave Himself for it. (Ephesians 5:25) Jesus didn't merely pity the Church, or merely desire good for her; rather He loved the Church with an undying love. Our view of Calvary's tree, and the One Who died there, will be enough proof that He loves us that much; and this fundamental truth will last for all eternity. There with His arms spread out, writhing in pain, we see the distance Jesus would go to secure our salvation. The transaction between Father and Son was one that no human eye could see or ever understand. The love of Christ for His Church is such that He counts Himself incomplete without her: "Which is his body, the fullness of him that filleth all in all." (Ephesians 1:23)

Thought to ponder: "The Church has been ransomed and will never be put up for sale."

July 21

"Thy word have I hid in mine heart, that I might not sin against thee." Psalms 119:11 (KJV)

How much is your Bible worth? I'm not asking how much you paid for it, or the amount of sentimental value you place on it. I have the Bible my maternal great-grandmother took to church with her, read from daily, and cherished all her earthly years. My mother passed it down to me, and there is no amount of money that could buy it. I also have my dad's Bible which he preached from for 25 plus years. It will be passed down to my family members as a keepsake, but the one that I cherish most is the one my wife gave to me after I surrendered to preach the gospel. It is a well-worn Scofield Reference Bible. I preached my first sermon from it, have studied from it, and have had to retire it because it is well-used. I treasure it as I would a rare diamond. How much is my Bible worth to me? So much that I have followed the Psalmist's plan for the Word of God.

The best thing in all the world is the Word of God; so says the Psalmist. To him it was a lamp unto his feet, and a

JULY 21

light unto his path. It was such a vital a part of his everyday life that he never left home without. The law of God was better unto him than thousands of gold and silver. The precepts of God were more to be desired than gold; yes, than much fine gold; sweeter also than honey and the honeycomb.

The best place for the Word of God is to hide it in our heart. The Psalmist would say that he has more than heard the word, or read it, but he has stored it up in his heart. He understood that the only safety he had from a surprising sin was to have the word entrenched in his heart; for when sin came knocking at his heart's door, he would send the Word of God to greet him, and he would flee.

The best reason for hiding the Word of God in our heart is that we may not sin against God. When we realize what sin did to our Saviour, we will lay aside every weight and the sin that so easily besets us. As we realize that our sins separates us from the sweet fellowship with Him Who loves us more than we love ourselves, we will gladly forsake anything that comes between us and our companionship.

Thought to ponder: "You can save the Word of God for a rainy day."

July 22

"Forever, O LORD, thy word is settled in heaven."
Psalms 119:89 (KJV)

I have a GPS (Global Positioning System) for my vehicles that I can plug into a power source, punch in a particular address, press the "GO" button, and off to my desired destination I drive. There are on the screen directions which will take me wherever I want to go. From a local point of interest or to one which is a thousand miles away, I am in the hands of a capable overseer. These instruments are so finely tuned that they will take you to the exact location of your choice, and not simply to a general area. On the horizon are new gadgets which will allow me to see on a screen what my termination point looks like--a house, a business, or a church. That takes away any guesswork on my part. These equipment toys were only dreams 25 years ago.

I have grown a little devious in my approaching senior years. Some have called it "Senior Boredom," and what I have begun to do is to have some fun with my GPS. If I am going to a place that I know the directions for, I will punch in the

JULY 22

address anyway and start out in the opposite direction, just to hear what the female voice will say. One particular statement is hilarious: "Re-calculating your destination point."

Could I strongly suggest to you that when it comes to the Bible, God's Word, it's a dangerous thing to choose to go in a different direction than which God has directed. We take our well-being into our own hands when we deliberately take another path, diametrically opposed to the one the Bible leads us in. Choosing to disobey God is detrimental to our spiritual health. It may be amusing and fun for the moment, but it will have many sorrowful repercussions for the rest of our lives. According to the Psalmist, God's Word, or Law, is eternal and unchanging. The revelation of God to us is fixed and established forever in the heaven of heavens, and if we opt for another route, we are treading on a path to destruction.

Thought to ponder: "God says what He means, and He means what He says."

July 23

"Then shall the lame man leap as an hart, and the tongue of the dumb sing: for in the wilderness shall waters break out, and streams in the desert." Isaiah 35:6 (KJV)

I was watching a professional football game between two staunch rivals. They have been enemies as long as they have been teams. One of them was a perennial favorite to be in the play-offs, while the other had not been to post-season play for the past 15 years. As the game progressed, there were several changing faces which could be easily seen; the competition was fierce and getting more fierce, tempers were raging and getting out of control, and the rain fell continuously. From the opening play to the end, the water drenched the players and the field. When the game ended, the perennial team advanced to the next round of play, while the loser had another year of frustration added to its disappointment. One of the last things the announcer stated about the blighted hope of the loser was, "The drought doesn't end on a rain-soaked night!"

JULY 23

We all go through the droughts of life, and they seemingly have no end. There are times when we become parched by the heated times of difficulty. Hardships have a way of draining us of our momentum, and we find ourselves lacking in the desert of doubt. The scorching sun of heaviness seems to drench us with its unending fervor. There seems to be no cessation to the onslaught of intense heat. Our tongues become sapless and silent with the pangs of hurt. If we remain here in these deserts of life, we will die, but the good news is that there is deliverance from these droughts.

Isaiah spoke of a time when streams in the desert would flow with the life-giving waters of deliverance. That is the promise God has made to us. When the ground is cracked and gaping and the thirst pangs overtake us, we can rest upon the assurance that the thirst-slacking waters will find us. Dry as everything may be around us, those fresh waters of redemption will come with a burst of sustaining relief. Later in Isaiah's prophecy, he would extend this gracious invitation: "Ho, every one that thirsteth, come ye to the waters, and he that hath no money; come ye, buy, and eat; yea, come, buy wine and milk without money and without price." (Isaiah 55:1)

Thought to ponder: "Don't pray when it rains if you haven't prayed when the sun was shining."

July 24

"And whosoever shall give to drink unto one of these little ones a cup of cold water only in the name of a disciple, verily I say unto you, he shall in no wise lose his reward."

Matthew 10:42 (KJV)

Recently in our area, some frigid temperatures came calling. Twenty degrees, with a wind chill factor at nineteen degrees, became bone-chilling. As the day came to a close, the wind died down and we settled into twenty degree temperatures. A group of people from a local business took to the streets to put scarves, gloves, and hats on branches of trees. Their goal was to help as many people as they could who would be spending the night on the streets. There was a note attached to the items hanging from the limbs which read, "Take one or two if you like them; take as many as you want if you need them." What a blessing it was for those who received the goods, but what a greater blessing it would be for those who took those items and made them accessible. The superior blessing will always be for those who are willing to do what Jesus would have done.

JULY 24

It is not only our duty to love the Lord our God with all of our heart, but also to love our neighbor with all our hands. God gave us one hand to feed ourselves and two hands to help feed others, and we can show our concern for those in need by helping meet their deficiencies. Those who are less fortunate than we, are at the top of our priority when it comes to ministering in the name of Jesus. What may be small and insignificant to others looms large in the eyes of God. When we as disciples of Christ are willing to give a cup of water to someone who is destitute and poverty-stricken, then we are assured that our reward will not be lost. A cup of cold water is regarded as a phrase used to express the least favor or benefit. The act is one which all of us, regardless of our situation, may give.

Thought to ponder: "Little becomes much when God has His hand in it."

July 25

"Little children, keep yourselves from idols. Amen."
1 John 5:21 (KJV)

I read an interesting quote from a well-known author who stated: "Idolatry is taking 'good things' and making them 'god things.'" There were no further comments on the quote so I took the liberty to evaluate it myself. From the vault of my acquired knowledge, I reasoned from the words that when we take the good things which God has given us to feast on, and force them into a god thing, we distort our view of a loving heavenly Father. That in turn will corrupt our behavior and ultimately lead us away from God. What He intends for our good, our enjoyment, and our well-being, should be left at that. God is the One Who has given us abundantly all things to enjoy; however that does not give us the license to turn those good things into idols.

Sex is a wonderful gift from God. It finds its fullness within the context of marriage--that is to say a Biblical marriage between one man and one woman for a lifetime. When we allow the sexual pleasures to circumvent its intended

JULY 25

purpose, it becomes a full-faced idol with all of its hideous features.

Money is another extraordinary profit from God. When it's used in the appreciation of our stewardship responsibility, our proper use of it becomes an extended hand of a loving Father. If we allow money and the love of it to take priority, then wealth can and will become the root of all evil intents and purposes.

Beauty, brains, success, and ambition are all good qualities in and of themselves, and when we bring all of these God-given dispositions into proper focus, they bring out the best of God in us. It's when we put these affections ahead of pleasing and serving God that will lead us down some unhealthy paths. These trends will only bring us to dead ends with no place to turn but back to Him, Who lovingly waits for our return.

Thought to ponder: "It's the 'God Things' of life which make for the 'good things' in life."

July 26

"Thou wilt shew me the path of life: in thy presence is fullness of joy; at thy right hand there are pleasures for evermore."
Psalms 16:11 (KJV)

There is a sign at the base of a rather steep incline that forecasts these warnings to would be travelers: "Soft Shoulder--Blind Curves--Steep Grade--Big Trucks--GOOD LUCK!"

That reminds me of some roads we travel in life. Most of those connections will reveal to us the splendor and beauty of God's creation, while others will bring us face to face with some passage ways looming as mammoth setbacks. If we get too close to the shoulder of these roads, we will bog down. When we travel these gateways, we will have to face some blind curves, and they most likely will bring too many surprises. As we take a path that has a steep grade to it, we will grow weary and faint. If we take a certain pathway, it may very well bring us face to face with some large trucks.

The roads we travel in life have not been paved with easiness, nor have they been promised to be free of roadblocks.

JULY 26

Setbacks have a way of bringing out the best or worst in us. The highways of daily living are strewn with challenges. Sometimes they become so many that we tire of them. These routes have a set direction; and if we stay faithfully on them, as tiresome as they may be, we will find our way to a richer and more meaningful life. There will be challenges along these paths, but they are not given to weaken us but to make us stronger; not to drive us away from God but to draw us closer to Him; not to discourage us but to encourage us along the rough and tumble way. Our roadmap is the Word of God, and within its pages, we find the directions which will lead us through the gateway to life. It is narrow and difficult, and only a few ever find it. As we set our faces like flint toward these challenges, we will be the over-comers.

Thought to ponder: "The bumps in life are what we climb on."

July 27

"To every thing there is a season, and a time to every purpose under the heaven:" Ecclesiastes 3:1 (KJV)

A pastor friend of mine shared his upcoming sermon outline with me about how the troubles of life are a lot like the season of winter. I listened intently as he gave me three points about the subject matter. I was drawn into his analogy as he pointed out the similarities. The more I heard him share his heart, the more I was convinced of the truth he talked about. He said that we could better understand how and why the troubles in life come if we compared them to wintertime.

He said first that winter is a season and will come around at its appointed time. It will find us not one day too early and will not be with us one day too long. Winter has been given its assignment and parameters and will remain faithful to its Creator. In Genesis 8:22, we read these words: "While the earth remaineth, seedtime and harvest, and cold and heat, and summer and winter, and day and night shall not cease." Just as winter is expected, we too can anticipate that

JULY 27

troubles will come. It should come as no surprise to us when we encounter the difficulties of life. They are going to come our way regardless of how faithful we may be. So, as surely as winter will come, so will the troubles.

My pastor friend also stated that winter may be severe. Living in the south, our winters may not be as unpleasant as those in the extreme north. Nonetheless, our weather can become frigid and frightful at times. Biting temperatures and howling winds can become an unsavory opponent as we try to maintain our comfort. So, too, can the troubles of life become serious. Some of the problems in life may come and go with only a minimal amount of pain. On the other hand some of the pesky troubles will come to make their homes with us. So, as winter may be severe, so may be the troubles.

Number three on my friend's outline was that winter will not last forever. The exact number of days in winter depends on whether it is leap year as well as the dates of the winter solstice and vernal equinox. That means that winter will last for 89 or 90 days. The heartwarming truth about the troubles we encounter is that they, too, will not last forever. There is a determined time for the sore trials of life, and they are noted in the master plan that a loving heavenly Father has for each one of His children.

Thought to ponder: "Don't waste your sorrows; they are the tears that bring joy in the morning."

July 28

"He (the devil) was a murderer from the beginning, and abode not in the truth, because there is no truth in him."
John 8:44 (KJV)

I was watching a mom try her hardest to get her child to behave so that the photographer could take her picture. The discontented youngster squirmed, cried, and gave her mother every reason to give up. The photographer was at his wits end, and one more outburst from the toddler would probably put an end to the effort of taking a picture. I watched as the patient mother worked with her child, slowly but surely assuring her that this was going to happen, but matters seem to grow worse. When the mom had done everything, she could think of, she evidently had an ace in her hand. She picked the child up, and said to her: "Honey, Ronald McDonald is watching you, and he is about to eat your "Happy Meal" and steal your toy." With that, this darling of terror became as quiet as a church mouse. No more tantrums because she did not want that to happen.

JULY 28

The enemy of our souls wants to do something more serious than Ronald McDonald could ever do. He wants to eat away at our "Happy-ness meal and steal the toy of our joy" if we allow him to do that. If there is one thing that Satan will most likely do, it will be to chip away at our joy and bring it to an abrupt end. If there is one thing he cannot tolerate, it is a joyous Christian. Our joyful tones are blaring screeches in his ears. His intentions are only evil and murderous, and he will do anything in his power to accomplish the task of terminating our cheerfulness. Jesus points out that he was a murderer from the beginning; he has not changed his colors since; nor does he intend to. There is no truth abiding in him, and we should know that no truth will come from him, only lies. Our only arsenal with which we can fight him is to have on the whole armor of God, and when we are dressed in that equipment, we can stand against the fiery darts of the enemy. Without that wardrobe of protection, we are easy and open targets for his onslaughts.

Thought to ponder: "Truth be told, the devil is full of lies."

July 29

"His lord said unto him, Well done, good and faithful servant; thou hast been faithful over a few things, I will make thee ruler over many things: enter thou into the joy of thy lord." Matthew 25:23 (KJV)

A former pastor of mine had some humorous ways to express biblical theology. He would take a profound truth and illustrate it in a simple way that a child could easily understand. For example, he would say, "When I get to heaven, I want to be a cook; and the reason being is that I want to walk up to the Lord Jesus, my Savior and Lord, and ask Him how He wants His steak cooked; and I want to hear Him say, 'Well done, good and faithful servant.'"

Well, there are many words that I anticipate hearing when I arrive in heaven, most of which this world has no human expression or vocabulary to convey. Heaven is a place that we not only will see, but will also hear in a way we have never before. Not only will we see the splendor and glory of this paradise, but also hear sweet voices never heard in our earthly existence. I long to hear the Lord Jesus speak. I

JULY 29

have wondered all these years what His voice would sound like. When He sat and taught the people, I know He spoke with conviction. When He scorned the religious for their daily mundane approach to their doctrine, I am positive that they knew He was serious. On my first day in heaven I want to hear the consoling words, "Welcome home My child," or hear the first phrase from the Lord Jesus, "Here is the mansion I have been preparing for you," and the congratulatory words, "All that you see is yours for an eternity."

Of all that I may hear on that appointed day, I want to give audience to these words: "Well done, good and faithful servant." Just to hear those reassuring words will be worth all the effort and labor in my earthly life. The stress and strain down here cannot be compared to the eternal weight of glory that awaits us in heaven. "Well done" will be a word of compliment. "Good and faithful servant" will be a phrase of congratulations. "You have been faithful over a few things" is a portraiture of confirmation. "I will make you ruler over many things" is an expression of commitment.

Thought to ponder: "Heaven holds all that we could ever imagine, and one day we will handle all that heaven is."

July 30

"The LORD hath appeared of old unto me, saying, Yea, I have loved thee with an everlasting love: therefore with loving kindness have I drawn thee." Jeremiah 31:3 (KJV)

My mother loved each one of her grandchildren as much as any grandmother could love her grandchild. She would do anything within her power for their well-being. She would sacrifice her time and effort to see that they were all taken care of. As she has said so many times that what she would do for one, she would do for the other without any hesitation. A friend of hers who knew that once asked her, "Of all your grandchildren, which one do you love the most?" Without hesitation she responded, "I love them all the same; but some of them I have loved longer."

Our loving heavenly Father does not love any one of His children any more or any less than the other. His care is not merely for the needy, who know their need, but also for the full who see no need. His amazing grace is not simply for the down and out, but also for those who see in themselves self-sufficiency. Our Lord does not make any distinction

JULY 30

between young and old, rich or poor. He loves each one with an unconditional love; a love that will never change or end; a commitment which will last an eternity; a connection which can never be broken. This is a radical kind of affection that the world knows nothing about, and can never fathom apart from God's revelation through His Son, Jesus. This is love so amazing, so Divine, that God could love me with an everlasting love. I am thankful that the Lord loves me in this manner, as unworthy as I am. I can never merit this kind of preference from a righteous and holy God; it is all of grace. Though God loves us all the same, there are some who have experienced this fullness of love longer than others. Truly it can be said that the longer I serve Him, the sweeter He grows.

Thought to ponder: "Love doesn't ask why, it states how."

July 31

"And he spoke a parable unto them to this end, that men ought always to pray, and not to faint;" Luke 18:1 (KJV)

During the winter of 1777 to 1778, General George Washington camped with his troops at Valley Forge, nearly twenty miles north of Philadelphia. Images of bloody footprints in the snow, soldiers huddled around lonely campfires, and Washington on his knees, praying that his army might survive, often come to mind when people hear the words "Valley Forge." One of the soldiers in Washington's army who had witnessed the General on his knees in prayer remarked, "We pray to God; and we keep our powder dry." What this soldier did was to reflect on his belief that God would answer their prayer, and the responsibility the soldiers took upon themselves was to keep their gun powder dry, because that would help defeat the enemy.

God expects us to pray. In Luke 18:1 Jesus encouraged His disciples to maintain a vigilance of prayer that would see them through to the end. He said, "that men ought always to pray, and not to faint." All of God's people should be

JULY 31

praying people. We should always be in a spirit of prayerfulness. From the time we awake in the morning, till the moment we close our eyes in the evening, our day should be consumed with solicitous prayers. When we begin to pray, it should awaken in us the need to embrace a propensity to give all that we are so that God can give all that we need. As our prayers rise up to heaven in the ear of a listening God, our hands should also be raised in a willingness to be prepared for the coming engagement. Prayer and activity go together like a hand and a glove. The glove takes on a new dimension when a hand is placed into it. The glove comes alive and can do what it could not otherwise do without the hand. Our prayers, as sincere as they may be, takes on a new fullness when we engage our all into the endeavor before us. There is nothing so valuable that we cannot give into the hand of a gracious God, Who in return will accomplish great things in and through us.

Thought to ponder: "Prayer and activity produce great answers, which in turn produces glory to God."

August 1

"If I then, your Lord and Master, have washed your feet; ye also ought to wash one another's feet." John 13:14 (KJV)

At a local fast food restaurant, not known for its courteous service, I made an order and promptly thanked the lady for helping me get my morning started off in a positive direction. Her response caught me off guard when she said, "No thanks required, sir; it's my pleasure to serve you." Now, that's not the kind of congenial service you would expect in this day. Most employees begrudge having to serve other people when it's not in their own interests, and most often they take their frustrations out on the customer.

That kind of reaction from those who serve begs some pressing questions to the Christian servant. Why do I serve other people? Do I minister to them simply to discharge some function? Am I under any obligation to look out for the better interests of others? Do I perform acts of kindness gladly when others have nothing to offer in return?

We are taught in scripture that the servant is not above his master, and the follower of his director will have the

AUGUST 1

proper example to follow. If the Lord Jesus, our Master, helped others expecting no profit or advantage to come His way, our reaching out to the needy and serving them will be done in a selfless way. If we only love those who love us in return, how different are we from the world around us? We are to be difference-makers in this earthly sojourn. As salt and light, we are to be set apart for this one primary objective--to share the love of the Lord Jesus in ways that the world cannot understand and for which there is no explanation. When the love of Christ and the light of Jesus are banners we carry proudly before us, the world will see the real Jesus living His life through us. Our call of ministry is to follow our Leader.

Thought to ponder: "Following our Leader will never lead us wrong."

August 2

"Blessed is the nation whose God is the LORD; and the people whom he hath chosen for his own inheritance."

Psalms 33:12 (KJV)

Someone asked a friend of mine how many country-western singers it takes to change a light bulb. Not knowing the answer, he shrugged his shoulders, shook his head, and responded that he did not know. The response from the questioner drew a broad smile from my friend and me. The answer was, "4: 1 to change the bulb and 3 to sing about how it used to be." As silly as the question and answer may sound, there is some merit in the last part of the answer, "sing about how it used to be!"

As I look back over the years, I find myself lamenting over the way things used to be. I have begun to realize that the United States of America today is not the one my grandmother knew. There was a time when we were a Christian nation, founded upon Judeo-Christian values. Times when I felt safe and secure in the laws of our land now seem to be a distant memory. There was a segment of life when we as a nation stood in strong support for the dignity of human life, the traditional family, the right to a God-centered education, common decency, and an accountability to God. We have removed ourselves from the conviction that a nation is only as strong as its belief in God and the practice of His commands.

Because of the influx of the masses who do not embrace our ethical value system, we can no longer make the claim to be a Christian nation, as a whole, who look to the Bible for Godly wisdom and instruction. The Bible does not seem to be the "Book" that we reach for when life spins out of control. We have been deceived into believing that the Word of God is no longer relevant in our society. Rather than looking to the church-house with its message of hope and love, there is now a tendency to cast our eyes to the White House, which can only promise hope and change but cannot fill the void. Our political system and laws of the land may promise this wealth of help but can only hope against hope that the change comes. There is only One Who can do that; and that is the Lord Jesus Christ, Who is the hope of glory. So, as the times are changing, we still remember and sing about how it used to be!

Thought to ponder: "Yesterday, all the troubles of my life seemed so far away."

August 3

"And when the day of Pentecost was fully come, they were all with one accord in one place." Acts 2:1 (KJV)

My mother had a number of old sayings she used when she wanted to make a point. She told me that these maxims have been handed down to her from her daddy and mother. They were pithy little phrases that conveyed a deep truth. She said that they seemed to work for her, so she in turn handed them down to the next generation. Mother was real careful not to insult anyone with her witty sayings. I have come to appreciate those words of wisdom over the years. Her use of them would be suited for the moment and on the spot.

I have heard her say, "Don't look a gift horse in the mouth, son." What she insinuated was that I should not be ungrateful when I received a gift. She would also declare, "He who lies with dogs, will wake up with fleas." Her point was that if I stayed around people who had a bad reputation, my way would become corrupted with the same report. Mother would also bring to light, "That's like the pot calling

AUGUST 3

the kettle black." The disclosure of truth here was the notion that a criticism that I would make of another could equally well apply to myself. The one that has stayed with me over the years is, "Many hands make light work."

As a Christian, I have tried to put that proverb into practice. With mother's encouragement to join my brothers and sisters in Christ, who have a like mind and spirit, I have committed myself to help spread the good news of the gospel. I have come to realize that no one individual can do it all. God has placed others in our company whose hearts beat for the same cause. Hand in hand with other believers, we can do more with less than one can do with much. Jesus was only One Who came to minister to the needs of others, and He was successful in every respect. We have the opportunity to consolidate our resources and accomplish more for the cause of Christ than ever before. When our hands are in agreement, harmony, and conformity, the world will see the reality of the gospel in our efforts.

Thought to ponder: "Many hands make light work."

August 4

"By this shall all men know that ye are my disciples, if ye have love one to another." John 13:35 (KJV)

Your vehicle tag will tell people what state you are from. A name label at a gathering will allow others to know your name. When law enforcement agents ask for your identification, they want to make sure that you are the one pictured on the license and that you are the owner of the automobile. When you use your charge card, or write a check for an item you purchased, the cashier will usually ask for your driver's license or some kind of proof that you, your credit card, or your check go together. If you pay a visit to a doctor's office and receive treatment, you will be required by the receptionist to provide insurance cards bearing your name. If you expect to receive a senior citizen's discount you may be asked to prove your age. When it comes to the proof that you are a disciple of Christ, the only badge you have is your love for the brethren.

When we love one another and acknowledge it, our enemies are pressed to concur that there is something different

AUGUST 4

in the way we live. Self-sacrificing love is not something common among those who practice the selfish love of what others can do for them. So, if the world is to see the love of Christ, they will see it in us. Our foes will be inspired when we pass along the street, and meet and express our affection to each other; and they will confess, "See how they love one another." The distinguishing badge and character of a disciple of Christ has nothing to do with outward garb, or any pretentious show, but has everything to do with an exercise of unconditional love to brothers and sisters in Christ. Our path of sacrificial service is paved with a unique love that looks out for the welfare of others. The well-being of the brotherhood and sisterhood depends upon our willingness to take our badge of discipleship out of our pockets, where it may be hidden, and display it in a respectable manner, which will in turn say to others, "I love you in Jesus."

Thought to ponder: "When we lose our honesty, we have nothing else to lose."

August 5

"Not as though I had already attained, either were already perfect: but I follow after, if that I may apprehend that for which also I am apprehended of Christ Jesus."

Philippians 3:12 (KJV)

A repeat offender in crimes, which had accumulated for years, was asked whether he had committed all of the criminal acts for which he was charged. In his response, he gave this amusing answer, "I have done still worse! I have suffered myself to be apprehended."

The apostle Paul would approach being apprehended of Christ in a purely positive way. Rather than bemoan his seizure by the Lord in a begrudging manner, he took the high road of determination. This effort of being possessed of the Lord would produce the most noble effort in the history of the gospel ministry. His own words sum up the intensity developed within his call to reach the world for the gospel sake in Philippians 3:12. It wasn't that Paul had reached his goal, or that he was fully mature; it was that he made every

AUGUST 5

effort to take hold of his sacred calling because he had been captured by his Lord.

Paul would say that he had not reached the conclusion of his life's goal, or that he had completed the course set before him. The road map to those destinations was intact in the scripture, but his extraction point from this world was not known. Though the path he travelled was filled with potholes and detours, he had the sense of a job that would never be finished in this earthly realm. There was so much more that he would give to the cause of Christ: more of the gospel message to share with a lost and dying world; a sense of urgency that the Lord Jesus could come at any moment; and a realization that today could be his last day in which to share the love of Christ. He never perceived that he would reach perfection here on this earth, but it would be this life-long goal of maturity that would keep him focused and driven.

Thought to ponder: "With our eye on the prize before us, we set a watch around us."

August 6

"I have fought a good fight, I have finished my course, I have kept the faith:" 2 Timothy 4:7 (KJV)

Someone has suggested that when we come to the end of life's journey, we can best describe that momentous event by using a punctuation mark. Because life has a beginning and an ending, we have the opportunity to make our mark on life. When we come to the conclusion of our pilgrimage, we can choose which indicator best describes our excursion. There are 14 punctuation marks commonly used in American English. Three of those fourteen marks are appropriate for use as sentence endings. They are the period, question mark, and exclamation point. By using one of these three markers, and we cannot use more than one, we can best personify the kind of life we have lived.

One expression we will use is that of a period (.). In grammar, a period is used to make a statement or end a sentence. In our earthly sojourn, we too will end life with a statement--we have lived and we have died, period. The Bible teaches us that we have an appointment to keep and an appearance to make. We all will die, and that's our appointment. We will appear before the judgment seat of Christ, and that's our appearance. There is no escape from these two events. So, life will end for us all with a period.

There is also the imprint of a question mark (?). A question mark is used at the end of a direct question. This mode of expression begs these questions that all of us will face when we find ourselves at the end of this earthly life: "Did I do all that I could possibly do for the kingdom's sake?" There is more than likely a "No" to this scrutiny. "Was there anything of importance I left undone?" Our likely answer will be an emphatic, "Yes!"

There is also the use of an exclamation mark (!). These indicators are utilized at the end of sentences to make an emphatic statement. When the weariness of this life draws to an end, and we have lived a life for Christ alone; and we have run the race faithfully and patiently; and we have kept the faith; and we have finished well; we, then, will have an exclamation point, or shout of victory, to put on our earthly life, as we rise to meet our Lord in the air.

Thought to ponder: "Happy are they who have eternal life; happier are those who live it to the fullest."

August 7

"Pray without ceasing." 1 Thessalonians 5:17 (KJV)

"Take a knee" is an American football term for when the quarterback drops to one knee immediately after receiving the snap, thus ending the play. The use of this play comes only near the end of the game when your team is in possession of the ball and holds a narrow lead. If you execute a run or pass play, you risk turning the ball over and allowing the opposing team to take possession and have a chance to score. By taking a knee, you are able to run down the clock without putting the ball at risk. As someone has said, "It's a boring, if strategically important, play."

In the world of daily pursuits, which include living every day for the Lord, the perfect play to call is that of taking a knee in prayer. There will be the struggles of life we face every day. Challenges to our well-being await us at every turn. These difficulties call for an offensive game plan that will counteract the aggressive enemy. That call will be to take a knee. When we get out of bed in the morning, or before we go to bed at night, the perfect play will be to pray; and taking

AUGUST 7

a knee is more than a stall tactic, or an end to a situation. It's an offensive way of winning the battles of life.

When we take a knee in prayer, it shows an act of humility in approaching the throne of grace. The Lord is close to those who are of a broken and contrite spirit. We are promised that when we draw nigh unto God, He will draw near to us. It has been said that we are as close to God as we are when we take a knee before Him in supplication. The fitting way to finish off putting on the armor of God is, "Praying always with all prayer and supplication in the Spirit." Paul would say, take a knee when you have armored yourself with God's provision.

Thought to ponder: "To win the battles of life, take a knee."

August 8

" For my thoughts are not your thoughts, neither are your ways my ways, saith the LORD." Isaiah 55:8 (KJV)

I enjoy watching a chess match between two talented players. The thought process between the two heighten the anticipation of what move would be made next. If you are an excellent chess player, you will make certain moves which I deem as being incomprehensible, because I don't understand the complexities of the game. This universe in which we reside is more infinitely complex than a chess game; but fortunately, God is considerably wiser than the best chess player, and we should not be too surprised in the least when we don't understand the "moves" He's making.

I am thankful that God's thoughts are not my thoughts. He is holy, I am sinful. I have the cataracts of sin covering my eyes; He alone is the all-seeing God. He sees ahead every move and every motion which takes place in my life. There is not a nanosecond of activity that passes the eye of God. He never sleeps, nor does He slumber. He is always in the hustle and bustle of my life. My thoughts are driven by the

AUGUST 8

fleshly nature; His are in the realm of the Spirit. His ways are not my ways. The ways which God prescribes and directs us to walk are different from ours. His ways are plain, ours crooked; His are ways of light, ours are the ways of darkness; His lead to life, ours to death. When it comes to the postures of life of which I have no explanation, He knows all about the conditions and has brought me to a place where I walk out with my head held high.

Thought to ponder: "Sleeping on the job can never be said of our God."

August 9

"And ye shall be witnesses unto me both in Jerusalem, and in all Judaea, and Samaria, and unto the uttermost part of the earth." Acts 1:8 (KJV)

"You have the right to remain silent" are the opening words and a part of the verbiage to the Miranda Rights of every United States citizen. It is a right to silence warning given by police in the U.S. to criminal suspects in police custody before they are interrogated to preserve the admissibility of their statements against them in criminal proceedings. The closing words of this right are equally telling: "You can decide at any time to exercise these rights and not answer any questions or make any statements."

Every citizen of this great country is protected by this law. It is a part of the reason why America is the greatest nation on this earth. When it comes to the citizenship of the kingdom of God, the opposite can be stated: "As Christians, who are bound for the celestial city, we do not have the right to remain silent. We do not have the prerogative to decide at any time to witness or to give an answer for the hope we have,

August 9

or not." As a matter of fact, it is our privilege and responsibility to share the good news of the gospel. What the heavenly Father has done for us should be our passion to share that with a darkened world. Our voices must be lifted up with clarity and sharpness to proclaim freedom to the captives. We must be the ones who share a burden to function as the hands and feet of Jesus. The resonance of our words ought to be so powerful that people will be drawn to the hope we have to offer. A word of personal testimony will go a long way in shedding light on a darkened path, so the next time we have the opportunity to share our faith, we do not have the right to remain silent.

Thought to ponder: "In the possibility of sharing Christ with others, silence is not golden."

August 10

" And let us not be weary in well doing: for in due season we shall reap, if we faint not." Galatians 6:9 (KJV)

At one of our local banking institutions I noticed a small marker that read, "Funds from deposits may not be available for immediate withdrawal." The impression from the sign said to me that I cannot expect to make a deposit of certain monies and then immediately make a withdrawal from the initial deposit. That can also be the subject of a spiritual investment and withdrawal. Some of the investments we make in our endeavors in the kingdom of God may not pay in immediate dividends. Some will find their way back to us, while others will only be known in eternity.

There are certain sponsorships which we need to make in this earthly sojourn. The godly actions of which we author will make for some future returns. There will be earthly benefits and heavenly rewards attaching themselves to our behavior. The law of sowing and reaping takes on the face of future compensation. This truth will be seen upon the

AUGUST 10

landscape of satisfaction in knowing that the seeds I plant will come to harvest; though they may not come instantly, next year, or before I pass from this life, I am fully persuaded that in God's timing there will be a harvest time.

One of the investments we can make which may not give us an instant return is in our children. They are the future of our nation. Someone has said that we are one generation of children away from extinction. Whatever resources we can muster up should be pointed toward bringing our children up in the nurture and admonition of the Lord. For many of us who have children who are married with children of their own, we take on the face of granddaddy and grandmother. We have the opportunity to do more for them than we did with our own children, and we can continue our parental skills with them in leading them in the right way.

Thought to ponder: "Know what you own; and know Who owns you."

August 11

"For Christ sent me not to baptize, but to preach the gospel: not with wisdom of words, lest the cross of Christ should be made of none effect." 1 Corinthians 1:17 (KJV)

While riding through a small rural town in our area, I was taken aback at a sight just off main street on a small dirt road. A church building was being renovated and the steeple had been removed and placed in an area where there were weeds and other rubbish. It was a strange sight to say the least. One expects to see a steeple sitting on top of the church with its spiral reaching towards the heavens, but instead it seemed as if the steeple had been carelessly tossed to the side. I was assured, though, by the members of the congregation that the steeple would once again find its rightful place on top of the quaint little church.

What I saw that day reminded me of how many people in our society look upon the cross. For most of them it's just a piece of wood or fiberglass that looks attractive perched on top of an edifice. Its beauty is only seen in the fabrication of and the cost of the lumber or in the color of paint applied

August 11

to it. The impressiveness of the cross to the world can be measured greatly by its height, weight, or beauty. When it comes to the preaching of the cross, the Bible says that it is foolishness to the world.

On the other hand, the proclamation surrounding the cross of Christ is the power of God to us who are the saved. The word "power" in the language of the New Testament is the word, "dunamis," from which we derive our English word, "dynamite." According to the scripture, the cross of Christ is the dynamite of God to those who love the Savior and who are involved in spreading the good news. The sum and substance of the Gospel is the crucifixion of Christ, and that becomes the foundation of all our hopes and the fountain of all our joys.

Thought to ponder: "The cross of Christ will 'X' out our sins."

August 12

"Without natural affection, trucebreakers, false accusers, incontinent, fierce, despisers of those that are good."

2 Timothy 3:3 (KJV)

The story is told of a man named John who was driving home late one night when he picked up a hitchhiker. As they rode along, he began to be suspicious of his passenger. John checked to see if his wallet was safe in the pocket of his coat that was on the seat between them, but it wasn't there! So he slammed on the brakes, ordered the hitchhiker out, and said, "Hand over the wallet immediately!" The frightened hitchhiker handed over a billfold, and John drove off. When he arrived home, he started to tell his wife about the experience, but she interrupted him, saying, "Before I forget, John, do you know that you left your wallet at home this morning?"

That is a case of false accusation. Paul, the apostle, spoke of the last days in which perilous times would come. One of the precarious situations during this unsettled period would be that of many people being false accusers, or devil,

AUGUST 12

being like Satan." In Revelation 12:10, Satan is viewed as the "accuser of the brethren;" that is to say, "false accusers, or devil, being like Satan." That statement should cause each one of us to sit up and take notice and stop to consider what we become like when we bring false accusations against the believers in Christ. The term "false accusers" is one word in the language of the New Testament. It is the word "diabolos" from which we derive our English word, devil. When we falsely accuse, or slander, a brother or sister in Christ, we share the same traits and desires of our arch enemy, the devil. With such actions, we will imitate that diabolical malignity which renders the great enemy of mankind so justly odious. Rather than denouncing our brothers and sisters, like the enemy of our soul does, we should be speaking with high regard of them whom our heavenly Father loves.

Thought to ponder: "Speak well of the people of God, less harsh words return to you."

August 13

"Let the word of Christ dwell in you richly in all wisdom; teaching and admonishing one another in psalms and hymns and spiritual songs, singing with grace in your hearts to the Lord." Colossians 3:16 (KJV)

The "No Child Left Behind Act of 2001" was a U.S. Act of Congress which reauthorized the Elementary and Secondary Education Act (which was former President Lyndon Johnson's war on poverty). The "No Child Left Behind Act" included the provisions applying to disadvantaged students. The Act requires all public schools receiving federal funding to administer a statewide standardized test annually to all students. Schools that receive funding must make progress reports in test scores each year. There have been pros and cons to the administration of the activity itself. There is a spiritual application that can be made from the "No Child Left Behind," and that is that no child of God should be left behind when it comes to teaching them the principles and practices of kingdom work.

AUGUST 13

As Christians we are all teachers in the sense of leading others down the straight and narrow path. We are instructors whether we have a degree in teaching or not. If there would be a degree required, it would be only a B.A. degree, and that would be a born again diploma. Our teacher is the Master Himself. We take our instructions from Him and pass them along to other believers. Our classroom is the world. Where ever we find ourselves in the course of life, we have a membership to help grow toward maturity. The truths we share as educational matters are from the Bible, the textbook of life. The lessons we teach others are drawn from the experiences of our life. Our passion is to not only make disciples of all nations, but also to teach them to observe all the things commanded by Jesus. The legacy of any teacher is to pass along the knowledge they have accumulated over the span of life. It has been said, "When an older person dies, it's like a library has burned to the ground."

Thought to ponder: "Teachers of the Word are not only heard, they are seen as well."

August 14

"Howbeit when he, the Spirit of truth, is come, he will guide you into all truth: for he shall not speak of himself; but whatsoever he shall hear, that shall he speak: and he will shew you things to come." John 16:7 (KJV)

While listening to the radio, I heard a rather interesting advertisement come over the air waves. At first I started to change stations, but something said to me that I should listen. The broadcast was an announcement concerning an important disclosure of information that was to be made within the next few minutes. Those who took advantage of the revealed knowledge would be guaranteed some incredible results. Toward the end of the announcement there were five words spoken with emphasis. They were: Get It? Got It. Good! The spokesman wanted to make sure that the news was understood: Get It? He also wanted to make evident that listeners had gotten the message: Got It. The announcer then took the lead and said with an exclamation: Good!

AUGUST 14

Our Teacher is the Holy Spirit Who has been sent by the Father. He is called the Spirit of Truth, and His mission is to guide us into all truth and keep nothing back that will profit us. His mission is to reveal the Father and the Son. The Holy Spirit is our Guide, not merely to show us the way, but to go with us throughout our earthly tenure. It is His desire to speak those things that the Father would have us to know. Whatever the Holy Spirit hears from the Father, He in turn speaks to us. The Father wants to make sure that we have come to an understanding of His revealed will. That to Him is the most important pursuit of His children, so He asks this question: Get It? Then it becomes our turn to answer Him with a statement of faith by saying: Got It. From that the Father will take great joy in hearing that His child has come to a realization of this great love: Good!

Thought to ponder: "Get It? Got It. Good!"

August 15

"Hast thou found honey? eat so much as is sufficient for thee, lest thou be filled therewith, and vomit it."

Proverbs 25:16 (KJV)

Each year on the fourth of July the Nathan's Famous Hot Dog Company sponsors a hot dog eating contest. In 2013 Joey Chestnut won the competition for the seventh year in a row, setting a new record by eating 69 hot dogs and buns in just ten minutes. According to news reports, Chestnut received a prize of $10,000 for his eating performance and consumed over 20,000 calories during his eating spree. Chestnut consumed hot dogs at a pace of seven a minute for ten minutes straight. To see him dispose of that much food, leads one to ask, "How much is enough?" That is a good question when it comes to the pursuit of creature comforts. How much do we really need to bring a lasting satisfaction? There is a God-shaped vacuum in every person, an emptiness that only God can fill.

Many people devote their lives to acquiring wealth and possessions, living with a focus only on the temporal.

AUGUST 15

The norm of the day is to stuff all the gusto of life into a short length of time without the realization of eternity. Contentment seems to be a lost word in the dictionary of today's society. "Get all you can" is the motto of the greedy. "Can all that you get" is the proverb of the hoarder. "Set on what you cannot can" is the maxim of the ill-content. As a result of this fanaticism, rather than living in contentment, people live in a perpetual state of dissatisfaction. Yet, after garnering all that the material world can afford, people of this ilk can never enjoy a moment of peace. The only one who can satisfy the human heart is the One who created it, and that is the Lord Jesus Christ, the Lover of our souls.

Thought to ponder: "What a Friend we have in Jesus."

August 16

"Who are kept by the power of God through faith unto salvation ready to be revealed in the last time." 1 Peter 1:5 (KJV)

One New Year's Day, in the Tournament of Roses parade, a beautiful float suddenly sputtered and quit. This particular float was larger and more decorated than the others, but as ostentatious as it was, it ran out of gas. The whole parade was held up until someone could get a can of gas. Seconds seemed like minutes, and minutes appeared as hours, as the rush for fuel was on. The amusing thing was this float represented the Standard Oil Company. With its vast oil resources, its truck was out of gas. Even though we, as Christians, have access to God's omnipotence, we too will run out of power if we do not avail ourselves of it.

There is a constant day-by-day, minute-by-minute power source from which we can draw our strength, and that stoutness is from the Holy Spirit of God. He has made available to us His enduring capacity. Our energy to do the work of ministry comes from His abiding presence. We are strengthened with His might in our inner man as we draw from His

AUGUST 16

never-ending source of energy. Though our walk may slow as a result of weariness in well doing, we have this confidence that the Spirit of power is ever present in a time of need. Even in the storms of life when the winds rage against us and our bodies are depleted from energy, the Holy Spirit is a force of power, always available to supply us the needed refreshment. He is not affected by any turbulence surrounding our plight, nor is He disturbed by destructive devices hurled against us. He stands ready, willing, and able to supply whatever invigoration is necessary.

Thought to ponder: "As the Power of God comes our way, so we can walk that way."

August 17

"But God commendeth His love toward us, in that, while we were yet sinners, Christ died for us." Romans 5:8 (KJV)

I read some amazing figures about planes and super-tankers. It was astonishing to learn how far each one of these behemoths could travel on a single gallon of fuel. A Boeing 747 (jumbo jet) can travel a distance of 280 yards, carrying 385 people at an altitude of 39,000 feet on one gallon of fuel. The length of three football fields is as far as this jet could travel while burning a single gallon of fuel. If that's not incredible enough, an ultra-large crude-oil carrier (supertanker) 31 feet long, travelling at 17 miles an hour and fully loaded, needs 10 gallons of fuel just to travel its own length of 31 feet. Those figures are mind-boggling, but could I tell you something that is even more extraordinary: God so loved the world that He willingly gave His one and only Son to die for our sins!

In Romans 5:8 we see the determination of God. When God commended (introduced) His love toward us, it revealed His set course of the extent He would go to save us.

AUGUST 17

While we were steeped in our sins, without any hope of getting out from underneath them, not seeking God for relief, He came to where we were to redeem us from our wickedness. God could have given up on us a long time ago. In the garden of Eden God could have washed His hands clean of Adam and Eve. They willfully, willingly, and wantonly disobeyed God. Yet we see the searching Father, walking in the cool of the day, knowing what had transpired, to have fellowship with His creation. Both Adam and Eve hid themselves from the presence of God, not wanting to face Him. We see the Father's determination to renew fellowship with His fallen creatures. It is truly an amazing grace that sought us while we were yet sinners. Jesus died for our sins so that we could have fellowship with the Father.

Thought to ponder: "Christ died so that we could live."

August 18

"Be not deceived; God is not mocked: for whatsoever a man soweth, that shall he also reap." Galatians 6:7 (KJV)

A little boy told a salesclerk he was shopping for a birthday gift for his mother and asked to see some cookie jars. At a counter displaying a large selection of them, the youngster carefully lifted and replaced each lid. He was looking for the perfect container, and he was bound and determined to find one. His face fell, though, as he came to the last one. Summoning for the cashier to come and answer a question, the youngster asked, "Aren't there any covers that don't make any noise?" That reminds me of some Christians who want to live any way they want to and not face the consequences of their sinful actions.

There is a law of sowing and reaping given in life. It covers every aspect of our journey in this occupancy. From the day we are born till the day we draw our last breath, we are faced with this regulation. We are told in the scriptures that what we sow, we can expect to reap. Every farmer understands the meaning of this principle: We reap what we sow, more than

AUGUST 18

we sow, and later than we sow. For the Christian there is the maxim that states, "If we live only to satisfy our own sinful nature, we will harvest only decay and death from that sinful nature." We are responsible for and will be held responsible for every action in our daily travels. If we think we can gloss over some harsh or critical activity, we are setting ourselves up for a judgment process from God, for God will not allow any word or deed to go unpunished. When we speak or do things outside the will of God, we invite His displeasure, and it is an awful thing to fall into the hands of an angry God. God does not take lightly our attempt to negate this law of sowing and reaping.

Thought to ponder: "Sowing Godly things will harvest eternal things."

August 19

"As every man hath received the gift, even so minister the same one to another, as good stewards of the manifold grace of God." 1 Peter 4:10 (KJV)

A rich man was determined to give his mother a birthday present that would outshine all others. He read of a bird that had a vocabulary of 4000 words, could speak in numerous languages and sing three operatic arias. He immediately bought the bird for $50,000 and had it delivered to his mother. The next day he phoned to see if she had received the bird. "What did you think of the bird?" he asked. She replied, "It was delicious."

God has gifted each one of His children. His desire is that we take what He has appropriated and utilize it for His honor and glory. The moment we came to saving faith in Christ, we were endowed with a spiritual ability. It becomes our right and privilege to facilitate that proficiency to further the cause of Christianity. The knowledge and wisdom to exercise this gift comes from the Holy Spirit. He takes the truths of God and makes them known to us. Behind the revealing of the truth is the reminding that we are to share that same truth. Again the Word says everyone has received a gift, so there is no excuse; we must minister this gift to one another. It is imperative that we serve each other with our gift. The danger we face is after having received the gift, we put it on a shelf to let it stay there until we think it's time to take it down and employ it for our benefit. Every gift we have received is to be used as a profit to the body of believers.

Thought to ponder: "It's time to unwrap our spiritual gift and use it."

August 20

"He that believeth on me, as the scripture hath said, out of his belly shall flow rivers of living water. (But this spake he of the Spirit, which they that believe on him should receive: for the Holy Ghost was not yet given; because that Jesus was not yet glorified.)" John 7:38,39 (KJV)

The body needs about three quarts of water a day to operate efficiently. Water helps break up and soften food. The blood, which is 90 percent H2O, carries nutrients to the cells. As a cooling agent, water regulates our temperature through perspiration; and without its lubricating properties, our joints and muscles would grind and creak like unused parts of some old rusty machinery. Without this constant supply of water, our physical body would slowly deteriorate and die. Jesus spoke of the Holy Spirit as "rivers of living water, gushing out from our belly." Out of our life can flow this life-giving and life-changing water we so desperately need.

It is our innate desire to be happy and blessed; and if any one of us desires to be truly and forever happy, we must

AUGUST 20

allow the living waters of the Holy Spirit to bathe over us as a rushing flood. The Spirit, dwelling and working in us, is as a fountain of living, running water, out of which plentiful streams flow, cooling and cleansing as water. Our spiritual well-being depends on this stream of life-giving water. Just as the physical part of our being cannot go without water, our spiritual portion cannot survive without the refreshing waters of the Spirit. There is an ever-flowing river of restoration and revival coming to us at every bend in the road. This life-giving relief helps us to operate efficiently in our ministry. It soothes our weary path. It lubricates our spiritual muscles, freeing them to exercise our gift. Without this river of living water, we would grind to a halt or creak like an unused part.

Thought to ponder: "Using God's H2O shows me 'How 2 Order' my life."

August 21

"Make a joyful noise unto the LORD, all the earth: make a loud noise, and rejoice, and sing praise." Psalms 98:4 (KJV)

One of the newer members in our church asked me what it meant to have "special music" in our congregational worship. They wanted to know what was so special about our music. Whether it be the choir singing a lyrical song, or an individual who brings special music, they were curious as to why we called it, "special." My response to them was that it's not the music we sing which makes it special, but the Person whom we extol when we sing; that's what make our music unique. I continued by saying that it's not even the type of music we sing--Contemporary, Southern Gospel, or some other Christian style of music. When we lift our voices in praise, it is the sweet sound of our melody in worship that makes our reverence all about Him.

The Psalmist said that we are to make a joyful noise unto the Lord. A joyful noise is a bold declaration of God's glorious name and nature, with shouts, clapping, and other outward expressions of praise. Because of the manifold blessing

AUGUST 21

of God so richly bestowed upon us, we gladly direct our voices of praise toward Him. The music we sing is all about the Lord, not about us. Every word and note sounded from the instruments and voices are all in the direction of exalting the King of Kings and Lord of Lords. He alone is worthy of our praise and adoration. While there is a time for quiet reverence in the presence of the Lord, God also delights in our outward displays of a joyful abandon as we worship Him with all we have. So, our "joyful noise" is directed upward to the heavenly Father.

Thought to ponder: "O for a thousand tongues to sing of God's greatness."

August 22

"He that saith he abideth in him ought himself also so to walk, even as he walked." 1 John 2:6 (KJV)

My mother was the consummate seamstress. She did all of our family sewing in our house as we grew up. It wasn't that we couldn't afford new clothes; mother preferred to do our sewing. She could take cloth with thread and needle to make a dress for my sister or a shirt for my brother and me. She had the knack and patience to sit down at a sewing machine and produce some incredible clothing. If mother needed to sew something beyond the basics, she would buy a pattern from one of the local fabric stores, lay it out and pin cloth to it to cut out a pattern. She was meticulous when using the pattern, and I remember her saying that it was important to follow the pattern. The clothes were always beautifully made.

Our heavenly Father has given us a pattern to follow, and that convention is found in the earthly life of the Lord Jesus. He is not only "The Way," but He shows us the way we are to go. When life becomes entangled with the thorns of misgiving, we have an example to follow. Life was never promised to be easy for us; and when we encounter the snags along the roadways, we have a standard by which we can follow. The excellent life of our Lord paves a path we can follow daily. The dark times will come and shelter the sun from our journey, but the light of the Lord Jesus' countenance will shine brightly upon us. We never have to worry that the path will change, because He never changes. If we follow Him, we will never be in the dark, will have no occasion to stumble, or have any need to doubt His goodness to us. Each step we take can be with the assurance that it will take us to His desired end.

Thought to ponder: "Walk like a man! Like God's man or woman."

August 23

"So likewise, whosoever he be of you that forsaketh not all that he hath, he cannot be my disciple." Luke 14:33 (KJV)

Fifty-six men signed the Declaration of Independence. Their conviction resulted in untold sufferings for themselves and their families. Of the 56 men, five were captured by the British and tortured before they died. Twelve had their homes ransacked and burned. Two lost their sons in the Revolutionary Army. Another had two sons captured. Nine of the fifty-six fought and died from wounds or hardships of the war. Carter Braxton of Virginia, a wealthy planter and trader, saw his ships sunk by the British navy. He sold his home and properties to pay his debts and died in poverty. There was no price too great to pay for their calling.

The Lord Jesus issues one of the hard sayings to His followers. It wasn't one that the disciples wanted to hear. He did not mince words when He extended to them the reality that it would cost them to follow in His steps. There is a call for sacrifice on the part of every believer. It is a surrendering of everything we have. There is no holding back or giving up

AUGUST 23

99% and keeping 1% for ourselves; it is a total relinquishment of all we possess. The word "forsaketh" means, "to bid farewell to, or adieu." Those things which have become a hindrance to us, we are to bid each one "farewell," and stay the road of commitment. Those affections which have cooled our love for the Lord, we are to say, "adieu." The confidence we have is that the Lord does not ask us to give up something that He will not give us something better in return. What we may give up is a paltry amount on our part as compared to what He has given to us in His Son.

Thought to ponder: "Our meager shovels of goodness cannot compare to the mega shovel of God's graciousness."

August 24

"Put on the whole armour of God, that ye may be able to stand against the wiles of the devil." Ephesians 6:11 (KJV)

My wife and I attended an event that we knew would be crowded with people. Many had been invited and the response was promised to be overwhelming. Almost everyone who had received an invitation was there. It was to be what many had dubbed as "shoulder to shoulder people." As we arrived, I noticed the parking lot was full and that a sign had been placed at the entrance which read, "Standing Room Only!" I knew we would be in for a long evening of standing.

In the realm of our spiritual warfare, as we wage the battle against the enemy, it will be "Standing Room Only." In our combat ordeal, there is no room for cowering, admitting defeat, and running away. No need to bend the knee to the opposition and admit defeat. There is not space for doubt and despair when it comes to waging war against the competitor for our very lives. We can take no breaks or respites from our mission, for the adversary is ever ready to engage

August 24

us. Because our standing is on the solid rock of Jesus, we can march into battle knowing that our footing is secure and our victory is assured. When we have put on the protective armor God has provided us, we are commanded to take our stand. As a robust soldier, with every provision made, with confidence in our Commander, and protected by the Holy Spirit, we can take our stance as a stalwart soldier of the cross. When it comes to worshipping the Father, we can bend the knee in submission; but when it comes to our struggle against the combatant of our souls, we can stand in the power of God.

Thought to ponder: "When it comes to our warfare, it is 'Standing Room Only.'"

August 25

"And he said unto them, Come ye yourselves apart into a desert place, and rest a while: for there were many coming and going, and they had no leisure so much as to eat."

Mark 6:31 (KJV)

Working with our children's ministry in church can be a rewarding time as well as amusing at other times. The truth that children can say the most entertaining things was never more evident than at one of our Wednesday evening meetings. During our prayer time when our leader asked for prayer requests, one of our six-year-old girls asked prayer for her dad. She was pressed to be more specific; and her response brought a smile from all of our leaders. She said, "Pray for my daddy because he is worn out." She was serious and concerned because her daddy is a farmer and oftentimes works from sun up to sun down.

On a more serious note, if we are not careful as Christians, we can experience "burn-out." We can become so worn out with the pressing issues of life that we can have a slow burn. Jesus recognized that His followers could reach a point

AUGUST 25

where they could possibly give in to the pressures of ministry, give over to the daily grind of constantly giving out, and eventually could give up. To safeguard against spiritual burn-out, Jesus extended an invitation to those who followed Him. He wanted them to join Him as He took time out of a busy, earthly ministry. He well understood that we all grow weary at times. He said to His disciples, "Come ye yourselves apart into a desert place, and rest a while." Our bodies need rest and can only take so much pressure before it succumbs to a blow-out. In that condition we are of very little good to others, ourselves, or to the Lord Jesus. It's better to be in one "peace of mind" than to be in many pieces of confusion and disorder.

Thought to ponder: "Come apart with the Savior, or come apart at the seams!"

August 26

"But he saith unto them, It is I; be not afraid." John 6:20 (KJV)

"I love you" are three words that can make the difference in an individual's day or life. This tiny sentence can change everything in a relationship when spoken in sincerity; and once it is uttered, there is no going back. These words should not be given out lightly but with honesty and sincerity. This phrase can have a lasting effect on marriages, as they are expressive of feelings. Every individual, regardless of who they are, should hear at least once in life those words, "I love you." As important as these three little words are for the welfare of love and marriage, there are three little words for the Christian which will serve as a reminder that we are protected by the mighty hand of God. Those words are, "Be not afraid."

These words were spoken to the disciples of our Lord as they faced a monumental storm in their life. As seasoned sailors on the Sea of Galilee, there came a time when their fears became larger than their faith. The anxiety they faced was so thick that it seemed to have a choke hold on their

AUGUST 26

very being. Their lives hung in the balance, and they were frightened out of their wits. There seemed to be no hope for them because the Lord was not with them during this time of emergency. They were alone on the raging sea with no physical strength to stem the tide of panic. It seemed as if they had led the last expedition for fishing, or said their last goodbyes to their families, or eaten their last meal. Then the Lord Jesus came walking on the sea; and as He drew nigh unto the ship, they were frightened even more than before. Jesus said unto them, "It is I; be not afraid." Immediately the ship was at the land where they were going. The Lord is always with us when the times of fear and uncertainty invade our privacy and peace. His words are always before us if we take the opportunity to remind ourselves of them: "Be not afraid."

Thought to ponder: "When fear comes knocking at your heart's door, send faith to answer and you will find no one there."

August 27

"What shall we then say to these things? If God be for us, who can be against us?" Romans 8:31 (KJV)

My wife and I came out of a local restaurant which specialized in serving seafood. As we made our way to the car, we noticed a truck pulling a boat through the drive-through window at the eatery and making an order. My wife commented, "He has gone fishing and probably caught nothing; so he has stopped to order fish to take home." I chuckled and said, "It certainly looks so." The thought came to me that some Christians have set out in their own strength to do the work of ministry. They have strengthened their determination to carry on at all costs. The approach is that when the going gets tough, the tough get going. In the process of taking that advance, they have failed miserably. They are invited to pull through God's drive-through window to stock up on some fresh repentance and renovated commitment. This will allow the Lord of strength to infuse spiritual power into them.

AUGUST 27

Our path to victory will not come through the multitude and strength of men and their fortitude. The gateway to pulling down strongholds will not come as a result of our prowess or determination. The channel by which the enemy will be held at bay will not be the outcome of strategy or formulas. The triumph of achievement will take place only when we allow the Holy Spirit of God to so invade our very being and every movement. With that plan of attack, there is no enemy looming so large who can withstand the power of God working in us. When the Spirit of God animates us, excites us, encourages us, and strengthens us, we can do any work we are called upon to do. Step by step, moment by moment, we are empowered by the omnipotence of our God. If God be for us, then who on earth can be against us? Greater is He Who is in us than he who is in the world!

Thought to ponder: "Whom God calls, He also equips for ministry."

August 28

"And whatsoever ye do, do it heartily, as to the Lord, and not unto men;" Colossians 3:23 (KJV)

A retired buddy of mine told me about a friend of his who became interested in the construction of an addition to a shopping mall. Observing the activity regularly, this friend was especially impressed by the conscientious operator of a large piece of equipment. Day after day this friend had his eye toward the work and the accomplishments of this individual. The time finally came when this friend had a chance to tell this man how much he'd enjoyed watching his scrupulous work. Looking astonished, the operator replied, "You're not the supervisor?"

That reminds me of some who only do what is right when it's convenient, or while someone of consequence is watching them. It seems that the higher in authority the onlooker is, the greater the steadfastness of effort. The self-worth of these free spirits seems to revolve around doing a job for the sake of earthly recognition. If it is not someone of significance, then the job is diluted with a half-hearted

August 28

effort, but as Christians we take a different approach to our search for meaning and fulfillment. What we do, how we do it, and why we do it, have the constant voice speaking into our ears and reminding us that what we strive to accomplish is done to please the Lord. Of all the rewards that men may give our way, they pale in comparison to what the Father gives to us--the promise of life here on earth, and the assurance of eternal life in heaven. Whatever work we may aspire to do, we are taught to do it as though we were working for the Lord of Heaven rather than for the adoration and praise of people.

Thought to ponder: "Our work for the Lord will have God's silent applause."

August 29

"To him the porter openeth; and the sheep hear his voice: and he calleth his own sheep by name, and leadeth them out."
John 10:3 (KJV)

One of my assigned church duties is that of extending a welcome to guests who come to worship in our sanctuary. Visitor's cards are handed out by our ushers and guests are requested to fill them out with some personal information. At the end of the services I have the opportunity to call out each name so that they can be recognized and welcomed. There are times when I struggle to make out the names on the guest cards. Some folks have poor penmanship qualities, and coupled with my weakness in being able to decipher someone's writing, it becomes a challenging time to get every name pronounced correctly. Most of the time I get the names right while at other times I stumble over them.

God knows each one of us by name. He doesn't have a memory lapse when it comes to His family of believers. Once a member, always a member; the family of God is ours for eternity. Because of our identity with Christ and

AUGUST 29

His finished work at Calvary, we will never face the quandary of having a name change. When our name is recorded in the Book of Life, no eraser is too large or too sturdy to blot it out. Our standing with the Father is based upon His unfailing love, not on our determined effort to love Him at all times. We will forget at certain seasons; fall in the midst of adversity; fail to love unconditionally; forsake the brethren in the time of need; or freeze when the enemy attacks. Our great and mighty God will never be found divorced from His creation, nor His child. His hand can reach down to our fallen state. His ear is always open to the cry of His own. His eye is fixed upon each and every one of us. He knows us by name and will always call us His own unique possession.

Thought to ponder: "The family of God shares the same name: Saint."

August 30

"Wherefore he is able also to save them to the uttermost that come unto God by him, seeing he ever liveth to make intercession for them." Hebrews 7:25 (KJV)

Recently I heard a pastor comment on a passage of scripture from Hebrews 7:25. His take on this Bible passage was to put an emphasis on what God did for us that we could not do for ourselves. God went beyond the pale of what we deserve. His grace reached much farther than we were entitled to. The minister stated that God did more than save us to the "uttermost." He emphatically said that God delivered us from the "guttermost!" I would say "Amen" to that because it rightly describes what the Father did.

God's hand is not too short that it cannot reach down to where we are and save us. Our deliverance comes from the strong hand of a Divine Creator. Down into the mud of sin, where we were, is the area that the Lord's hand was extended. These mighty and energetic fingers of a loving God are not so weak that they cannot deliver us from our sin. As defiled

AUGUST 30

as we may be, and as tangled up as our life may appear, this tender touch from the Master's hand brings about liberation.

Also, His ear is not too heavy that He cannot hear our cry, as feeble as it may be at times. What may be inaudible to others, the Father's super sensitive ears are bent toward His child to pick up the faintest of cries. Our Lord is touched with the feelings of our infirmities. He was in all ways tested as we are, yet without sin. When we hurt, He knows the pain we suffer. When we cry out to Him, His ears are not so dull that He cannot hear.

Thought to ponder: "From the uttermost to the 'guttermost,' God delivers."

August 31

"But every man is tempted, when he is drawn away of his own lust, and enticed." James 1:14 (KJV)

One of the intriguing parts about watching how anglers lure fish into swallowing a hook is to observe the habits of the fish. They seem to be swimming around the neighborhood waters, minding their own business and not looking for any trouble. Then plop comes the baited hook with its enticing nourishment. There's just something tempting about a morsel of food that seems to be swimming around. The unsuspecting fish nibbles around the edges of the bait, then swims away for a few seconds, returns to take a larger bite, and finally throw caution to the wind and swallow hook, line, and sinker. For a split second there is a kind of utopia in the act; but the end results are less than what was expected. What a picture of James 1:14 and the allurement of sin.

How like fish we are when it comes to a tantalizing nip of sin. We assume that we can nibble around the edges of immorality and consider the action to be harmless indeed.

AUGUST 31

We feel as though we can stop at anytime without any repercussions. Our initial thought may be that if no one else is involved in the act, then I am only hurting myself. The reasoning behind this action is that I can press the edge of the envelope without opening its contents. Our rationalization of dining on tidbits of sin here and there will only give us indigestion which can be cured with an antacid of good works. We may have a smitten conscience of wrongdoing and leave the enticement alone for a while, but eventually come back to the consumption of more sin. That has ever been the sequence of events put forth by the enemy of our souls: the temptation, then the drawing away from God by our own lust, and the enticement that follows. Ultimately we will find ourselves diving headlong into the wickedness and being consumed by its overwhelming power.

Thought to ponder: "When we flee temptation, we should leave no forwarding address."

September 1

"As the heavens are higher than the earth, so are my ways higher than your ways and my thoughts than your thoughts."
Isaiah 55:9 (KJV)

One of our church associational leaders was talking about some of the failures in our church and why they happened. He talked about the lack of leadership among those who oversee the ministry. There was the need for more training in the area of evangelism, and He spoke about the prerequisite for a more committed group of men and women in the pew. In the process of his sharing his heart, he used a word that immediately caught my attention; it was the word "stradegy." Now that is not a word in the dictionary, and it was the first time I had heard someone use it. I came to realize what the brother was talking about as he continued. He said that when the church utilizes a worldly strategy to reach the lost, it will lead to a tragedy--thus the combination of a strategy and a tragedy equals a "stradegy."

We should know by now that using the world's conduct and practice will only lead us down the dark trail of tragedy.

SEPTEMBER 1

There is only one end when it comes to this type of pursuit. It's not what the Lord has planned for our endeavors, and there is no heavenly good that will come out of a worldly undertaking. When we depend upon what man can do for us, we will have a man-made result--which may be strong for a season but has no lasting endurance. On the other hand, when we depend upon the guidance and execution of the Bible, we will achieve by God's help what only an omnipotent God can do--which will last through this lifetime and carry over into eternity. God has promised to show Himself strong on our behalf when we fully obey Him, embrace His leadership, and depend upon Him for the lasting results. The only remedy for a "stradegy" is for us to refuse the ways of the world and fully embrace God's judgments.

Thought to ponder: "When we get 'down' to God's way, we will always be 'up' for any day."

September 2

"Every way of a man is right in his own eyes: but the LORD pondereth the hearts." Proverbs 21:2 (KJV)

At one of the main intersections of our town, there was a "Road Closed" sign resting on its side, with some of the wooden pieces missing, while other fragments had been damaged beyond repair. One of the workers for the highway department said to me, "It looks like somebody couldn't read or they were not paying attention when they ran into the sign." Someone else spoke up and remarked, "Well, that doesn't surprise me because people are going to be people, and they aren't likely to change their ways." God uses the Bible to position certain road signs along life's highway to help us navigate through the terrible terrains of a crooked world, and there are times when we blindly run over them or through them to our hurt. Those warning signs are not placed in our path to keep us from something, but rather to protect us from the dangers of disobeying them.

One of those protective exhibits is that of a "Stop Sign." God uses these to warn us of an impending wreck if we keep

September 2

pursuing our own way. He strategically places these signs to warn us of the dangers up ahead if we continue. Obeying a "Stop Sign" will save us many heartaches and sorrows.

Another evidence of God's direction is that of a "Yield Right Of Way." Holy Spirit is our guide and teacher. He is the agent by which any great work will be accomplished. We are to yield to Him our time, our talent, and our treasure so that the work can be finished properly.

There is also the testimony of God that speaks of a "Merging Sign." This sign speaks to us that we are to join others in the work of the Lord. We can multiply the results while dividing the work. No man is an island. We are a fellowship of believers who share a heart for ministry, and together we can accomplish much.

There is one final sign God has placed in our path, and that is a "Green Light." This reference teaches us that as we go to all nations we are to make disciples of many; we are to bring them into the fellowship of other believers; and teach them to observe all the truths which our Lord has taught us.

Thought to ponder: "When we walk the narrow path, we will find wide open opportunities."

September 3

"Let us therefore come boldly unto the throne of grace, that we may obtain mercy, and find grace to help in time of need."
Hebrews 4:16 (KJV)

There may have been a time when the most complicated computations people needed to do could be performed on their fingers and toes. In these days, it's all but impossible for many people to imagine doing anything involving numbers, from math homework to tax returns or tipping servers in restaurants, without the help of at least a basic pocket calculator. In fact, electronic calculators are so widespread now that it's hard to believe they didn't become commonplace until the late 20th Century. Some of the most complex equations known to man have been solved by a personal calculator which cost less than fifty dollars.

The Bible is the source which enables us to work through the most confusing times in life. The muddy and dim periods that bring darkness to our souls can have the light of the Word of God shone upon them to bring clarity. Though the way may seem dark and strewn with dangers, there is a

September 3

brightness of daylight that shines through the precepts of the Bible. It doesn't require a rocket scientist to figure out where we need to turn to in a time of need. We know the way we must go, and we are invited to take the road of obedience to bring us to an expected end. God's word has the answers and directions to our complexities if we are willing to put forth the effort and time to seek them. We are invited to come boldly to the throne of our gracious God. He awaits us there in the throne room for our entrance into His presence through prayer and supplication. The promise is that there we will receive His much needed mercy, and we will find His marvelous and amazing grace to help support us when we need it the most.

Thought to ponder: "His invitation to come is our privilege to respond by coming."

September 4

"Get thee hence, and turn thee eastward, and hide thyself by the brook Cherith, that is before Jordan." 1 Kings 17:3 (KJV)

"And it came to pass after many days, that the word of the LORD came to Elijah in the third year, saying, Go, shew thyself unto Ahab; and I will send rain upon the earth."
1 Kings 18:1 (KJV)

Hide-and-seek is a popular children's game in which any number of players conceal themselves in the environment to be found by one or more seekers. The game is played by one player chosen (designated as being "it") closing their eyes and counting to a predetermined number (such as counting to 10) while the other players hide. After reaching the number (such as reaching 10), the player who is "it" attempts to say, "Ready or not, here I come!" and then to locate all concealed players. The game can end in one of several ways. In the most common variation of the game, the player chosen as "it" locates all players as the players are not allowed to move; the player found last is the winner and is chosen to be "it" in the next game. There is a biblical application to this child's game that is appropriate for the Christian.

God came to the prophet Elijah and gave him some marching orders. These instructions would ensure that the man of God would be successful in his pursuits. Elijah faced some trying times in his life and these two instructive commands would enable him to be strong as he stood before wicked King Ahab. Rather than running away in fear from the evil king, Elijah had to put himself in a place that would prove to be the groundwork for the conquest. The Lord said first, "hide thyself." After a period of time in which the prophet would be prepared to take the next step, God instructed Elijah to, "shew thyself." The application here is simple but profound. If we are going to show ourselves strong on behalf of the Lord, we must hide ourselves in submission to the Lord.

It is imperative that we steal away to pray in some secluded place. Being secluded with the Lord in the quietness of the morning, or in the middle of the day, or at the close of night is God's design for His servant is to be alone with Him. Prayer helps shape our perspective of who God is and whose we are. Prayer doesn't necessarily change God's mind, it changes us. It helps mold our faith which is vital in standing firm in the face of adversity. So, before we show ourselves, we must hide ourselves.

Thought to ponder: "Hiding with God and seeking His face is the path to well-being."

September 5

"Whatsoever thy hand findeth to do, do it with thy might; for there is no work, nor device, nor knowledge, nor wisdom, in the grave, whither thou goest." Ecclesiastes 9:10 (KJV)

One of the local radio stations advertise their music as, "Standing on the shoulders of giants." Their genre of music covers the easy listening sounds of the 50s, 60s, and 70s. When you tune in, you can hear crooners like Frank Sinatra, Dean Martin, and Bobby Darin singing their big hits. At other times you can listen to the silver voices of Johnny Matthias, Roy Orbison, or B.J. Thomas streaming out their chart toppers. There are the instrumental hits from Ray Conniff, Lawrence Welk, and Percy Faith who made relaxing music. All in all in the area of performing artists, it could be said that we, today, are standing on the shoulders of these giant musicians.

As Christians, we are not so much standing on the shoulders of the past giants of our faith as we are standing shoulder to shoulder with the saints of today. Knowing who the apostle Paul was and knowing his wealth of spiritual

SEPTEMBER 5

insights is a must for the servant-teacher; but to know who my brothers and sisters are in the faith is of greater wealth than knowledge of the saints of old. Being inspired by the lives of the apostles Peter, James, or John is of unequaled worth; but to join the fellowship of other believers who have responded to the call of discipleship will make our ministry fully rewarding. Our work and labor in the fields of the world are strengthened by our coming together, hand in hand, shoulder to shoulder, with one mind and one pursuit, to accomplish the task of winning the lost to Christ. With our shoulders joined together in full commitment to the Lord, the world can see the mighty force of an army marching toward its goal. As we draw strength from the saints of old, may we translate that inspiration into a determination to focus our efforts on the saints of today who can be our marching partners.

Thought to ponder: "Great teamwork yields great results."

September 6

"He that goeth forth and weepeth, bearing precious seed, shall doubtless come again with rejoicing, bringing his sheaves with him." Psalms 126:6 (KJV)

One of the men in our church made an interesting recommendation to me. He suggested we remove all of the "Exit" signs in our sanctuary and replace them with "Enter" signs. His point was that as we walked out of church we would not be exiting into the world but rather entering the world. His rationale made sense. When we end our worship time in the auditorium, we don't leave our celebration there, but we take it with us as we enter the world. What we have experienced during our time of praise and worship can be taken with us because we have the opportunity to show men and women what honoring God is like. Leaving a time of worship with a determination to take it with us will be our mark of commitment to the cause of Christ. We are salt and light; we can and must make a difference.

If the Lord has given you a song to sing in church, don't silence your voice as you meet people out in the public. We

SEPTEMBER 6

can say that, "in my heart there rings a melody, a melody of love." This world has enough static and clamorousness that a fresh vocal harmony will drown out the noise. If the light of the Lord Jesus has shined into your heart, let that radiant beam so shine in your daily life that others may see your good works and give glory and honor to Him who deserves it. The darkness of this world will always be with us, but we can lighten up our little spot in it. If the Lord has blessed you beyond measure in corporate worship, let those blessings flow forth from a heart of gratitude into a public celebration of life. The truth is that the only God some may ever see will be in us. Let us walk in a worthy fashion that so pleases Him who has commissioned us to "Enter" the world with a song in our heart, a light for the path, and a blessing for those we meet.

Thought to ponder: "A new perspective is an entrance sign leading us out of worship into the world!"

September 7

"And that knowing the time, that now it is high time to awake out of sleep." Romans 13:11 (KJV)

I was riding down Interstate 75 the other day when an eighteen wheeler cruised by me. It was one of those transporters that one could not miss. It was bedecked with lights, advertisements, and other ornaments. I noticed on the passenger side, just below the door of the truck, a sign that read: "In case of emergency, awake driver." I knew what the notification meant. In case of an emergency in regard to this vehicle you can awaken the driver who is sleeping inside. I trust the operator of the vehicle never had such an emergency that would rouse him from his sleep.

I thought of a spiritual slant to the notice on the truck concerning an emergency. We are living in what the apostle Paul called, "perilous times." The Bible teaches us that in the last days before the coming of the Lord, there would be a spiritual lethargy which would descend on those whose heart has grown cold and indifferent. We are warned to be sober and vigilant during these days. There is a sense of

September 7

crisis in these ending times; and the last thing we need is for Christians to be asleep at the wheel. We do face emergencies in these closing days of grace, and maybe we need to take heed to the issues of this life by posting our own sign and then mobilizing our efforts to be alert. Rather than waiting for someone else to take action, our sign could read: "We are facing alarming matters of lukewarm living. You don't have to awaken me for I am wide awake and taking these precarious days seriously."

Thought to ponder: "An idea is a funny little thing that won't work unless you do."

September 8

"Out of the same mouth proceedeth blessing and cursing. My brethren, these things ought not so to be." James 3:10 (KJV)

A lady who has a booth in a local antique mall walked into the business and wanted to know how much she had made for the month. The owner looked up her sales report and told her that she had sold quite a bit. In her excitement of grossing over $250, she let a mild expletive slip from her mouth. No sooner had she spoken the word, that she looked up to the ceiling and said, "Thank you Lord!" My mind raced to a verse of scripture that I had recently read that speaks of the silliness of such remarks.

James, the apostle, speaks of the absurdity of blessing and cursing which pour out of the same mouth. In his spirit of ebullience he says, "This is not right!" The rationale he uses in the utilization of words is the imperativeness that we guard our speech. What is in our heart will eventually find its way to our mouth, and through the expression of language we speak wisdom or foolishness. James says that it is considered implausible to do both. Jesus said that a man's words

SEPTEMBER 8

will always express what has been treasured in his heart. If we store away those wholesome words of life and use them at the right time and for the right reason, we are considered to be wise with our speech. If we have reserved evil words of harm and use them to defame others, we are considered to be unwise in our conversation. Out of the same mouth come blessing and cursing; these things ought not to be.

Thought to ponder: "Kind words and unkind words cannot live together."

September 9

"That ye may be blameless and harmless, the sons of God, without rebuke, in the midst of a crooked and perverse nation, among whom ye shine as lights in the world."
Philippians 2:15 (KJV)

Travelling south of Atlanta, Georgia on a cold and wet evening, I had to take a second and third look at a car that raced past me. I had watched in the rear view mirror as the car made its way toward me. It was covered with salt residue and could barely be seen in the twilight. The only clean place on the car was the driver's windshield. Everything else was covered with slime. One of the distinguishing marks on the automobile revealed the manufacturer of the car. It was the timeless and iconic Rolls-Royce Phantom Coupe'. A $450,000 prized collectible looked as if it had come out of the junk yard. What should have been a shiny silver steak for all to admire was encased with grime and filth.

As Christians we are to come out from among the worldly things and be a separate people. We are to be different from those around us who have no claim of kinship

September 9

to our Lord and Saviour. As grimy and filthy as this world is, we are to be sparkling saints among the muck of life. Jesus reached down into the miry pit of sin and brought us up and out of the quagmire of deprivation. He washed us in His own blood and made us one of His own; a private and unique treasure are we to the Father. We are the apple of His eye. He gave us a new change of clothing that we are to wear as the righteousness of the Lord Jesus. We are, according to Philippians 2:15, to be blameless and innocent as a child of God, living in the world above reproach, because we find ourselves in the midst of a crooked and perverse nation. We are to shine as beacons of light in a darkened world. Rather than blend in with the world and behave like petulant children, we are to rise to the standard God has set for us in His Son. We are timeless and iconic, much like a Rolls-Royce Phantom Coupe', and should live in a way that would parallel our Christian standing.

Thought to ponder: "As children of the heavenly Father, we are to act the part of kinship."

September 10

"And as it is appointed unto men once to die, but after this the judgment." Hebrews 9:27 (KJV)

I was reading a list of items we are well acquainted with and how long they last. A lightning bolt lasts 45 to 55 microseconds. A hard pencil can write up to 30,000 words or draw a line more than 30 miles long. Most ball-point pens will draw a line 4,000 to 7,500 feet long. The longest authenticated life-span of a human being is 113 years, 215 days. A 100-watt incandescent bulb will last about 750 hours; a 25-watt bulb, 2,500 hours. A one-dollar bill lasts approximately 18 months in circulation. The average running shoe worn by the average runner on an average surface will last 350 to 500 miles. Eternity on the other hand has no end. It will go on forever and ever.

The two most solemn facts of our being is that it has been appointed unto each one of us to die, and after our death comes the judgment. We all have an appointment with death that we cannot escape. The commission of every living individual will be that of physical demise, unless the

September 10

Lord comes to rapture the saints away. What we do with Jesus, His sacrifice and death on the cross, will determine where we spend eternity. Many shall go away into everlasting punishment, but the righteous into life eternal. (Matthew 25:46) There is a judgment awaiting us all. The young, the old, the rich, the poor, the men, the women, all have a day of exposure--a time when we stand before the Judge who will appoint each and everyone his or her destiny. For some it will be the Great White Throne judgment, while for others it will be the "Bema Seat" judgment. For an eternity we shall be with the Father or separated from Him.

Thought to ponder: "When our time on earth is spent, eternity begins."

September 11

"Some trust in chariots, and some in horses; but we will remember the name of the Lord our God." Psalms 20:7 (KJV)

Early on the morning of September 11, 2001, nineteen hijackers took control of four commercial airlines (two Boeing 757 and two Boeing 767) en route to California (three headed to LAX in Los Angeles, and one to San Francisco) after takeoffs from Boston, Massachusetts; Newark, New Jersey; and Washington, D.C. Large planes with long flights were selected for hijacking because they would be heavily fueled. On the evening of the attacks, President George W. Bush addressed the nation. His closing remarks are worthy of our consideration. He said, "This is a day when all Americans from every walk of life unite in our resolve for justice and peace. America has stood down enemies before, and we will do so this time. None of us will ever forget this day. Yet, we go forward to defend freedom and all that is good and just in our world."

There is a sense of 9/11 urgency in our God-fearing churches throughout this country, a day when all Christians

September 11

from every walk of life will come together to unite in a resolve for justice and peace within the confines of church fellowship. The history of Christ's church standing down the enemies of the cross are well-known and need to be kept in perpetual memory. Jesus promised that the gates of hell would not prevail against His church. The fulfillment of that promise can be seen through the One who has the keys to death, hell, and the grave. We, as Christians, can live in the calmness of everyday life with that assurance. Peace rather than enmity must prevail among the brothers and sisters in Christ. It is the life line to our fulfilling the Great Commission. Every Sunday is an opportunity to pay homage to our great God and Savior. We must never forget this day because the Lord, Himself, has deemed it the "Lord's Day." We can go forward with confidence in our sure victory to defend the freedom given to us by the Lord Jesus. We can amplify all that is good and just within the church of the Lord Jesus.

Thought to ponder: "Peace is not merely the absence of war, but rather a quality only God can give."

September 12

" So we, being many, are one body in Christ, and every one members one of another." Romans 12:5 (KJV)

Someone asked me what I thought an ideal church would resemble. The questioner evidently thought that I would have a pat answer and would give my humble, subjective opinion. I thought for a moment and responded, "An ideal church would have strong biblical preaching, sound teaching from the scriptures, and stalwart members who would be willing to do whatever was needed." I then hastened to add that I had something even better than the description of an ideal congregation. If I could choose members who had last names that would depict this "ideal church," I could make a better presentation of my view. The following names are real people who are active in a church I know or have heard about. Their last names depict what a church should be like.

There is Ben and Jean Churchwell. Ben is the chairman of the deacon body and has a heart for the deacon outreach ministry in his church. His heart beats for the welfare of

SEPTEMBER 12

the saints. I also know Calvin and Betty Workman. Betty is responsible for teaching and leading the children of her church. She works in one of the most under-appreciated ministries of outreach. I have met Bob and Glenda Goodwill. Both of these saints are leaders who oversee the weekly visitation in their fellowship. Bill and Betty Senior felt the call to represent their last name by ministering among the senior citizens in the meeting house they attend. Mable Watcher is a single mom who has a heart for the clothing and food ministry at her local chapel. She is constantly watching for those who are living through some rough and tough times. Interestingly, Jim and Barbara Youngman are leaders in their local youth group and have proven their last name by working with teenagers. They have no children of their own, so they reasoned that they could have surrogate children to whom they could give their parental guidance. Give me a church who has these names, and I will show you how this body of believers is living out the life of our Lord Jesus.

Thought to ponder: "Everybody is somebody in His body, the body of Christ."

September 13

"And brought them out, and said, Sirs, what must I do to be saved? And they said, Believe on the Lord Jesus Christ, and thou shalt be saved, and thy house." Acts 16:30, 31 (KJV)

A lady recently shared with me that she had started a basket list, not to be confused with a bucket list. A bucket list is a series of actions to accomplish before one dies, and as each activity is completed, they are checked off. According to this lady, her basket list is a series of questions she wants to ask God when she gets to heaven, and she is storing them in a basket of sorts. She shared a few of the inquiries: Why did God allow Satan to do his menacing work on earth? Why did God permit many people to linger in their suffering before they die? Why did God allow the righteous to suffer and seemingly the unrighteousness to prosper? And the list went on. Most of us have questions we would like to ask God. There is a question, though, we will not have to wait till we get to heaven to ask, because then there will be no reason to. The question is, "God, what must I do to be saved?"

September 13

The answer to the inquiry is, "Believe on the Lord Jesus Christ, and thou shalt be saved." Believing is an act of faith. Faith has to do with a person. Putting our faith, our trust, and our confidence in the finished work of Jesus on the cross and realizing the need of a Savior will bring the gift of salvation, better translated into heavenly language as eternal life. This question of salvation, or eternal life, must be answered on this side of eternity. What we do with Jesus in this life will determine where we spend the next life. Only two choices are given to us--heaven or hell. There is no time to waste as we face the imminent return of the Lord Jesus for His saints. Those who have embraced the answer by repenting of their sins and through faith inviting Jesus into their heart, will have no need of eternity to inquire about salvation. If there are questions in heaven, then this particular one will have no need to be asked. So, if this enquiry is in your basket list, take it out.

Thought to ponder: "All of our questions can be answered through Jesus, God's Son."

September 14

"Jesus saith unto him, I am the way, the truth, and the life; no man cometh unto the Father, but by me." John 14:6 (KJV)

I oftentimes see a person with a cell-phone in hand moving about and asking, "Can you hear me now?" They are trying to find the right spot where the reception is clear enough to hear. Some of the cell-phone companies don't have all the areas covered, so that means a user has to be in the right place to get a strong signal. Being in a dead spot and having an emergency is not one of the choices anyone would welcome. There is also technology that allows an individual not only to talk to the person on a phone, but also to see them at the same time. I am waiting for someone to be moving around and asking, "Can you see me now?"

Someone has well said, "I would rather see a sermon than to hear one." There may be a strong sermon proclaimed from the pulpit, but if the individual who delivered the homily is not walking the straight and narrow way, the teaching simply becomes as the apostle Paul would say, "a sounding gong or a clanging cymbal." There is much confusion when

September 14

words and actions are not married. To deliver lectures may be a wise thing to accomplish, but the lessons learned from the doctrines presented will be through observation of how those works compliment the instructions. Having sound words divorced from right actions is like taking a bath in dirty water. The idea sounds valid, but the results are not ideal. To say one thing and do another is the epitome of self-delusion. To see a sermon is not only to take note of the words spoken but to see the reality of the expressions lived out honestly. Words are empty when they are not backed up with the right actions. Jesus not only said, "Follow Me," He showed the way by the measure of His walk. His was a union of words which He spoke and a wedlock of works that gave light to the way people should follow. Jesus truly is the way, the truth, and the life.

Thought to ponder: "Jesus knew the way. He showed the way. He lived the way. He was the way. He is the way."

September 15

"Wait on the LORD: be of good courage, and he shall strengthen thine heart: wait, I say, on the LORD."

Psalms 27:14 (KJV)

A doctor's office is not a place you want to visit when you are in a hurry. Time slows down to a crawl when you find yourself in a waiting room. Medical personnel and physicians seem to be in slow motion when you want to be in and out of the office in a few minutes. I do give the doctors and nurses the benefit of the doubt when it comes to their time because they have no control over the circumstances when emergencies and human factors are involved. I recently overheard a lady who was waiting patiently for two hours for her appointment with her doctor say, "He's the best doctor I have ever had, but one thing he was not taught in medical training is to be on time." We were not born with the virtue of waiting patiently.

It takes the right kind of discipline from the Father to develop patience in our life. We have microwave expectations of God. We feel that God should instantly answer our

September 15

prayer or come to our need. It's our life, we reason, and God should conform to our wishes, work on our timetable, and accept our terms of agreement. When He doesn't follow our whims, we feel as though He doesn't care about our well-being, and if He lags behind in coming to our rescue, then God is not as awesome as we thought He was. Regardless of how we feel about the circumstances surrounding our life and God's activity or lack of the same, He is still omnipotent, omniscient, and omnipresent. He does not need a lecture from His creature to inform Him of what He is to do with His creation. He has been in the business of taking care of His own longer than we can think, and God doesn't need our finite input into His infinite plan.

Thought to ponder: "Losing our wait and our patience are one in the same."

September 16

"Neither is there salvation in any other: for there is none other name under heaven given among men, whereby we must be saved." Acts 4:12 (KJV)

Have you ever wondered how much information really exists online? New data suggest that 1.2 Zettabytes (1.3 trillion gigabytes) is now stored in cyberspace--which amounts to 339 miles of fully-loaded iPads stacked to the sky. The International Data Corporation estimates that by 2020, business transactions on the Internet will reach 450 billion per day. With numbers like this, it boggles the mind to make sense of how much data are in existence and accessible at the stroke of a key on a computer keyboard. Someone recently suggested that there is so much data stored in the world that we may run out of ways to quantify it.

With all of the mind-boggling numbers to rationalize on the internet, there are 1,189 chapters in the Bible, which includes 31,103 verses and having 807,361 words that tell us all we need to know about God. God has revealed Himself through the scriptures and ultimately has made Himself

September 16

thoroughly known and approachable through His one and only Son. It doesn't take a rocket scientist with knowledge of or access to the internet to reveal to us that there is only one passage through which we come to the Father, and that is through the Lord Jesus Christ. There are not many ways to heaven, only one. Even though people perpetuate the notion that there are a plethora of ways to come to God, the bottom line is that there is no other path than through Jesus. All other roads will lead away from God and will only bring the emptiness of eternity. God in His master plan to redeem a lost and dying world to Himself gave us the road map to follow that would bring us safely to Him. There can be no salvation in anyone else but Jesus, because God has not given another name whereby we can be saved.

Thought to ponder: "The road to safety is paved with the precious blood of Jesus."

September 17

"Notwithstanding in this rejoice not, that the spirits are subject unto you; but rather rejoice, because your names are written in heaven." Luke 10:20 (KJV)

One of the laughing matters during the 50s & 60s was to buy an item marked, "Made In Japan." The figure on the merchandise signified that it was cheaply made and in abundance. Into the 70s & 80s items marked, "Made in Hong Kong," took on the same token of being inexpensive. Through the 90s and into the new century, "Made in China" has taken over as being economical and thrifty. Down through the years products marked with one of these indicators were considered to be poorly made and in quantity. Some may consider products manufactured oversees as a way of saving money for the companies stateside. However we may look at these products, they are made as cheaply as possible.

It 's no laughing matter when we as Christians realize that our names have been written down in the Lamb's book of life. We have a home reserved in heaven just for us, and

September 17

we can rejoice in that gift. The Lord Jesus works now on the completion of our mansion. Our salvation and eternal home are both products made in heaven, and that makes our experience here on earth and in glory one of the most precious qualities of life. I know many people who like to see their names written down, whether it be a recognition of an achievement or a celebration of some performance. Many relish hearing their names called out and the accolades which follow. Our names are written down in heaven and one day soon the Lord Jesus will confess us before the Father in heaven. We will be recognized as good and faithful servants. Our eternal rewards will be the crowns of our earthly accomplishments. Having our names entered into the heavenly book of remembrance is the gift that keeps on giving for all eternity.

Thought to ponder: "Salvation is the key that opens the door of eternal life."

September 18

"Return unto thy rest, O my soul; for the LORD hath dealt bountifully with thee." Psalms 116:7 (KJV)

Standing behind an individual as they waited to pay for their purchased items, I listened as they complained about everything under the sun. The line was too long at the check-out counter. The cashier was slow as Christmas, or as another commented, "Slower than grandma." Some of the items they wanted were sold out. The weather had been too cold too long. The prices of certain items had gone up but their salary stayed the same. On and on the whining and grumbling continued. Rather than causing a scene and arguing with them about their impatience, I bowed my head and said a brief prayer of thanksgiving for the manifold blessings the Lord had richly bestowed upon me.

It seems to many that it's easier to complain about situations than to pause and give thanks for the showers of unseen benefits which come our way every day. Sometimes the rainy weather comes our way to water the seeds of disappointments to bring a harvest of hope. Oftentimes the wind blows

September 18

not to damage our treasures but to blow away the chaff of idolatrous ways. What many fail to realize is that God causes it to rain on the just and the unjust, and He causes the warm winds and howling winds to come our way in order for us to encounter His great love for us. Whether we can see it or not, His hand of protection is around us as we travel the dangerous roads of life. When things don't go our way, it gives us an opportunity to thank the Lord for being in control. He guides us through all sorts of encounters to strengthen our walk and develop our faith in Him, and He will be with us through all of the times of life--good and bad. He is a loving Father who looks out for the welfare of His child. There is not a place we can go to escape His presence. There is not an action we can take that will cause Him to stop loving us.

Thought to ponder: "It takes more facial muscles to frown than it does to smile."

September 19

"But by the grace of God I am what I am: and his grace which was bestowed upon me was not in vain; but I laboured more abundantly than they all: yet not I, but the grace of God which was with me." 1 Corinthians 15:10 (KJV)

Watching the 2016 Republican Presidential debate, one of the candidates boasted of his ability to make a deal. He claimed that he had been making them all of his life, and he had gotten good at it. He wasn't cut from the fabric of a politician, so he boasted that he could strike up a deal better than anyone on the platform. One of his counterparts spoke up and said, "We don't need somebody in the White House who will make a deal; we need a president in the oval office to make a difference. With that response, the audience broke out in an applause that lasted for a minute, much to the chagrin of the self-proclaimed deal maker.

When Jesus came to this earth, His entrance was not to make a deal. Deals were not what was needed for mankind. Man is born a sinner, not by choice but by birth. He does not have enough goodness in himself to raise himself up to God's

September 19

standard of virtuousness. Our righteous acts, according to Isaiah 64:6, are as filthy rags in the sight of a holy God. A Savior who would be born of a virgin, live a sinless life, be nailed to a rugged cross, shed His precious blood, be buried and raised again on the third day, were the needs of a lifetime for men and women. Jesus left the royal throne of heaven to come and dwell among humanity with the full intent and purpose of making a difference in our life, and what a difference He has made in humankind. His presence among us became the light of the world, and this world has never been the same from the moment the cry of a virgin born baby was heard in Bethlehem. His path of holy living becomes our course to follow. Pursuing Him in holiness as His disciples did will prove to this world what a difference Jesus will make in a person's life.

Thought to ponder: "The difference between sin and righteousness is Jesus."

September 20

"There is a way that seemeth right unto a man, but the end thereof are the ways of death." Proverbs 16:25 (KJV)

During his time with the Minnesota Vikings professional football team, Jim Marshall was involved in what is considered by many to be one of the most embarrassing moments in professional sports history. On October 25, 1964, in a game against the San Francisco 49ers, Marshall recovered a fumble and ran 66 yards with it in the wrong way into his own end zone. Thinking that he had scored a touchdown for the Vikings, Marshall then threw the ball away in celebration. The ball landed out of bounds, resulting in a safety for the 49ers. According to Marshall, when he approached Vikings head coach Norm Van Brocklin afterwards, Van Brocklin said, "Jim, you did the most interesting thing in this game today, you ran the wrong way, thinking that you were in the right with every step."

Solomon spoke of an individual who thought he was on the right path. All the circumstances seemed to point in a positive direction. Every step he took was considered

September 20

to be the accurate way. Moment by moment he journeyed the pathway of morality. Things seemed to be looking up in his excursion. There were no stop signs or detours along his way. Every circuit seemed to be one of freedom and clearness, but the end of the way for this thoughtless and careless individual, according to Solomon, would be his tragic death. There is a path before each person, and if it's not the way that leads to righteous living, the latter end will be that of destruction. Our search for the right way can only be discerned through the leadership of the Holy Spirit of God. He has been sent by Jesus to be our Guide. When we set our compass upon Him and pursue the way He leads, it will bring us to life everlasting. Our journey with Him will move us in the right direction, and when we come to the end of life, we will discover that the proven path that Jesus gave us was the right one after all.

Thought to ponder: "Check to make sure your ladder is propped on the right wall."

September 21

"For in him we live, and move, and have our being; as certain also of your own poets have said, For we are also his offspring." Acts 17:28 (KJV)

I saw a sign in a local restaurant that gave the inspiration for this devotional. It read, "I'm so busy I don't know if I lost my horse or found a rope." There are seasons in life when we seem to lose our proper perspective. As someone has said, "We find ourselves at times not knowing whether we are coming or going." Oftentimes, out of the "busy-ness" of life, we lose our focus. Our eyes have a tendency to follow the bright lights of success and drift away from the more important things. The outlook we have on life is driven largely by the values we place on spiritual things. An improper view of the importance of our relationship with Christ will do a disservice to Him who gave His all, so we could have it all. It's important that we keep the main thing the main thing.

Jesus should the focus of our life. He deserves to be number one in every aspect of our being, and He expects us

SEPTEMBER 21

to honor Him in all our ways. In our walk, our talk, our service, and our love, the Lord is to be supreme in our thoughts. If Jesus is not Lord of all, He is not Lord at all. For in Him we live and move and exist. He truly is the reason for our living. We are not our own; we have been bought with a price, and we are to glorify God in our body and in our spirit which both belong to God. Even though we give our best, there are those times we allow our perspective to become blurred by the fanciful things of this decaying and dying world. We are to keep our eyes focused on the Lord Jesus, because He is the author and finisher of our faith. He has blazed the path of perfect faithfulness, and by His example we can be in step with the Holy Spirit who is the agent sent by the Father, to be our guide. As we walk with Him, the Spirit of God illuminates our path and gives us the proper focus.

Thought to ponder: "With Jesus, keep the main thing the main thing."

September 22

"He shall call upon me, and I will answer him: I will be with him in trouble; I will deliver him, and honour him."

Psalms 91:15 (KJV)

As Christians who have been entrusted with the gospel, we are called upon to dispatch the good news to others who are in desperate need of a personal relationship with Jesus Christ. We could look upon a witness to the Lord Jesus as a 9-1-1 emergency dispatcher. We have been strategically placed in an emergency situation. People are crying out for help in life-threatening matters. Their anguish comes ringing over the telephone lines during our encounters with them. There is a sense of impending trouble and their need is for someone to hear them. The cry is troubling and unless someone will hear and respond, there will be little or no peace. Their world is in chaos and they are pleading with someone to help them. We have the calming words of assurance that Jesus will speak through us to address their turmoil.

September 22

In many cases our rapid yet calm response as a dispatcher will make the difference between life and death for the frantic caller. Once we have a sense of the crisis they face, collect the necessary information about their need, and share the calming news of the gospel, our ministry as "dispatchers of grace" will then come to full fruition. The consignment and charge we have come from the empowerment of the Holy Spirit of God. He has delegated the news of deliverance to all "dispatchers of grace," and as trustees of this good news, we cannot relinquish our positions as guardians of truth. Our effectiveness in this ministry and the ability to see it through to the end, will be seen in our willingness to feel the pain that others have. God has promised that if we call upon Him, He will answer; He will be with us in our trouble; He will deliver us; and He will honor us. If God is willing to do that for us, then we have no excuse not to do it for those who call upon us. We will stay on the job 24-7 until the Lord calls us home, and only then will we be relieved of our duty to others.

Thought to ponder: "The good news is God's news of Jesus."

September 23

"Our fathers trusted in thee; they trusted, and thou didst deliver them." Psalms 22:4 (KJV)

A popular game show, in the course of the contest, offered its contestants a series of lifelines. These "game savers" were used as a means of giving the individual an aid to answer difficult questions. After using a lifeline, the contestant could either answer the question, use another lifeline, or walk away and keep the money earned so far. The show's original three lifelines were "50:50" in which the computer eliminated two of the incorrect answers; "Phone-a-Friend," in which the contestant made a thirty-second call to one of a number of friends and read them the question and answer choices after which the friend provided input; and "Ask the Audience," in which audience members used touch pads to designate what they believed the correct answer to be. There were times when the lifelines provided the correct answers while other responses were not so kind to the contestants. Like the lifelines in the game show which were intended to help those who had lost their way, we as

SEPTEMBER 23

Christians should be using the lifelines the Father has given to us to help the lost find their way.

The refrain to a familiar church song challenges us to, "Throw out the lifeline! Someone is drifting away. Throw out the life line! Someone is sinking today." When we think about the men and women we meet as drifting away from the shore of God and sinking into the miry pit of sin, it should challenge us to do for them what someone did for us. Somebody loved us enough to throw out a life vest for us. Their patience and endurance with us in our time of great need were the turning points in our deliverance. Had it not been for them, we, perhaps, would be lost and undone without hope. Our lives would be like a ship drifting on an ocean filled with adversaries who would sink us at the blink of an eye. People without Christ need other people to lovingly care for them and offer them the life-changing truths of the gospel. We will be held accountable for what we do and fail to do in leading others out of darkness into the light of the Lord Jesus. Our lifeline may be the only one someone may ever see.

Thought to ponder: "Our challenge today is to have a lifeline for a lifetime."

September 24

"Now before the feast of the passover, when Jesus knew that his hour was come that he should depart out of this world unto the Father, having loved his own which were in the world, he loved them unto the end." John 13:1 (KJV)

A senior citizen was once asked what had robbed him of joy the most in his lifetime. He paused for a moment, as if to evaluate the question, and responded, "That which has been a thief of my joy all these years are the things that never happened." It has been well said that worry is like a rocking chair; it gives us something to do but doesn't get us anywhere. The biggest thief in life is the lack of faith on our part in fully embracing the consistent truths that God loves us, holds us, and keep us with His powerful and unchanging hand. Someone has cited these three keys to happiness: "Fret not--God loves us (John 13:1); Faint not--He holds us (Psalm 139:10); Fear not--the Lord keeps us (Psalm 121:5)."

Fretting is not letting God have full control over our situations. When we are overwhelmed with the uncertainties

September 24

of present events, we have a tendency to feel that we can control the small issues of life; and if we come to a point where things whirl out of control, then, and only then, will we turn to God for secondary help. God loves us with an everlasting love, and we have no reason to agonize over the uncontrollable issues, because He will see to our every need. Fainting is not waiting on the Lord to fulfill His plan in our life. We have a proclivity to feel that we know what's best for our life, and with this attitude, we fall far short of God's expectation for our well-being. God holds us in the palm of His hand, and with this assurance, there is no purpose to be apprehensive when we face the unknown. Fearing is not facing our enemies with the authority given us by the Father. All power has been given to the Son, and by virtue of our kinship, we can share in that same dominion. The Lord keeps us near Him every step of the way, and our confidence is in His unchanging word.

Thought to ponder: "Our waiting on the Lord will never disappoint."

September 25

"He that hath the Son hath life; and he that hath not the Son of God hath not life." 1 John 5:12 (KJV)

Erma Bombeck was once quoted as saying, "Never go to a doctor whose office plants have died." Likewise it would be unwise to attend a church that is dead. Their deadness would soon rub off on us and we would become like they were in all of their dearth of life. How does one know that a church is dying or is deceased? There are some sure-fire symptoms of a group of people devoid of life. The following are just a few out of many. You might be in a dead church if:

The Bible is not given its proper place in the preaching and teaching of its timeless truths. The lack of Bible knowledge in a struggling church will suck the very spiritual life out of what may be left.

The altar is empty after the sermon has been delivered and the invitation to action has been given. It's easier to remain stoic in the pew rather than make your way down to the old fashioned altar and pour your heart out to a merciful God to breathe life into the congregants.

September 25

There is no Holy Ghost fire in the pulpit which translates into no burning passion in the pew. A lack of fire cannot give fire away. It has to be burning hot in order to pass it on.

Prayer becomes something to recite rather than an intensity to excite.

I begin to look at other people and compare myself with them in order to solidify my significance, rather than allowing God to finger my heart and point out my shortcomings.

My needs become more important in the scheme of life rather than seeing the privation or difficulties others face and refuse to minister to those who are starving.

The members have lost their vision of a destitute and dying world on the precipice of hell ready to tumble into an eternity without God.

You might be in a dead church if any of the above are true in your church!

Thought to ponder: "In God's work, life can come out of death."

September 26

"Charge them that are rich in this world, that they be not highminded, nor trust in uncertain riches, but in the living God, who giveth us richly all things to enjoy."

1 Timothy 6:17 (KJV)

Recently a friend of mine shared with me a letter he received from his insurance company announcing some updates on his policies. It outlined the new benefits he would be receiving as a result of a recent visit by his agent. During the visit my friend was shown several diagrams and sketches of his upcoming retirement options and was offered a plan that would take care of him and his wife for the rest of their life. He said to me that the offer was almost too good to be true but was assured that everything shown to him was legitimate and on the level. He checked the offers from the insurance company with the Better Business Bureau and found that the proposals were factual. He grinned and said, "I am set for life!"

I am glad for my friend that he feels comfortable with his present situation and his future, but I am reminded of a better standing that I have with the heavenly Father. I am rich beyond compare, not simply in the material things of

September 26

this life, but rather in the spiritual riches. Listed below are just a few of the treasures which belong to me:

I am an heir of God and a joint-heir with the Lord Jesus Christ. (Romans 8:17)

I am loved unconditionally. (John 13:1)

Goodness and mercy are pursuing me now and for the rest of my life. (Psalms 23:6)

My body is the temple of the Holy Ghost. (1 Corinthians 6:19)

Every need I have is met by a loving God. (Philippians 4:19)

I can enter the throne room of God to obtain mercy and find grace to help in my time of need. (Hebrews 4:16)

I have been gifted by the Holy Spirit to minister the same one to another. (1 Peter 4:10)

As I engage the world with the gospel, I can do all things through Christ who infuses strength into my life. (Philippians 4:13)

I am never left alone but have a companion who stays with me to the end of my life. (Hebrews 13:5)

Thought to ponder: "What God gives to His child, the world cannot match nor take away."

September 27

"Do all things without murmurings and disputings."
Philippians 2:14 (KJV)

Someone gave me a plastic ruler with this advertisement on the front, "You can expect more from us (business name) and you get it...even this ruler has an extra inch." Rather than the twelve inches on a normal ruler, this example had thirteen inches. That little ad reminded me of a passage of scripture that speaks about going about our daily business without complaining or arguing. As Christians, we are to do more and make a greater effort in the endeavors we undertake; we are to try harder to get the task done correctly; we are to do more than we are required to do to reach a goal; and we are to pursue every labor with vigor, energy, and a joyful attitude.

There are many things in our walk which become somewhat laborious and disagreeable, but we are instructed to comply with them and be joyous in the performance of our duties. When disputes and strife tangle our way with the vines of oppression, we are to avoid them, take the high road,

SEPTEMBER 27

and tolerate them, while being lenient with those who disagree with us. We are to suffer any injury that can be borne, for the sake of peace, committing our well-being to our Lord's keeping. Our journey here in this life will not be free of any impediments. There will always be those things which will come our way to test our faith. When we commit our way to the Lord, He has promised to direct our path. Some of those avenues will take us down alleys fraught with hostile and antagonistic attitudes, but as we face each crisis, we are assured of being more than conquerors through Christ who loves us. Our approach to the challenges of life is to face them head on with joy in our heart.

Thought to ponder: "A smile is a frown turned upside down."

September 28

"Boast not thyself of tomorrow; for thou knowest not what a day may bring forth." Proverbs 27:1 (KJV)

I saw a bumper sticker that read, "Don't worry about tomorrow; God is already there." Those words are as true as any could be spoken when it comes to the experiences of our life. There are three days most of us fear the most: yesterday, today, and tomorrow. Yet God is in all three days. He makes Himself a part of all the activities of our life: past, present, and future. He was with us in the yesterday of our mistakes; He is in the today of our uncertainties; and He will be with us in the tomorrow of the unknown. As someone has well said, He is the I AM of yesterday, today, tomorrow, and forever.

God is the God of yesterday when it comes to our shortcomings and our sins. When our feet become defiled with the muck and mire of sin, we have a path to follow to cleansing. When we come to Him with a heart of repentance, agreeing with Him about the nature of our sin, He has promised to forgive us of our sins and to cleanse us from all the

September 28

unrighteousness. That is a promise we can carry with us all the days of our life. He is the God of today guiding us each step we take. Again He has assured us that if we acknowledge Him in all our ways, He will direct our path. Those roads which are filled with the potholes of trouble will become smooth passages as we follow His ways. That is an additional commitment He has made for each one of His children, which has never been broken. Lastly, He is the God of our tomorrow when it comes to the unknowns. We don't know what tomorrow holds, but we certainly know who holds our tomorrows. It is the Lord Jesus Christ who brings all of our unknowns into sharp focus with the eye of our faith. When we can't trace His hand, we can trust His heart.

Thought to ponder: "Yesterday, today, and tomorrow all belong to God; let Him handle them."

September 29

"But I fear, lest by any means, as the serpent beguiled Eve through his subtilty, so your minds should be corrupted from the simplicity that is in Christ." 2 Corinthians 11:3 (KJV)

Someone explained the game of baseball with the following illustration: "You have two sides, one out in the field and one in. Each man that's on the side that's in goes out and when he's out he comes in and the next man goes in until he's out. When three men are out, the side that's out comes in and the side that's been in goes out and tries to get those coming in out. When both sides have been in and out nine times, including the not outs, that's the end of the game." That description of the grand old game of baseball reminds me of some ways we try to explain the simple gospel message to those in need.

The simplicity of the gospel is the message that God will pardon us from our sins and give us eternal life with Him in heaven, if we will turn away from our sins and turn to Him, accepting His Son, Jesus Christ, as our Savior and Lord. When we speak the unvarnished truth of the gospel, we do

September 29

so with an intention of allowing the Holy Spirit to put the finishing touch of grace on the message. Our call as messengers is to enunciate with clarity the virtues and uprightness of the gospel. We can trust the raw power of the good news of the gospel to permeate any darkness and stronghold present. It doesn't matter how dark the night may be, when we shine the light of the Lord Jesus, the darkness must flee. This simple message of salvation by grace through faith is not for the few, but rather for all the world. "For God so loved the world" is what John makes known to us, and with that love for the lost permeating our hearts, we go forth with the determination to let others see the Lord Jesus living His life through us.

Thought to ponder: "The plain and simple fact is simply the fact of the gospel."

September 30

" I have no greater joy than to hear that my children are walking in the truth." 3 John 4 (KJV)

A friend of mine gave me a rather interesting lady's watch knowing that I was a minister of the gospel and would appreciate what it stood for. It's unique in the sense that it had the ten commandments on the wrist band. Every time you looked at the face of the watch, you would see those instructions staring back at you. How many times have you seen someone wearing a watch with the most important injunctions God has for people? It's a special, one of a kind, unique time piece. I made the remark that with this watch you can not only tell the time, you can also know how to best utilize the time by following the precepts of the Decalogue. This watch is one of the best conversation pieces that we could use to start a verbal interchange with others.

The ten commandments are not suggestions from God but rather ten freedoms which if followed would release us to the fullest life possible. There can be no greater joy known to us than when we fully embrace what God has intended for

September 30

our good in giving us these commandments. When we maintain a heart desire to have no other gods before us, to make no idol, to not misuse the name of God, to remember to dedicate the Sabbath day, to honor our parents, to not murder, to not commit adultery, to not steal, to not give false testimony, and to not covet what our neighbor has, our pathway to heaven will be filled with the overwhelming pleasure of knowing that we are well-pleasing to the Father. When we love God supremely, with all of our heart, mind, and soul, and our neighbor sacrificially, we have fulfilled all that God has desired of us. It could be said of Father what the apostle John said of his children in 3 John 4, "I have no greater joy than to hear that my children are walking in the truth."

Thought to ponder: "The best that God has for us is when He says, 'Thou shalt not.'"

October 1

"Neither is there any creature that is not manifest in his sight: but all things are naked and opened unto the eyes of him with whom we have to do." Hebrews 4:13 (KJV)

When our world seems to be falling apart, it's actually God who is seeing to it that our world is falling into place. God has some unique ways in which He works. We may not understand the procedures He uses but we can trust His plans, for He knows what is best. Our perspective may be jaded by the pain we bear. The thought of suffering being beneficial for our spiritual well-being is somewhat foreign to our thoughts. As unique as God is, so are the experiences we encounter in life. To sharpen our focus on the plans God has for us, we need to see God as a "know-it-all!"

You have probably been around people who think they knew everything, and they wanted you and everyone to know it. People of this ilk may think they make positive contributions, but in the end more harm is done than good. On the other hand, God knows everything about us and has some good things in store for those who love Him. God

OCTOBER 1

knows our frame. He knows what we are made of and realizes we are made of clay. He will not put more on us than we can handle. When we come to the point when we think we have had enough, God has measured out what we actually need. His grace will forever be sufficient for our every need. He knows our future. The light, temporary nature of our suffering is working for us to produce an everlasting weight of glory which will be beyond any comparison. He who loves us far more than we could ever love ourselves will always express His love for us in ways which will bring abundant benefits. God knows our feelings. It is said of the Lord Jesus that as our High Priest, He is touched with the feelings of our infirmities, and that He was in all points tested as we are. When we hurt, He can sympathize with us in our agony. No human being ever knew the incredible suffering and vexation He endured on our behalf. He did it in part to fully identify with our suffering.

Thought to ponder: "We know God because Jesus has revealed Him in His life."

October 2

"It is of the LORD'S mercies that we are not consumed, because his compassions fail not. They are new every morning: great is thy faithfulness." Lamentations 3:22, 23 (KJV)

A trip of a thousand miles begins with the first step; and the other million steps are taken one at a time. Each step brings us closer to our anticipated end. Heaven is just on the horizon and the progress we make through each movement brings us ultimately to our goal. Rome wasn't built in a day, and we can't expect everything to be microwave ready. Maturity takes time, and God's time is on our side. Our problem seems to come when we try to take two steps at a time. When we attempt to take multiple steps, our feet become tangled, and we fall on our face in shame. It's always harder to get up after we fall than it is to fall. When we take one small step for ourselves toward God's appointed destination, it will become a giant leap for Christendom.

The question may arise, though, as to how we can take one step at a time and reach our expectation? How can we trust God to the point of casting all our need upon Him?

October 2

We may think that we don't have the necessary resources to arrive at our goal. Our earthly reserves may run out too soon, and at some point they will, but God's provisions have no end. God is the only resource we will ever need. His bountiful supplies not only come every day, they will be fresh every morning. The Lord's loyal kindness never ceases toward His people, and His compassions have no end. We can trust Him to provide for our every need, every step of the way, every waking minute. The mercies of our Lord will never be wiped out, and His favor has no limits. As we walk in the ways He has established, we will find that our life takes on a radiance of its own which will become an everlasting encouragement. We will never be left alone; we will not be forsaken; we cannot cause the Lord to love us any less; we are the apple of His eye; and we will be taken care of.

Thought to ponder: "Day by day with the Lord will take care of our weakness."

October 3

"Vanity of vanities, saith the Preacher, vanity of vanities; all is vanity." Proverbs 1:3 (KJV)

Riding up an interstate highway reminds me of our trek through the wilderness of this world. The road ahead is one long, black ribbon of asphalt, going on and on seemingly having no end. Along the roadway there are exit signs. Some are dark and foreboding, while others are inviting with bright, flashing lights. As Christians we are called to walk the straight and narrow path, while keeping our eyes on Jesus our leader and protector. Along the way we are tempted to take our focus off the Lord and take one of the attractive exits ramps because we see better and brighter things.

As someone has said, "The grass is not always greener on the other side." The physical gratification may appeal to our senses as lush and pleasurable, but in the end our actions will leave a bitterness of spirit. That which may be sweet to the taste at first loses its flavor slowly and surely. If we aren't careful, we will exchange the best things in life, the spiritual,

OCTOBER 3

which have enduring value, for those items, the physical and temporal, which devalue as the days go by. Our eyes are naturally drawn to the thrilling sights which sparkle with interest but can't keep the promises they make. Beauty soon turns to ashes in the end with the disappointment of broken oaths. Our only hope for lasting fulfillment is in the unchanging Christ. The one avenue that will take us to great achievements will be the road less travelled--the journey of self-surrender to the Lordship of Jesus Christ.

Thought to ponder: "Self-surrender is a choice we make for our own good."

October 4

"But sanctify the Lord God in your hearts: and be ready always to give an answer to every man that asketh you a reason of the hope that is in you with meekness and fear."

1 Peter 3:15 (KJV)

My grandson asked me what Daylight Savings Time (DST) meant. I was caught off guard by his question and struggled to give some kind of answer that would make sense to him. I said to him, "DST was the practice of setting our clocks one hour ahead during the summer months so that evening daylight lasts an hour longer." At the moment that was all I could say to him until I got home and went to the internet to see what else I could learn about DST. I discovered that DST can save energy, promote outdoor leisure time activity in the evening (in summer), and is therefore good for physical and psychological health, reduce traffic accidents, reduce crime, and is a good tool for business. I feel like I have a better answer the next time someone asks me what DST means.

October 4

As members of the body of Christ, we are taught in the scriptures that we are to be ready to honor the Lord Jesus as holy and be prepared always to give a defense to anyone who asks us for a reason for the hope that is in us. This action is to be done with gentleness and respect. People in our midst are seeking for some answers to the issues of life. In their search for solutions they may turn to us for help in the endeavor. It may be a silent cry, or it may be one loud and clear, and it is imperative that we have a biblical response. It's not that we have to have all the answers to their problems, but it is incumbent upon us that we point them in the direction of the Scriptures, which in turn will reveal the Lord who does have the answers. Our ear must always be open to the cry of the discouraged and the down and out. Our eye must be on the look-out for those who are struggling with a load of care. Our heart must go out to those who battle the consequences of a sin-filled world.

Thought to ponder: "When we set the Lord Jesus apart in our heart, it will set us up for great things."

October 5

"Wherefore the rather, brethren, give diligence to make your calling and election sure: for if ye do these things, ye shall never fall." 2 Peter 1:10 (KJV)

My wife found a recipe for a carrot salad that sounded delicious. She made a list of the different ingredients that would go in the tasty treat and went to the grocery store to purchase the various items needed. When she returned home from shopping, she began to lay out the contents on the counter which would go into the salad. She then realized that she had forgotten to purchase the most important part of the carrot salad. It wasn't the oil, the spices, or the other seasonings. The carrots were what she had forgotten to buy. After taking a deep breath, she said, "What good will all the ingredients be if you don't have the carrots." I am reminded of something of greater importance when it comes to life, and that is taking every effort to work hard to prove that we really are among those God has called and chosen.

OCTOBER 5

We are challenged in the scriptures to make sure that we have taken care of the most fundamental part in our salvation experience, and that is the Lord Jesus. That comes in the form of repentance and faith in the finished work of Christ on the cross. He alone is the pre-eminent figure in God's plan of redemption for mankind. As good as good works are in the scheme of working out our salvation with fear and trembling, they are not the salient features in the gift of eternal life; nor is striving to keep the commandments of God a pathway to salvation. Our feeble attempts to live godly lives with grit and determination are not the road that will bring us to heaven. Our path may be filled with all the necessary components of living a godly life, but if Jesus is not factored into them, they avail nothing. Not everyone who calls out the name of Jesus will be saved; only those who call upon the name of Jesus will be delivered from eternal death. Having all the integral parts of a godly life will be of no lasting value if we don't have the most important foundation--JESUS!

Thought to ponder: "Jesus is the main ingredient to the sweetness of eternal life."

October 6

"I went by the field of the slothful, and by the vineyard of the man void of understanding; and, lo, it was all grown over with thorns, and nettles had covered the face thereof, and the stone wall thereof was broken down."

Proverbs 24:30,31 (KJV)

An iconic house in our neighborhood is undergoing some much needed restoration work. Back in its heyday, this dwelling was owned by a wealthy businessman whose son would become a United States Senator. Over the years I have watched the evolvement of this residence from its glory days to its demise. Slowly but surely the life and beauty of this mansion was drained as a result of neglect. It seemed at first that no one had a heart for such a graceful looking house. For the past several months my heart has been broken when I drove by and saw what had taken place as a result of negligence. Thankfully someone has a heart to see that the glory of this house can be restored. I am reminded of a scene in Solomon's experience which he shares in one of

OCTOBER 6

his proverbs. He said, "I walked by the field of a lazy person, the vineyard of one with no common sense."

There must be constant labor in the vineyard of good if our lives are to be productive for the kingdom's sake. The day must not find us trying to figure out if today is a good day to labor or an evil day to take our ease. What comes of our efforts can be clearly seen in how we view our work ethics. We must constantly be on guard to overcome the tendency to become careless in our conduct. Dereliction of duty and inactivity are the twin sisters of sure failure. Inattention to the daily demands of prayer, Bible study, and fellowship with the Father will bring about a broken wall of harmony. Those sweet moments of praise and adoration will come to a screeching halt when we fail to keep our daily quiet time with the heavenly Father. Where there is a spiritual vacuum, the enemy will try to fill it with his devious activities. The picture Solomon paints here is a warning not to allow the weeds of our evil habits to spring up in the garden of our daily living. If we are not careful, we will allow the thorns of failure to mar our deeds and weaken our behavior, and the broken wall will allow the enemy a resting place.

Thought to ponder: "The book of Proverbs brands laziness as the most prolific source of poverty."

October 7

"The Son of man came eating and drinking, and they say, Behold a man gluttonous, and a winebibber, a friend of publicans and sinners. But wisdom is justified of her children."
Matthew 11:19 (KJV)

I recently attended a "Leadership Day" at my grandson's school. Scores of kids marched into the gymnasium to take their seat and await the activities. While we waited, I looked across the mass of boys and girls and envisioned that maybe one of these children would be one of our next instrumental leaders--someone like Billy Graham who could be influential in bringing about the next great awakening. I wondered if the next Lottie Moon or Annie Armstrong who would touch a continent for God was present on this day. Maybe another Martin Luther King, who would stand strong for equality among the masses, was in my presence. Could there be a Senator, Governor, or even a President in the group? After the hustle and bustle of the events of "Leadership Day," it was a satisfying time to say the least.

OCTOBER 7

For the Christian, every day is a leadership day. It is our duty to be active in the kingdom of God and be found faithful in carrying out our many mission-related activities. We have the privilege to take the lead in witnessing to the masses who are lost without Christ. Our great commission becomes even greater with intention as we realize that eternity for the lost is forever. The opportunities to encourage and support the down and out with a hand to lift them up is within the scope of our ministry. No needy person left behind should be our ongoing motto. Every day should find us reaching out to the destitute with no thought of anything in return. As we follow the Master's lead in striking a balance between the needy and their needs, we are enabled to reach out to those who are different from us. We can make inroads into the most difficult of circumstances. Jesus was the "Friend" of sinners, and we should emulate His passion for those who are rebuffed. We can represent the One Who gave Himself for us by leading the way in giving of our time, our resources, and ourselves to further the kingdom's enterprise.

Thought to ponder: "Every great leader has been a good follower at some point."

October 8

"I must work the works of him that sent me, while it is day: the night cometh, when no man can work." John 9:4 (KJV)

I remember learning this well-known prayer as a youngster:

"Now I lay me down to sleep, I pray the Lord my soul to keep. If I should die before I wake, I pray the Lord my soul to take."

I have come to realize that there is an addition to this prayer that goes like this:

"Now I wake me up to work, I pray the Lord my day not shirk. If I should die before the night, I pray the Lord my life is right."

The image our Lord paints here in John 9:4 is that of life and death when it comes to the activities of the day. Life gives us numerous opportunities to work the works of the Father. There are 24 hours in every day, not one less not one

OCTOBER 8

more. We have all been given the same amount of time; some know how to best utilize their time and squeeze more out of a day than others. It's not how much time we have as it is how we use the time we have. God has given to each one of His children the gift of time, and He expects us to master it with great authority. It is the foolish one who wastes his time. Solomon said of the slothful, "A lazy person is as bad as someone who destroys things."

On the other hand, death puts an end to all human activity on earth. There is no flurry of action in the grave. While we have air to breathe, we are to be diligent in the sowing and reaping in God's vineyard. Whatever we do, we are to do it well; for when we go to the grave, there will be no work or planning for knowledge or wisdom. Our occasion to do good on this earth will come to an end one day, and what we have done up to that time will draw a curtain on any future plans.

Thought to ponder: "Work for the night soon falls upon our labors."

October 9

"The steps of a good man are ordered by the LORD: and he delighteth in his way." Proverbs 37:23 (KJV)

"Watch Your Step" is a warning sign posted in a prominent location on most all public transportation vehicles. There are a number of accidents just waiting to happen for the thoughtless and inattentive. All kinds of injuries can take place if we choose to disregard the notice. If we fail to obey the imperative means, we take responsibility for what happens, and it puts us in some embarrassing situations. I have seen people trip, stumble, and fall over a "Watch Your Step" sign. It's no laughing matter to see this unwise decision played out.

The Bible teaches us, "The steps of a good man are ordered by the Lord." Ladies, that includes you as well. Men, women, boys, and girls who keep their daily devotionals and quiet times up to date will find that the Lord opens certain doors of opportunity and closes other doors of danger. We can be assured that the Father will not lead His child down a dark road without providing adequate light for the

OCTOBER 9

journey. Our passage through the deep waters of life will not go without sufficient strength to take us to the other side. The venue through the rough and rocky places will be with more than enough stamina to endure the challenges. When we make our way through the turbulences of life, we must guard our steps with vigilance because we don't know where the next step may take us. When the Lord has established our steps, we can make it through any device formed against us. His guiding hand excels any Global Positioning System (GPS) known to man.

Thought to ponder: "Established steps are secured for the life of the Christian."

October 10

"And we know that all things work together for good to them that love God, to them who are the called according to his purpose." Romans 8:28 (KJV)

It's a bummer to be on vacation and get sick. To not feel well at any time is an unwelcomed visitor, but to be in a place where you should be relaxing and enjoying the scenery can be unsettling when you feel nauseous. The thought of having to be taken to the emergency room for treatment can be unfortunate when your heart is set on having a time of fun in the sun or an occasion to have a go in the snow. Winter, Spring, Summer, or Fall are times to hit the road for vacation, and the one thing we never invite along for the trip is sickness.

A fast food restaurant was razed for a newer and better facility. There was a sign in front of the bare ground that read, "Rebuilding to serve you better." This became an object lesson for the troubles of life. When God allows the uninvited to invade our peaceful and serene moments, He is doing it for our good. As uncomfortable as the process may be, God does

October 10

have our best interests at heart. He is working according to a divine plan that brings to the surface decisive results. God is always looking ahead to the end game when the final moves will direct us toward His best. Without the hands of a disciplining Father's love for His child, we would be less than the best for service in His kingdom. Problems are never welcomed in our walk. They seem to us to be a distraction, and we could be better without them. With God the detours become His "main attraction," for out of the troublesome times there will come the quiet periods of contentment. May we ever keep our eyes on the Author and Finisher of our faith.

Thought to ponder: "Rebuilding takes time and patience but the results are rewarding."

October 11

"I know thy works, that thou art neither cold nor hot: I would thou wert cold or hot." Revelations 3:15 (KJV)

An opening line in a recent announcement in our church bulletin caught my attention. It read, "If anyone is interested in playing church..." The second and third lines fully explained the intention for the information. It stated, "League co-ed softball." The intent of the announcement was for those who had an interest in playing softball for our church to sign up. I'm certainly glad there was enough room on the paper and sufficient ink to finish the full announcement. Otherwise our church could be looked upon as members who endorse an interest in just playing church.

I wonder how many churches in America today are going through the motions of having church. When the doors are opened it becomes a time to play rather than a time to pray. It seems evident on every Lord's Day there is a segment of Christianity who pretend to be pious and religious with a matter-of-fact attitude. They approach their worship with

OCTOBER 11

an intention to placate the demands to remember the Lord's Day and to keep it holy. Using the covers of religiosity to shade their true colors, they go about the business of "busyness." They show no Holy Spirit power and have the look but not the latent force of the Divine. The pulpits of these churches, along with the pews, have no resemblance to the early New Testament church. The Acts church turned their world upside down for the Lord. No foe was too formidable to stop them. When the church of the first lethargy wakes up from it ceaseless activities of worldliness, maybe she can find her way back to God. The Father patiently awaits her return.

Thought to ponder: "Hot or Cold? That is the question."

October 12

"To the praise of the glory of his grace, wherein he hath made us accepted in the beloved." Ephesians 1:6 (KJV)

"Members Only" is a brand of clothing that became popular in the 1980s with its line of jackets and accessories. It became the stylish fad that swept across America and became an iconic trademark. To wear one of these jackets would set you apart as an owner of a much-sought-after product. The coats were costly and not everyone was privileged to own one. I remember my first jacket was the product of a hand-me-down from a close friend. Rather than donating it to Goodwill, he passed it along to me. When I slipped the jacket on, it became an advertisement to those around me that I was a part of the in-crowd who had reached a pinnacle of ownership to such a unique garment. I felt as though I was in my own little world and perhaps uniquely different from others who didn't have this prized possession.

As "Members Only" in the body of Christ, we all share in the fellowship of the saints. As believers we have the blessed privilege to join our hearts and minds in a unique

October 12

togetherness the world knows nothing about. We have an experience of companionship in the faith which befits the life and ministry of the Lord Jesus. He enjoyed the closeness of His disciples and intimacy with others who followed Him, and He spent much time with them because they were a part of His ministry. He reached out to all believers, of all ages, from all races, to convey His love for them. Our Lord didn't have any favorites whom He doted over. His was an acceptance based upon His unique love for each one of us. As Christians we have been accepted by Jesus unconditionally. We cannot merit His love by our actions. The apostle Paul said that we are to praise God for the glorious grace that God has poured out on us who belong to His dear Son. We share an intimacy within an inner circle of other believers, a good-will of affection.

Thought to ponder: "From the depths of sin, we as Christians have reached the pinnacle of wealth in Christ."

October 13

"And what I say unto you I say unto all, Watch."
Mark 13:37 (KJV)

Recently I encountered one of the strangest weather events in our area. It all happened within a range of 18 miles. In Warner Robins, Georgia there was tornadic activity over Robins Air Force Base. There were howling winds in excess of 90 miles per hour, while sheets of driving rain were blown sideways. It was a scary event for about 20 minutes for those involved as employees sought safety. Some workers texted their spouses to say that they were frightened and that they loved them. All the while 18 miles south in the sleepy little town of Haynesville, the sun was shining brightly and a gentle breeze caressed my face. All was peaceful and serene and 18 miles north there was such turbulent weather. I thought out loud, "How can winds be blowing so fiercely in Warner Robins, and a short distance south in Haynesville the weather could be so calm?"

The message in this frightening event was that all can be peaceful on the home front, while someone whom I rub

OCTOBER 13

shoulders with can be going through some alarming storms. I may have a calm time in my walk while someone close to me can be experiencing some stinging winds of sickness, and all the while I may be unaware of it. While life may be serene for me, there are those who are pummeled with the waves of woe. As peaceful as the times may be for many of us, there are those brothers and sisters in Christ who are facing some raging storms of fear. It could be that life couldn't get any better for some while many are engulfed with uncertainty. We can be in close proximity of each other and not be aware of what may be aggravating the one standing next to us. If we stay in tune with the Holy Spirit, He will give us the discernment needed to recognize those who are in need without a word being spoken. Without His help, we'll be unaware of the tumultuous times that many go through every day.

Thought to ponder: "A keen heart will give a clear vision for those in need."

October 14

"Be ye therefore followers of God, as dear children; and walk in love, as Christ also hath loved us, and hath given himself for us an offering and a sacrifice to God for a sweet smelling savour." Ephesians 5:1,2 (KJV)

When we simply practice our faith on the weekends, it becomes a hobby, not a passion. Jesus didn't suffer rejection, pain, and death for a mere Lord's Day activity. It's when we live out our faith every day, in an open and honest way, that we move from an avocation of faith to a passion of faith. When the things of God take a back seat during the week to the principles of service and worship, it becomes a mere profession of belief, not a possession of confidence. We deceive ourselves in the process of a "Sunday Only" worship and do damage to the kingdom purposes.

It's not merely faith of our fathers that we affirm, but rather faith of the everyday in the courts of the world when our faith is proven to be genuine. Our application of the principles of discipleship should reach out to others and expend that energy in winning the lost to Christ and

October 14

disciplining others. Following Christ every waking minute should consume our desire to serve and worship the Lord only. It's not only our privilege to worship the Lord on His appointed day, but also our responsibility to actively walk with Him in obedience every day. Our love for Him can be seen in our affection for His body of believers. When we believe that everybody is somebody in His body, the body of Christ, it will cause us to lose sight of ourselves and only see others with their many needs. This doesn't only happen on the Lord's day; it must take place every day!

Thought to ponder: "Don't let your worship on Sunday become a hobby; let it become a flame of fire."

October 15

"Persecuted, but not forsaken; cast down, but not destroyed;"
2 Corinthians 4:9 (KJV)

A church bus was sitting in a garage area awaiting repair because of a major fender-bender. Someone had carelessly rammed the bus from the side and left it unusable. As I looked upon the mangled mess, I wondered if this bus would ever be serviceable again. I also noticed that there was a sign in full view that read, "Heaven Bound." Because of the accident the bus was placed in what the owner called, "The Graveyard." Though the bus was in shambles, it was repairable. According to the mechanics and body repair men, a little work would put the coach back on the road again. "She's only down for the two count," joked the owner of the business. "She'll be stronger and more dependable than ever," was the word from the repair men.

That reminds me of a time when Christians run into the accidents of life. We are "Heaven Bound," but we can be derailed. Our standing can become damaged as a result of our careless efforts to guard our hearts and minds from the

October 15

carnal desires of the flesh. The enemy of our souls will seek to trample our attempts to live holy lives. A lack of caution on our part to turn a deaf ear to the deceiving lies of the adversary will sidetrack our faith into his playground. The enemy has more experience than we could ever have. He will cause more damage to our standing if we allow him, and if we are not careful in our walk, we will permit him to become our ring leader. When we are blind-sided in our travels, we can overcome the temptation to give up and give in. We may be knocked down, but we are not out of the battle. We can come back stronger than ever if we allow the power of the Holy Spirit to take control of our situations. Depending on Him will carry us through the toughest and most demanding times. We may be side-tracked for the moment, but our commitment to allow the Father to do His repair work on us will produce a stronger and healthier child.

Thought to ponder: "Our home is in heaven, but our feet are here on this earth."

October 16

"Let your light so shine before men, that they may see your good works, and glorify your Father which is in heaven."
Matthew 5:16 (KJV)

A well-known enterprise who has the world's largest budget motel chain with motels in the United States, Canada, and China has a catchy advertisement for their business. Their claim and promise are, "We'll leave the light on for you." As weary travelers make their way to their destinations, and night time overcomes them, those words are a welcome relief to remember. With weary eyes, sore backs, and aching feet, a promise of "keeping the light on" is an oasis in the midst of a desert of weariness. To think that someone would be kind enough to remember you in that manner is almost unheard of in today's society. Though the company offers these assurances to promote their endeavors, there is a message for the Christian who is the light of the world, and it becomes our responsibility to leave that light on.

Jesus said of His followers that they were the light in the midst of the world. He stated that they were beacons on a hill

OCTOBER 16

which should shine so that others may see their light and in the process glorify the Father in heaven. We, as Christians, are the only beacon of hope in this dark and dreary world. Though the Pharisees of the day set the fervor of the time, they were not the reflectors of the "True Light." The scribes had a good understanding of the light in the scriptures which were to excite and animate others, but they fell miserably short as translators of the "One Light." Other religious entities perpetrated the hold they felt they had on the truth of the light but failed in their feeble attempts as being escalators of the "Only Light." Jesus is the one and only true light who lights the way to eternal life; and His children, made in His likeness, are to be true reflectors, translators, and escalators of Him, who is the "One and Only Light."

Thought to ponder: "The darker the night, the brighter the light of Christ shining through us."

October 17

"In the day of my trouble I will call upon thee: for thou wilt answer me." Psalms 86:7 (KJV)

I recently saw a tee-shirt that had this admonition, "Take Two Tablets, And Call Me In The Morning." It was signed, "GOD!" The tablets on the shirt were the two tables containing the 10 Commandments of God. The first five directives were on the left tablet, while the other five were on the right side. The "call me" was in reference to calling God, the author of the Decalogue. The invitation from the Father to His child was to live by His precepts. The commandments were given for our good so that we could become His best. The call was for us to ingest and digest His requirements for us. If we follow the injunction, "Thou shalt not," we will not be bound up but freed up to become all we can be. Now I'm not a medical doctor who can give medical advice, but I can offer you a good prescription to follow when you become spiritually sick. When you have one or more of the following symptoms, you can take two tablets (obey the 10 Commandments) and call God in the morning:

October 17

If your life is sickened by unsettling news of disaster,

If your testimony is weakened by bad choices with the consequences stinging like an adder,

When your walk becomes weary because of the excess baggage of the carnal,

When your eyes start to lose their focus on faith,

When your heart becomes divided over mammon or God,

When your feet grow weary of running in front of or away from God,

When your ears lose the sensitivity to hear the whispers of God,

When your emotions rage out of control because of the seeming absence of God in your affairs,

When your life is turned upside down due to aging, sickness, or loneliness,

YOU CAN TAKE TWO TABLETS AND CALL GOD IN THE MORNING!

Thought to ponder: "God's perfect "10" is bound up in His 10 commandments."

October 18

"Therefore leaving the principles of the doctrine of Christ, let us go on unto perfection; not laying again the foundation of repentance from dead works, and of faith toward God."

Hebrews 6:1 (KJV)

I recently purchased a Mennonite cookbook at a local thrift store. As I was thumbing through the table of contents, I noticed a line that read, "Oriental Foods." At first I thought it strange that Mennonites would be interested in foods from other countries. I can understand the hunger for pies, pastries, soups, salads, and home-cooked meats, but to have an oriental recipe in a traditional home cookbook seemed a little odd. Then again it shouldn't be any different than Christians who have an appetite to grow and mature in the Lord by pursuing the greater things than simple salvation. There should be a hunger for the higher and deeper things of God.

We who have been saved by grace through faith should be thankful for the mercy of God, but the act of being redeemed shouldn't stop there. As great as the miracle of the

OCTOBER 18

new birth is, our zeal for a closer walk with the Lord should be our aim. There is more to life than simply living day to day. God has an extraordinary plan that will enable us to thrive in the midst of all circumstances. There should be a driving ambition to pursue God and His ideals. He has so much for us in the way of holiness of which we are unaware. Our passion to draw closer to Him should be constant. He has promised to slake our thirst for Him in revealing His Son Jesus to us, who is the living water. Every aspect in our life should have a goal in mind. Our aim is heaven, and as we pursue the eventuality of that final resting place, our pace should be one of steadfastness. Our eyes must be on the final goal of spending an eternity of bliss in the presence of a loving and merciful God.

Thought to ponder: "The higher things of God are for those who seek Him."

October 19

"If I regard iniquity in my heart, the Lord will not hear me."
Psalms 66:18 (KJV)

Have you tried to open your vehicle's car door or trunk with a remote key that resembled the one you used in the past, but for some reason the device didn't work? If the key fob is similar to the genuine key, but doesn't match the proper circuitry for your automobile, it matters not how many times you press the unlock button. Your mode of transportation remains locked and unusable. You will spend the rest of your day outside your secured vehicle with a sore thumb and frayed nerves. You may hear the beeping sound from the remote each time you press it, but if it isn't matched up electrically with the programmed lock in the vehicle, nothing happens. It becomes an exercise in futility.

The Psalmist speaks of a persistent problem in the lives of many Christians. We face an issue that disrupts the sweet fellowship of communication with the heavenly Father. Regarding iniquity in our heart has a devastating consequence. It's like having the proper words to speak but not

October 19

the right line of communication. We can pray and pray and not see any results. Harboring ill feelings puts an abrupt end to the Lord hearing our prayers. It's not that the Lord cannot hear our pleas because we know that He can. When we maintain sin in our heart, it is a well-defined truth that the Lord will not give attention to our supplications. We may have all the right words in the proper order of how they should be spoken, but if our heart has not been cleansed from the unrighteous acts of sin, those well-meant words fall on deaf ears. Our passion of speech in uttering the appropriate phrases of prayer may sound real to us as we speak them, but all is vain unless the Holy Spirit has prompted us with holy utterance. He will not abide in an unclean heart, and therefore will not inspire holy prayer. Our line of communication with the Father in making our appeals to Him rings only a busy signal. It's when we clean out all the clutter in our heart that we have an open line to heaven.

Thought to ponder: "Holding a grudge is tightening a rope around our prayer life."

October 20

"Say not ye, There are yet four months, and then cometh harvest? behold, I say unto you, Lift up your eyes, and look on the fields; for they are white already to harvest."

John 4:35 (KJV)

As I write today's devotional, the local farmers are beginning to harvest their crops of cotton. There are several farms in the area with massive fields of "Southern Whipped Cream" as some farmers call it. Tall cotton bushes loaded with white fluffy balls are spread out across the land. The fields resemble a patch of land where freshly fallen snow had descended. From one end of the tundra to the other, whiteness is magnified beyond belief. The whole landscape looks as it were a long ribbon of white, stretching for what seems like miles. It's during this period of the year that farmers are paying close attention to the ingathering of their precious crop. Cotton will not always be in the field for the farmers to garner so close attention becomes a priority.

The likeness of these cotton fields was used by our Lord as an opportunity to impress upon His followers that the

October 20

time had come for an ingathering of souls. The season was right; the occasion was now; and the privilege was underscored. Jesus wanted to convey to His disciples that a clear stage to cast the net of salvation out into the sea of humanity, and draw it to the shore of deliverance, was now. His call came to them as He pointed out that the harvest is the present day, not tomorrow, nor the next. The admonition was to wake up and look around at these fields of opportunity; they are white and ready for accumulation. This would be a challenge for these disciples. The harvest was ripe for the picking and these learners had to make themselves available for the task set before them. It would take a massive effort for these adherents to their Master's call to lift up their weary eyes and recognize the open field before them.

Thought to ponder: "Our responsibility is to rescue the perishing, and care for those dying in sin."

October 21

"The thoughts of the diligent rend only to plenteousness; but of every one that is hasty only to want." Proverbs 21:5 (KJV)

There is a road near my house that has a pond on each side. Both ponds are small but produce some interesting creatures, among whom are turtles. It's not an uncommon sight to see those creatures of God making their way from one body of water to the other. One afternoon I had to drive home from church to pick up some material and noticed that a turtle had just gotten on the apron of the road. Several minutes later as I made my way back to church, I recognized the same turtle as he finally made his way into the high grass along the roadway. My patience with these fellows is pressed to the limits. As someone has said, "Observing a turtle make progress is like watching paint dry!" I've never seen a turtle get in a hurry. If anything, it seems that they slow down and almost come to a complete stop.

There are some life-lessons which we can learn from a simple creature God created. We can glean much from the habits of these little creatures. If we are observant enough,

October 21

God can reveal some much-needed instructions as we consider the turtle. Not known for their speed, they make up in resolve, and what they lack in quickness, is found in their steadfastness. "No mountain too high; no valley too low to conquer," could very well be the motto of these incredible creatures. Turtles have determination. There is a sense of steadiness in the pursuit of their goal. The ambition they have, mixed with determination to stay the course, make up for any so-called deficiencies. Of course to them it's not considered a shortcoming to be slow of pace, but rather an opportunity to achieve its goal, whether quickly or slowly. We can also observe in turtles that they have a resilience in making sure that no obstacle can deter them from reaching their destination. Look to the turtle to learn the lessons of intention, resolution, inclination, and determination!

Thought to ponder: "Steady plodding brings prosperity; hasty speculation brings poverty."

October 22

"And if children, then heirs; heirs of God, and joint-heirs with Christ; if so be that we suffer with him, that we may be also glorified together." Romans 8:17 (KJV)

"Give of your best to the Master," are the words of a song which challenge me every time I hear them sung. When I sing the song and speak those words, I am reminded that the Lord wants nothing less than my very best. I am overpowered with a sense of debt to the Master because He gave His all for me. He gave up everything so that I could become heir of everything. All that was His in heaven He laid down and picked up the cross. Jesus took all of my hell so that I would never have to taste the hell of my sin. I may not know all that act includes, and the ramifications of His beneficent gift, but I am convinced that what He did, He did for me. I am richer beyond compare and more wealthy than a billionaire.

I owe Jesus everything, not every other thing. Giving Him my all brings out His best in me. Where at one time I was a poor sinner by birth, clothed in the rags of unrighteousness,

OCTOBER 22

steeped in the horribleness of my sin, I came and humbly bowed at the Master's feet and gave Him all of me. That has been the best gift that I could ever give to Him. He took me as His very own, clothed me in the righteousness of Jesus Christ, and gave to me the precious gift of the Holy Spirit. What I gave to Him was like small thimbles of myself compared to the large shovels of grace He poured into my life, and that grace has no end; it is given to me fresh every day. He grows sweeter to me as the days goes by, and I am forever indebted to Him for His marvelous act of mercy. His love for me is unconditional. His grace is free. His mercy is undeserved. His care for me has no end. His presence will always be my partner. His promises will never fail. His plan for me has an expected and rewarded end.

Thought to ponder: "When we do our best, we never rest until the rest becomes our best."

October 23

"The name of the LORD is a strong tower: the righteous runneth into it, and is safe." Proverbs 18:10 (KJV)

Some new medical technology innovations will be available in the near future. They make some incredible promises for those of us who have been badgered by sickness. Two in particular are, "Electronic Aspirins" and "Needle-Free Diabetes Care." An electronic aspirin is a patient-powered tool for blocking signals of pain at the first sign of a headache. Needle-free diabetes care allows the patient the freedom from poking the skin to draw blood and permits the use of a patch to read blood analytes through the skin. These breakthroughs are tremendous advancements in the fight against the pain and disease of the body. Along the way these turning points in medicine subscribe some fantastic aids.

We serve a God who not only has promised good things for His children; He has come through time and time again. When other people fail to keep their pledges of good-will to us, God keeps on giving out His best for us, even in

October 23

times when we are least deserving. His pledge to us is never ending. What He says, He will do. Where He sends us, He will go with us. What He asks us to achieve, He supplies the power to accomplish the task. He loves us, provides for us, protects us, cares for us, upholds us, encourages us, walks with us, feels for us, empowers us, anchors us, enriches us, embraces us, delivers us, shields us, holds us, and preserves us; and the list goes on. He truly is our shield and protector, always a strong tower we can run to in time of need. Our path is always before Him, and His attentive eye is constantly watching over us. We never come to a point where we lose hope or give up, because our great God will provide a way of escape. The promises of this life pale in comparison to what God will accomplish in and through us.

Thought to ponder: "A tower of strength is what our God is for those of us in need of shelter."

October 24

"And almost all things are by the law purged with blood; and without shedding of blood is no remission."

Hebrews 9:22 (KJV)

I have a collector friend who has amassed an incredible collection of pens and pencils. These writing instruments were manufactured as inexpensive ways of advertisements for businesses, churches, and other trades. Some of these collectibles have funny sayings on them; others have serious quotes; while certain ones are for collecting purposes only; and the rest are whimsical tools of art. The number of pens and pencils my friend has numbers in the thousands. He said that he had enough to use a different one each day for 18 years. My friend jokingly said, "I've never met a pen I didn't like."

One of his favorite pens is in the shape of a spike, like a nail of sorts. It's rough to the touch, uncomfortable to write with, and unattractive. It's not one you would choose out of a lineup to use, but the message on the pen is the clincher. The inscription written in red states, "3 nails, 4 given." That

OCTOBER 24

of course speaks of the cross of Christ and the forgiveness of our sins.

The "3 nails" didn't hold Jesus to the cross; His undying love for each one of us kept Him there. He could have called down a legion of angels to rescue Him. All the while Jesus was on the cross, we were heavily on His mind. Each blow of the hammer that drove the nails deeper into the hands of Jesus brought out an anguish of love with each strike. The blood that flowed from His hands, His feet, and His side was the guarantee of our forgiveness.

"4 given" are words which are forever embedded in our hearts. They sink deep into the fabric of our being and will carry us through the toughest times of life. The enemy may sow seeds of doubt as to the reality of God--forgiveness of our past, present, and future transgressions. We can stand upon the word of the God of all truth, the God of all assurance, and the God of all encouragement. His promise holds true throughout our earthly sojourn and will follow us into eternity.

Thought to ponder: "Nothing but the blood of Jesus!"

October 25

"Only be thou strong and very courageous, that thou mayest observe to do according to all the law, which Moses my servant commanded thee: turn not from it to the right hand or to the left, that thou mayest prosper whithersoever thou goest." Joshua 1:7 (KJV)

I have become wary of packages that carry the words, "Easy To Open." Many of those bags are anything but easy to pry open. Time and time again, I have become annoyed and frustrated with packages that are difficult to unseal, and what makes matters worse is, I can see those words, "Easy To Open" staring back at me as I struggle to get inside. Some types of these packages have the reputation of being particularly bothersome, and I believe that everyone one of them end up in my possession. Many forms of traditional packaging are awkward for some seniors who may lack the necessary strength or coordination. The older I get, the more sensitive I am for those who struggle to open the so called, "Easy To Open" packages.

OCTOBER 25

The Bible is the word of the living God, given to us as His preparation book. Someone has well used the acronym "BIBLE" to spell out, "Basic Instructions Before Leaving Earth." Those words pinpoint for us what the Father has in mind for His children in eternity. There is so much that we don't know and cannot know here in this earthly realm, so God has inspired men of old to pen those instructive words for the express purpose of preparing earthlings to be fitted for heaven's habitation. The Bible isn't difficult to open. There is no struggle to pry open the cover to expose the precious words written inside. All it takes is a commitment on our part to open every day the pages of Holy Writ and meditate on them. As the words of scripture make their way from our lips to our hearts, the Holy Spirit will anoint them for our mind's consumption. All that we will ever need to know about heaven will be found in the groundwork of God's Word. Our anticipation and education of heaven can be found in the rehearsal of the scriptures in our daily living.

Thought to ponder: "The Bible opens our minds to the heart of God."

October 26

"Howbeit when he, the Spirit of truth, is come, he will guide you into all truth: for he shall not speak of himself; but whatsoever he shall hear, that shall he speak: and he will shew you things to come." John 16:13 (KJV)

I inserted my key into the ignition of my 15-year old truck and was prompted with this message on the dashboard, "Caution, your battery source in your keyless remote is low." I am amazed that technology has advanced as far as it has. In newer vehicles, there are rear-mounted cameras to aid in backing your car out of a tight position. GPS vehicle tracking can be added, at a cost, to cars equipped with the device. There is technology that helps the driver to detect blind spots when he/she is not paying attention, and the list seems to be endless as new innovations are introduced each year.

The Holy Spirit is our Guide and Teacher. He has been sent by the Father to come alongside of us as we live out the Christian life. There are potholes of sin strewn along the road of life that are sometimes undetectable, and we need a

October 26

guiding hand to help us avoid them. When the Holy Spirit detects that something has gone awry in our life, or we have slipped to the side of the "heavenly road," He prompts us with conviction. Convincing work is the Spirit's work. He can do it effectually, and none but He. The Spirit of God will be our Guide into the fullness of truth. The Spirit of Truth will take us by the hand, and, step by step, give us the needed strength to follow. As we do, He guides us into the territory that God has established for us, and He then unfolds to us the treasures it contains. The only things He will speak are the things He has heard from the Father. As He reveals the will of the Father to us, we are able to discern that good and perfect will of God.

Thought to ponder: "God doesn't have new technology, only proven truth."

October 27

"Leave there thy gift before the altar, and go thy way; first be reconciled to thy brother, and then come and offer thy gift."
Matthew 5:24 (KJV)

In my grandson's grade school there is a list of seven effective habits which each student is encouraged to learn and practice. They are posted on the wall of the gymnasium for all to see. Almost every time I have been in the school, the administrator or a teacher promotes an atmosphere where these principles can be learned. One of the habits caught my eye as I thought about the importance of making my Christian walk more productive. Habit number three was, "Put first things first." That has a spiritual connotation to it. The Bible speaks of some priorities we are to maintain.

One of the leading pursuits we should embrace is to carefully preserve Christian love and peace with all our brethren. We should keep our eyes open for any deviation from the instructions Jesus gave us in Matthew 5:24. We are a family of believers, knit together in Christian responsibility, who

October 27

are instructed to love each other unconditionally. Our walk should be one of maintaining that kind of devotion to our brothers and sisters in Christ. If at any time during our journey there is a quarrel or misunderstanding, we should confess our fault, humble ourselves to our brother or sister, and make an offering of satisfaction for the wrong word or deed. This action should not be put off for a more convenient time. It should be done quickly, without delay. When the time comes when we are preparing our heart for any religious exercise, it's profitable for us to make the occasion a time of serious reflection and self-examination. Until this is done we cripple our fellowship with each other and are unfit for communion with God.

Thought to ponder: "Putting first things first will provide all things an avenue of success."

October 28

"Be not overcome of evil, but overcome evil with good."
Romans 12:21 (KJV)

I met a man in an antique mall that had an interesting tee-shirt on. It read, "Keeper Of The Bees." He was on vacation and couldn't wait to get back home so that he could take care of his little creatures. He talked enthusiastically about his love for the bees and their care. He said that there was no cost too much when it came to taking care of his hobby. He also said, "Most of my life is surrounded by taking care of every one of the needs these fellows have." With an air of joy he walked away knowing that in a few days he would be home.

As Christians we have some "Be's" to take care of. These are not the kind that make honey or sting when agitated, but those that the Bible speaks of when we are taught to "Be" something. Our time should be consumed with making sure that these "Be's" have their needs met. There is no one thing too good to keep back on lavishing our attention on these much needed requirements. These "Be's" can't take care of

October 28

themselves. They need constant attention and daily nourishment from family members who have made a commitment to seeing that necessities are filled.

There is the, "Be strong and of a good courage" in Joshua 1:6

There is the, "Be filled with the Spirit" in Ephesians 5:18

There is the, "Be of the same mind one toward another" in Romans 12:16

There is the, "But be ye doers of the word, and not hearers only, deceiving your own selves James 1:22

Thought to ponder: "To be or not to be is not the question. 'TO BE' is the solution."

October 29

"Now before the feast of the passover, when Jesus knew that his hour was come that he should depart out of this world unto the Father, having loved his own which were in the world, he loved them unto the end." John 13:1 (KJV)

While sitting and waiting for my oldest grandson's high school graduation to begin, little did I know what I was about to hear. In this day of political correctness and worry about offending someone, it is frowned upon by some to speak about Jesus in a public forum. The class president made no apologies about where he stood when it came to Jesus. He went above and beyond the call when he spoke in plain and simple terms about his faith. In a very simplistic way he said, "Whatever you may attain or achieve in this life, Jesus is better! You may become a millionaire, but Jesus is better! You may climb the highest mountain and have world acclaim, but Jesus is better! However you may come to greatness, Jesus is better!" When he finished, he received a loud and long applause.

I am grateful for that evening when I was reminded that whatever I may come to in fortune, Jesus is better. He is the

OCTOBER 29

One who satisfies all my desires. There is not one need that He cannot and will not meet. I am the benefactor of all His rich blessings. Whenever my pathway becomes obscure, He is always there with light for my journey to see me through to safety. My steps have been ordered by the Lord, and the way has been paved with His mercies. He has given me His word as a roadmap for my path. When I depend upon Him, He never disappoints me. My life is enriched beyond measure because of His unconditional love for me. His peace is better than all the absences of war. I cannot lose because He has declared me a winner. I am the apple of His eye. When I fall, the Lord is there to pick me up, dust me off, and send me on my way. Whatever good may come to me in this present life, Jesus is better!

Thought to ponder: "Life may hand me good and better, but Jesus gives me His best."

October 30

"For thou hast been a shelter for me, and a strong tower from the enemy." Psalms 61:3 (KJV)

While driving up a local Interstate highway, I came in behind an 18 wheeler. I noticed the name of the company, its logo, the promises they made, and a seemingly contradictory statement. The company's name was, "Strait Trucking Lines." The promise made, "We get you there faster and cheaper." Their overture of, "faster and cheaper" seemed to be discredited by these words underneath the promise: "Caution, we make wide turns!" What the company was so bold to advertise seemed to have this caveat: "We may not be able to keep the promise because we make wide turns." Of course the meaning of the "wide turns" was that the truck took a distance to make a turn, but many of the things this world may paint as promising and glamorous can and will fade into disappointment.

This is not so with our Lord Jesus. What He promises, He will do. There is no lack in His meeting all of our needs. He doesn't make a promise and then renege on it. His word is

October 30

forever settled in heaven. He loves us unconditionally. There is no changing, no turning back when it comes to filling our privations. Our security and peace of mind rest squarely on His dependability. His pledge to us far exceeds any kind of earthly love or favor. He has never, and will never, leave us in a pinch. He has not forsaken us and left us as orphans at any juncture. His track record is sterling. There are no recalls, reworks, reversals, or reconsiderations. Only in heaven, as we spend an eternity of bliss, will we come to fully appreciate the promises made and fulfilled while we were on earth. Our Lord Jesus will always be a shelter for us so that we can run to Him in a time of trouble.

Thought to ponder: "Kept promises, not broken promises, are what our Lord gives."

October 31

"I am a companion of all them that fear thee, and of them that keep thy precepts." Psalms 119:63 (KJV)

There is a stretch of road in our neighborhood that has 28 signs within a distance of a quarter of a mile. This averages one sign for every 50 feet. These markers include stop and caution signs, street signs, some billboards, and advertising signs among others. I was reminded of a song from the 1970s, "Signs, signs, everywhere a sign. Do this, don't do that! Can't you read the sign?"

Our heavenly Father wants to make sure that we are properly instructed in His ways. He has given us instructive signs along the way. Jesus has sent the Holy Spirit to be our Comforter and our Guide. We have the Bible as the inspired word of God to give us light for our path. God has gifted certain men and women with gifts to minister within the body of Christ. We have so many God-given endowments that it led someone to say that we, as Christians, are without excuse.

God wants us to take advantage of every opportunity He has made available. We are only limited by our willingness,

October 31

or unwillingness, to embrace His instructions. The light He has shone into our life can only be diffused if we choose to do so. Everything we need to know and should know about the Father can be found in His Son, Christ Jesus our Lord. We are more than fortunate to have the amount of information we have about the will of God and His ways. We can clear the sleep from our eyes to behold the wonders of the Lord. We can choose to center our heart on the Father and be filled with hope and joy. We can open wide our mouths to proclaim His great acts. We can tune our ears to hear the wonderful words of life.

Thought to ponder: "Wonderful doesn't adequately describe the Words of God."

November 1

"If my people, which are called by my name, shall humble themselves, and pray, and seek my face, and turn from their wicked ways; then will I hear from heaven, and will forgive their sin, and will heal their land." 2 Chronicles 7:14 (KJV)

A sign at a local church had this admonition, "Pray For America." Underneath the marquee was an electronic clock that had the time of "11:59." The thought occurred to me that the interval for praying for America was reaching its end because there will come a season when God will say "Enough!" The last thing I want to hear the Father pronounce is that it's too late to pray for our nation. We are one minute away from high noon when the morning of opportunity ends and the afternoon of judgment begins.

We still have what I call a minute of mercy from God-- sixty seconds in which we can plead to God to be merciful to His people. There is much we can do in 60 seconds to prepare ourselves to intercede on the behalf of our country. In 15 seconds we can humble ourselves before God. We can have a change of mind and a change of heart at the blink of

November 1

an eye. It's what I call an attitude adjustment for God. In 15 seconds we can pray. God is not impressed with the length of our prayer as He is in a clean heart who utters the prayer. One of the shortest prayers in the Bible was, "God be merciful to me a sinner." This man who spoke these impassioned words went home justified. In 15 seconds we can seek the face of God. With a heart-felt commitment we can set our eyes upon the Lord Jesus who is the Author and Finisher of our faith. He can point us in the right direction for intercessory prayer. In 15 seconds we can turn from our wicked ways. An about face from our evil doings can be done in a split-second decision. When our mind is set on Him, our heart can be set on our nation. In just 60 seconds we can do much to prepare the way for a revival here in America.

Thought to ponder: "Pray For America! It is 11:59 and counting."

November 2

"Bring ye all the tithes into the storehouse, that there may be meat in mine house, and prove me now herewith, saith the LORD of hosts, if I will not open you the windows of heaven, and pour you out a blessing, that there shall not be room enough to receive it." Malachi 3:10 (KJV)

A friend of mine was sharing with me about the passing of his dad. His father had lived as a widower for 20 years after the death of his wife. Following the funeral service, my friend was going through some of the paperwork of his dad's financial matters. He came to realize that he had made an investment in one of his friend's business pursuits. It was one of those adventures which had little return for the money invested. My friend said that his dad could have empowered his money in better stock options for a greater return, but because of the friendship between the two, his dad sacrificed thousands of dollars.

Think about the blessings of God we forfeit each day when we disobey Him. Living in constant fellowship with the Father brings an abundance of goodness to us. We are

November 2

filled to the brim and overflowing with the Father's best when we comply with His commands. The good fortunes of the Heavenly Father are unchanging and unceasing. What He says He will do without hesitation. The flipside to that is when we wander away from His sweet presence and yield to the thief who will steal those godsends.

God said that if we would obey Him, He would open the windows of heaven to bless us beyond what we could imagine. Those blessings would exceed any good that this world may give us. God is not stingy when it comes to covering us with His benefits. He has more to give us that we could ever receive. All that the Father has is waiting for us when we walk with the Lord in the light of His word. It would behoove us to trust and obey Him, for there is no other way to be happy in the Lord.

Thought to ponder: "The best has already come. It's ours when we obey."

November 3

"Whom having not seen, ye love; in whom, though now ye see him not, yet believing, ye rejoice with joy unspeakable and full of glory:" 1 Peter 1:8 (KJV)

Two precious little girls who attend our church have Biblical names. When they were born, their mom gave them the names of, "Hope and Joy." Being twins there were times when it was a challenge for me to tell them apart. The mom of these little jewels said that there was a way to tell the difference between the two of them. She said that Hope was a bit chubbier than Joy. Putting that criteria to the test, I did notice that there was a difference between them.

That got me to thinking about our hope and joy which we have in the Lord Jesus. Our hope in one sense is a bit chubbier than our joy. Our joy is in the Lord Jesus. In Nehemiah 8:10 we read, "The joy of the Lord is your strength." As we go from day to day, our joy is renewed continually. The new day doesn't bring us joy because Jesus is the only one who can do that for us. We can rejoice with joy unspeakable and full of glory because of what has been accomplished in the sacrificial death of Jesus. It is this type of joy that will get us through the toughest times in life. This kind of joy will see us through each day.

On the other hand, our hope in the Lord Jesus will take us to heaven, shouting every step of the way. Our hope is built on nothing less than Jesus' blood and righteousness, and our response to that reality is that we can lean wholly on Jesus' name, the name which is above every name. This hope will not lead us to disappointment. We know how dearly God loves us because He has given to us His Holy Spirit to fill our hearts with His love. Our hope is in fact a bit chubbier than our joy in the sense of where our hope will take us. Joy will see us through each day, but hope will see us into heaven, our eternal home.

Thought to ponder: "Joy gives us strength. Hope gives us stability."

November 4

"Behold, I stand at the door, and knock: if any man hear my voice, and open the door, I will come in to him, and will sup with him, and he with me." Revelation 3:20 (KJV)

Driving up Highway 400 north of Atlanta, Georgia, I noticed a sign on the roadway that read, "The Highway of Hospitality." At the time I read the sign, I was bumper to bumper in traffic. It was 97 degrees, nerves were frazzled, and people were growing impatient. I had just come out of downtown Atlanta where I had spent an hour working my way through gridlock. Highway 400 on a Friday afternoon was anything but hospitable.

I soon realized amidst the traffic jam that signs can be deceiving. As well intentioned as the one who placed the sign by the highway was, certain promises will fall by the way as being empty and unfulfilling. We have no control over events that happen. The sign, of course, had no rule or sway over the circumstances. Roadblocks, detours, and stalled vehicles happen, but God is in control of all things, at all times, through all circumstances. He is never taken by

NOVEMBER 4

surprise or caught off guard. There are no "got you's" with Him. He is sovereign and will do what He pleases, and we can trust Him completely that He will see us through all the gridlocks of life.

God's way is the way of true "hospitality." His promises are never broken. His ways are always right, and His ways are always the best. He is always munificent and will take care of all our needs. He is the perfect Host. He comes to knock on our heart's door and desires to have fellowship with us. He not only invites, but He spreads the table with all the spiritual good we will ever need. In the midst of chaos, perplexity, and turmoil our Heavenly Host comes with all the furnishings we need.

Thought to ponder: "Hospitality is our Lord's gift of service."

November 5

"Because strait is the gate, and narrow is the way, which leadeth unto life, and few there be that find it."
Matthew 7:14 (KJV)

In my neighborhood there is a thoroughfare known as "Perfect Road." A family by that name has owned land in the area as long as I can remember. When the dirt road was paved, it bore the name of the family whose land it went through: "Perfect." I asked one of the members of the family whose land it went through about the road and its namesake, and he laughed and said, "The road is anything but perfect. It's not a super highway; it will not lead you to a "Disney Resort;" nor will it bring you to a "Taj Mahal!" I chuckled when he said that and thought to myself that there is only one perfect road, and that's the one the Lord Jesus blazed for us.

The "strait and narrow" way isn't for everybody. It's not for the mild and weak at heart. It doesn't appeal to those who are walking the "broad way, and entering the wide gate." These are of the party of which the Lord said were in the

NOVEMBER 5

company of a great multitude who are going about their own pernicious way. Rather than discipline themselves to walk a fine line, they take the way that seems right unto them but will fail to realize that in the end, the road will became a path to death.

The "strait and narrow way" which leads unto life is for those who are living a life of total commitment and dependence upon the One who leads the way to fullness of life. This is the only pathway God has appointed His children to pursue. It will not always be the easy way, but it is the only passage by which we can enter a life of fulfillment. Our daily endeavor is to enter into this appointed gate.

Thought to ponder: "The road of God is the Heavenly Highway."

November 6

"I came that they may have life, and have it abundantly."
John 10:10 (KJV)

I had a great uncle who was an excellent storyteller. He could spin yarns that would leave your sides splitting with laughter because of his tales. He, my great aunt, and their son would visit my paternal grandparents on Sundays and have a meal. My grandmother would fix a Sunday lunch, and following the meal, the men would gather outside under an oak tree to hear the latest escapades from Uncle John. He chewed tobacco and would pause in the middle of his sentence, pick up his spittoon, and empty what seemed to be an endless flow of tobacco juice. I looked forward to the times when Uncle John came because I knew that my afternoon would be spent sitting next to him listening to those funny stories.

Jesus was the master storyteller. Out of the experiences of humanity, He could draw a story that would fit the need of the moment. He kept His audiences on the edge of their seats, speaking to them sometimes in parables, and at other

November 6

times in true-to-life experiences. His messages had one common thread. He came that Christians may have a life that would be filled with abundance, and the messages He imparted were divinely given by the Father. There are times when I yearn to have been one who sat and listened as Jesus taught His followers, and yet, I am more advantaged than those who heard Him speak. I have the Bible, the record of His messages, at my fingertips so that I can read and listen to Him speak at any time. In the morning hours, or at midday, evening, or midnight, I can refresh myself with the timeless and unchanging truths of God's Word.

Thought to ponder: "The power of the Word is in the power of God."

November 7

"But I will sing of thy power; yea, I will sing aloud of thy mercy in the morning: for thou hast been my defence and refuge in the day of my trouble." Psalms 59:16 (KJV)

When our girls were younger, Christmas morning for the entire family was a time of joy and festivity. Waking up early and racing toward the living room was like a two person race. There underneath the Christmas tree were the toys our daughters had asked for. The anticipation on their faces as they tore through the paper were looks which have captured my mind all these years. There is no sweeter sense and greater joy for a parent to see the look of amazement on the faces of their delighted children. One of the "gotcha moments" is when you pick up a gift and read the words, "Batteries Not Included." The aggravation comes when you realize that there are no batteries in the house. To add to the heartburn, all of the local stores are closed. For a child to wake up on Christmas morning and find a present they asked for and there are no batteries is a major disappointment.

November 7

God doesn't disappoint us when He give us the gift of His Son. We celebrate that offering as we gather around the cross to remember that God so loved the world that He gave to us the gift of Christ. His bestowal comes not only with a life-time guarantee but also with the Source of Power to live out the abundant life. Along with the benevolent gift of eternal life, God provides the energy through His Holy Spirit to embolden us to live the life of a Christian. This potent power which flows from the hand of God doesn't diminish over the years and never requires replacement or exchange. After years have come and gone, there will never be a time when that puissant power will cease to be. The God who created the world is the One who keeps the universe on its steady course. More power than our finite mind could comprehend is being supplied every waking moment of our earthly sojourn. Whatever the power we may need is always available. No need to wring our hands in doubt or worry our hearts sick over any quandary we face. A cry from the heart brings about the deliverance.

Thought to ponder: "The practice of our faith will give us the perseverance in our faith."

November 8

"As the Father hath loved me, so have I loved you: continue ye in my love." John 15:9 (KJV)

Brian Shaw, known worldwide as one of the world's strongest men, is commonly known as the most colossal Strongman. He has finished within the top four contestants every year since 2011 and has taken the World's Strongest Man crown on three explosive occasions--first in 2011, again in 2013, and the third triumph in Malaysia in 2015. He also holds an impressive set of world strength records, from the 825lb Squat, to the 880lb Deadlift, to the 1,140 strapped Hummer Tire Lift. It's mind boggling to realize that a human being can lift that much weight.

Love can lift heavier loads than any human could ever imagine. Think about the load of sin we once carried upon our backs. The weight of sin was so heavy it bowed us in despair. There was no amount of energy we could expend to unload the heaviness of sin. No earthly person could do what the Lord Jesus did when it came to our sinfulness. At one moment in time, our precious Lord carried the weight of our

November 8

sins on His shoulders. When He trod the way to Calvary's Hill, carrying His cross, He bore our sins. We once were separated from God because of those sins. We could do nothing to deliver ourselves from the penalty of sin and the plight of despair. What Jesus did once and for all on the cross, He did for all who will come to Him in faith and repentance. We were the reason Jesus went to Calvary. When He was on the cross, we were on His mind.

Thought to ponder: "Out of God's great love, He lifted me up."

November 9

"For the Lord himself shall descend from heaven with a shout, with the voice of the archangel, and with the trump of God: and the dead in Christ shall rise first:"

1 Thessalonians 4:16 (KJV)

A lady in our church is pregnant and expecting the baby to make his entrance into the world at any moment. She looks every bit the part of being with child, and it shows in the way she walks, or wobbles is a better descriptor. This will be her first child. She and her husband are learning the mechanics of child birth as they make their way through each day. Her husband said, "We don't know if the baby will come before we go to bed in the evening, or before we get up in the morning. One thing we do know for certain is that the baby will be here soon." Their expectancy grows each day. They are ready for the moment when the beloved boy will arrive.

We know that the Lord Jesus is coming soon. We don't know the day or the time. As with the couple and the coming of their baby, we don't know if the Lord will come in the

November 9

evening, morning, or afternoon. One thing we know for certain is that He is coming again, and it will be sooner than we think. Jesus is preparing a mansion for each one of His children; and when the last room has been completed and heaven is made ready, the Lord will descend from heaven with a shout, with the voice of the archangel, and we shall rise to meet Him in the air. The day, the time, and the method of Jesus' coming is known only by the Father, but as we observe the seasons of His promised return, we know that His appearance is on the horizon. Jesus is coming soon, morning, or night, or noon. Knowing that, our expectancy will grow each day as we await His return.

Thought to ponder: "Heaven is just a trumpet sound away. Be listening!"

November 10

"For we wrestle not against flesh and blood, but against principalities, against powers, against the rulers of the darkness of this world, against spiritual wickedness in high places."
Ephesians 6:12 (KJV)

David versus Goliath is a Bible story almost every Sunday School child knows or has heard. It seems to be one of those narratives of the Bible kids love to hear, not once, but many times over. Almost every child who has listened to the events of the story can tell you with great accuracy what happened and how David was able to overcome Israel's arch enemy. There is no missing the punch line when it comes to David's heroic efforts. Hero versus villain; Hero wins! Villain loses!

When our girls were younger, they heard about the shepherd boy, David, facing the Philistines champion, Goliath, and overcoming the odds. David's victory over Goliath is perhaps one of the most beloved stories in the Old Testament. It's such a powerful picture of what God can do with very little to overcome very much.

November 10

Though a well-known story for children, the victory over Goliath under impossible circumstances has an adult story-line. We all face the giants of everyday life. As we walk this earthly pilgrimage, our paths will cross with these behemoths. These giants must be slain each time they raise their ugly heads. There is no special time of the day when the goliaths of life make their presence known. It could be the first thing in the morning as we make preparations for the ensuing day. It could be at noonday when we reach the apex of the day, or it could be in the evening just before we ready ourselves for a night of rest. At any given moment between sunup and sundown, these giants can come against us to weaken our confidence in God; and if we are not carefully prepared to face our giants, they will run roughshod over us. With God on our side, we can use what He has placed in our possession to bring down the terrifying plots of the enemy.

Thought to ponder: "The Lord's coming--it could be today!"

November 11

"I delight to do thy will, O my God: yea, thy law is within my heart." Psalms 40:8 (KJV)

I have a Christian friend who likes to make his boast in the Lord by saying, "I want to be Jesus with skin on." His desire is that other people will see Jesus living His life in my friend's ways, in his personal, social, and spiritual life. When my friend speaks, he wants other people to hear him speak as if the Lord Jesus was speaking through him. When my brother in Christ does a deed of kindness, his goal is that those around him will see the act and attribute it to Jesus. As my acquaintance lives out his faith, he lets his light shine in such a way that others may see his good works and glorify God the Father.

If that's our passion, to be Jesus with skin on, there are a couple of things we must do in order to live the life of Jesus in our daily walk. We must spend time alone with the Lord on a daily basis to learn more about Him. To be like Him, we must know Him personally and intimately. Those two qualities will come about as a result of our prayer time and Bible

November 11

study. Using our time of private prayer will draw us closer to the Father's side and will be seen in our public time of worship. Having a daily time of being alone with the Lord in the Word will help shape our passion to be Christ-like. Learning more about Jesus through His Word will give us the garments of His likeness. His manners will become our ways. His words will be echoed through our speech. His love will be shown through our compassion for those less fortunate. His likeness will be woven into the fabric of our ministry.

Thought to ponder: "To be like Christ is to allow Him to live His life through us!"

November 12

"Beloved, believe not every spirit, but try the spirits whether they are of God: because many false prophets are gone out into the world." 1 John 4:1 (KJV)

My college English Professor was well versed in grammatical correctness. Whether speaking or writing, she impressed upon me the importance of speaking and writing well. She said that she makes no apology when correcting one of her students when it comes to their speech or writing. She had taught English in high school and college for 42 years. She was not bragging when she said to me, "I have studied and taught English long enough that when someone misspeaks, it's as if the volume is turned up on the word spoken. When someone doesn't get the subject and verb in agreement, it's as if it is written in bold, black letters!" I have profited from her teaching and her sensitivity to the English language, and I have tried to translate that into my daily walk with the Lord.

As Christians, we ought to be so in tune with the truths of the Bible that when someone says or writes something

NOVEMBER 12

which does not line up with the Holy Scriptures, the volume should be so loud in our ear, and the written error so bold and black in print, that we are able to reject it outright. Just as oil and water do not mix, truth and error cannot occupy a place in our faith. Jesus is the only Truth we will ever need, and anything outside that realm is perversion. We should be so sensitive to the Holy Spirit's leadership that we can easily detect if the word is truth or error. Jesus promised that when the Spirit of truth was come, He would guide us into all truth. He would not speak on His own but would tell us what He has heard. The Father will sensitize our hearts through His Spirit to enable us to determine if what we have heard or read is reliable or unreliable. Our Lord has only one frequency through which He reveals the truth of Himself, and that is the Bible, the Word of the living God.

Thought to ponder: "A lie by any other name is still a lie!"

November 13

"Order my steps in thy word: and let not any iniquity have dominion over me." Psalms 119:133 (KJV)

On my smart phone, I can do anything I choose to do that a phone of this sort can provide. There are apps at my fingertips to send and receive messages or email. There is a calendar to remind me of the day, and a camera that I can use to take photos. I can check the weather and made notes to remind myself of important dates. There are also apps that allow me to surf the internet, read the latest news, and if I am in the mood for music, I can call up a site that will satisfy my musical taste. If I have stocks and bonds, I can check the latest movement in the volatile stock market to see where I stand financially. There are very few things I cannot do with my phone in the way of convenience, but there is one area that this handheld device cannot provide: it cannot give me the inspiration I receive from reading the Bible.

The Bible is the infallible, inerrant, and inspired Word of God. It was breathed by the Father; and men of old times, under the inspiration of the Holy Spirit, penned the words

November 13

which give to us the Bible we have today. We can use the Bible as a flashlight of sorts to light our path as we make our way through a darkened world. The Holy Scriptures give us the proper instruction we need to make us wise as serpents and harmless as doves. Our faith is made stronger by hearing the Word of God, and prosperous by obeying it. Our daily steps are established upon the Word of the living God. The fowls of the air cannot devour this prevailing Word. The stony places will not keep the growth of the Word at bay. The sun cannot scorch it. Even the thorns cannot choke out the established Word. God's Word is settled in heaven forever, and we can stand firmly fixed upon this unchanging Word.

Thought to ponder: "The Word of God will outlast every word ever spoken."

November 14

"And the King shall answer and say unto them, Verily I say unto you, Inasmuch as ye have done it unto one of the least of these my brethren, ye have done it unto me."

Matthew 25:40 (KJV)

Back in the day when gas stations had attendants who checked the engine oil level, pumped gas, washed windshields, and checked tire pressure, the services were provided for free along with a with a smile. Customers were glad to have these exercises rendered. Devoted workers took great pride in knowing that a job was well done. Some of these stations were well known for their superior services. Many companies took great pride in knowing that their customers were satisfied with services well done. That kind of service with a smile seems to have vanished to a degree with time.

Each one of us has been called to a lifetime of service. The life and ministry of Jesus are the patterns we are to follow. What He did, how He did it, and when He did it are our customized design. This interval of time becomes a ministry

NOVEMBER 14

that has the welfare of others needs in mind. It is the kind of outreach that takes on great joy and pride in knowing that what has been done was in the name of the Lord Jesus. Jesus spoke of our consideration for others as an overture to Him. When we focus on the less fortunate and needy, our ministry of love and compassion becomes that for the Lord Jesus. How we treat others is how we would treat the Lord. We need to be careful what we say about others because in so doing we are talking about Jesus. Whatever we do with our words or our deeds must have the Lord Jesus at the center of our ambition. After all, it's all about Him, not us.

Thought to ponder: "True service is when our hands and our feet work from our heart."

November 15

"Thou hast enlarged my steps under me, that my feet did not slip." Psalms 18:36 (KJV)

By rearranging two words in a particular sentence, we can go from being reluctant in ministry to becoming reinvigorated when it comes to our work in the Lord. Oftentimes we ask the question, "Who am I?" Our thought is that we are just one among many, and we are tempted to think that we can have very little impact on the kingdom enterprise. It's when we rearrange the "am" and the "I" that we arrive at the statement, "WHO I AM!" We go from questioning who we are, and making a bold statement of whose we are!

It's when we realize whose we are that our identity is sealed in the Lord. When we rise to the plateau of understanding who we are in the Lord that we can attempt and accomplish the impossible. We can overcome incredible odds because of Who is on our side. Our victory has been secured in the person of Jesus Christ. All power has been given unto Him in heaven and earth, and He in turn has given us the

November 15

same potent help. There is no power on earth that can bring defeat to a child of God who is walking in the ways of God. His steps are ordered by the Lord and no enemy can bring to naught any God-ordained work. Nothing on this earth can stop us when our eyes are fixed upon the author and finisher of our faith. No foe can withstand the Spirit of Christ. He indwells us with His power and enables us to do what man can't do, but what God alone can do.

Thought to ponder: "It's a sin to be good when God says we can be great."

November 16

"But speaking the truth in love, may grow up into him in all things, which is the head, even Christ:"

Ephesians 4:15 (KJV)

In the course of a conversation I had with an elderly minister, he said, "It's not acceptable to say 'Amen' on Sunday and then say nothing Monday through Saturday to compliment your faith." Immediately I knew what he meant. If we utter an "Amen" on Sunday during the sermons and then say nothing positive about the Lord to the public the other six days, we are contradicting our good word of agreement during the services on the Lord's day. A good approach to responding to these statements would be, "My brothers and sisters, these things ought not to be."

There's nothing more encouraging for the speaker, during the course of a sermon, to hear someone say, "Amen!" It's a way of saying, "So be it! I agree with you!" It gives to the deliverer a sense of connection to the audience. I believe the Lord Jesus is pleased to hear someone echo an agreement during a time of worship, but to remain silent the other days

November 16

of the week will make us weak in our walk. We should be taking the truth we agreed to during the course of a sermon and expanding its truth and expounding the veracity of the Word of God. People may never come to a worship service to hear the scriptures explained and defined, but they will be more susceptible to hear a sermon, if it comes from a lay person who speaks of what they heard, believed, and agreed to after a time of proclaiming the Word in worship. For us to be energetic in our public worship and never follow it up in the public sector is to weaken our effectiveness in winning the lost to Christ.

Thought to ponder: "To agree with the Truth obligates us to speak the Truth."

November 17

"Behold, I was shapen in iniquity; and in sin did my mother conceive me." Psalms 51:5 (KJV)

Most people enjoy looking for a bargain even though some items may be marked up in order to be marked down, giving you the impression that you got a deal. There's just something about getting an item for less than the original price. Some people even enjoy the art of haggling for a lower amount, trying to get it as cheaply as they can. I believe a vast majority of people have embedded in their DNA makeup the prospect of a deal. We are all genetically different, but when it comes to negotiating, we want our greenbacks to go as far as they can. If we can strike a deal that is dirt cheap, we take great pride in knowing we have accomplished a monumental task. I must confess that I am among those in the ranks of being a bargain hunter.

God doesn't bargain with us when it comes to our sin. He doesn't give discounts in order to minimize our shortcomings. We have all sinned and fallen short of God's expectations for we were all born a sinner, yes, from the moment

NOVEMBER 17

our mothers conceived us. Not one of us is righteousness enough to barter with God for the free gift of eternal life. We all, like sheep, have gone astray to search out own way of acceptance. There is no 10% off the original price for the penalty of sin. Someone once said that 100% of us have 100% sinned. Though that may not make for good grammar, it does bring out the graphic nature of the hideousness of our sin. The good news about how God dealt with our sins can be seen in the cross of Christ. It was there that Jesus paid it all--100% of our sin debt. Through the shed blood of Jesus, we now have peace with God and the peace of God.

Thought to ponder: "The cross of Christ straightened our crooked sin."

November 18

"He that hath ears to hear, let him hear." Matthew 11:15 (KJV)

At the height of the Citizen Band (CB) craze of years gone by, I fondly remember the days when I would sign on using my handle, "Mosquito Hawk." It was fun to exchange conversations with other folks who had been hooked by the same bug. It was awkward in the beginning to master the lingo of those who would use the airwaves as a means of communicating. I was introduced to a whole different world of words that one uses when operating a CB. It took me a while but I learned what it meant when someone would ask, "What's your 10-20?" Or when someone would say, "That's a big 10-4." Or when someone finished the conversation, they would ask, "Do you copy?" The one that I used more than any was, "Does anybody have their ears on?" This meant, of course, "was anyone listening?"

As Christians we all have a spiritual ear that becomes a receptacle for the Word of God, His will, and His ways. It becomes our responsibility to keep our ears in tune with one of the most important gifts God has endowed us with, His

November 18

precious Word. When Jesus made the statement, "He that hath ears to hear, let him hear," it was a proverbial expression implying that the highest attention should be given to what was spoken." God is speaking to each one of us. Every day of our life He communicates to us His desire for our lives, and what He has to say to us is of utmost importance. We have a tendency to allow our ears to be overridden with other sounds. We are responsible for what lingers in our ears. We can easily press the "mute" or "end button" in order to cancel the prevailing sounds of the enemy. With our ears open to God's leadership, we can navigate the waters of trouble from start to finish.

Thought to ponder: "Do you have your ears on?"

November 19

"Therefore I take pleasure in infirmities, in reproaches, in necessities, in persecutions, in distresses for Christ's sake: for when I am weak, then am I strong."

2 Corinthians 12:10 (KJV)

A lady was brought into a restaurant in a wheel chair. I noticed that she had a scripture verse emblazoned on her tee-shirt that read, "No weapon formed against thee shall prosper." (Isaiah 54:17) Her hands and feet were twisted and gnarled. Her speech was slurred as she struggled to speak. She labored as she ate her meal. Someone had to assist her as she drank from a large glass. Nothing came easy for this dear lady. I blushed as I thought about my recent complaint of a sore neck and back. My pain seemed to be so insignificant compared to this brave lady who struggled each day of her life. For someone who may not have the insights of a just and righteous God, they would argue that the lady's daily trials and the scripture verse do not mix very well. On the surface that may appear true, but underneath the seemingly misconception is a much needed truth.

November 19

The Christian's response to situations like these would be in a matter of one's perspective on pain and suffering. The apostle Paul had the proper view about the discomforts and disappointments of life. He saw them as avenues of growing stronger, not becoming weaker. He looked upon them as opportunities to mature and not burdens to weigh us down. Paul's rationale was that the way forward would be through our sorrows. The hard knocks of life would give us a keener view of who God is and His ways. We can trust by faith that God will see us through each lamentable situation.

One of the positives of pain is that it makes us open our eyes wider. Distress causes us to focus more on God in the crisis of life than in the times of ease when we become too comfortable in our well-being. The Heavenly Father doesn't want us to walk through heartache with our eyes closed. He wants us to have our eyes focused upon Him when the dark times come. The darker the night, the keener our eyes should be in navigating through perilous times.

Thought to ponder: "The bumps of life are what we climb on!"

November 20

"The LORD is good unto them that wait for him, to the soul that seeketh him." Lamentations 3:25 (KJV)

While working with children in our church, we are constantly saying to them, among other things, "Be still." I am convinced that most kids have an extra bottle of 24-hour energy stored somewhere on their person. When they need it, and that seems like always, they pop the top and siphon off an extra measure of stamina. Some of these fast-paced kids seem to have more than one bottle of this power enhancer. As difficult as it is for most children to be still, many Christians struggle with a similar problem, and that is being still and experiencing the awesome presence of God.

We live at an accelerated pace in our day and time. We want what we want now, without any delay. Many are fast food junkies, visiting multi-billion dollar businesses, to get their nourishment at lightning speed. Some look to microwave ovens to give instant results. Others will do whatever is necessary to get their wishes instantly, but there are no shortcuts when it comes to having intimate relationships. There are

November 20

no overnight results when it comes to fostering friendships, and there are no microwave ends when it comes to having sweet communion and fellowship with the Heavenly Father.

The key to our maturing in the Lord is learning how to wait on God. Rather than running ahead of Him, or following from behind, it's incumbent on us to walk with Him at His speed. It takes time to develop an association with the Father, but the results will be "out of this world!"

Thought to ponder: "Waiting on God will give us all the energy we will ever need!"

November 21

"The righteous is delivered out of trouble, and the wicked cometh in his stead." Proverbs 11:8 (KJV)

My wife and I were travelling some back roads in our community and came upon a sign that read, "Caution, Rough Road Ahead." How true was that sign. Little did I know that we were in for an adventurous drive, not knowing what to expect. We encountered cracks in the road which seemed that all were just a few feet part. There were potholes in the pavement which you couldn't see until you were over them. I noticed pieces of the road were missing from the ribbon of asphalt. I couldn't guess what was up ahead of us. It was like trying to maneuver your way through a mine field of surprises. It wasn't very long, though, before we could see those rough roads in the rear view mirror. Up ahead, the pavement became smoother with no more surprises.

The Bible speaks of the rough roads of life ahead for all of us. It's not a matter of if they will come, but rather when they will commence. There are the cracks in our journey of faith

November 21

with the Lord which the enemy tries to use to steer us away from Him. Potholes are all around us as we make our sojourn to the celestial city. Some of them are quite deep, and if we chance to hit one, we can be sidetracked for a season. The enemy of our souls will try to take pieces of our fellowship with the Lord and weaken them into a mere acquaintance. We are cautioned to be on the lookout for these artillery shots taken by our foe. He will do everything in his power to spoil the sweetness of our Lord's presence. Though the road becomes rough and the night becomes dark with dread, there is one delightful thought: the way will not always be as oppressive as it may be now. There is coming a day when we will walk down the streets of heaven on golden avenues. There will be no cracks, potholes, or pieces missing from that golden pavement.

Thought to ponder: "One day the asphalt black road of this life will turn to the golden street of heaven."

November 22

"Then shall the kingdom of heaven be likened unto ten virgins, which took their lamps, and went forth to meet the bridegroom." Matthew 25:1 (KJV)

While I was in the public work force, my supervisor had the option of excusing my unpunctual arrival for work. It was a policy given by upper management that if an employee was tardy in punching the time clock, a reprieve of 29 minutes was allowed. On the time card were the initials "T.E.," which meant, "Tardiness Excused." If the tardiness exceeded the time allotted, the employee was charged with an hour of leave. After the many years of punching the time clock, I am thankful that the employer understood the issues of being late for work. More than once did the supervisor give me 29 minutes of relief.

There is coming a day on God's calendar when tardiness will have no legitimate excuse. Our Lord has given us fair warning that at His coming those who are not ready for His arrival will be left out. On God's timetable there is a moment in time when Jesus will come to take His Bride home. At that

November 22

specified point, there will be a "snatching away" of the saints of God. It may seem that Christ has tarried past that time, but it is for certain that He will not wait beyond the due time. In God's own way, He will send forth His Son at the appropriate season. The Father has given us enough time to prepare ourselves for His Son's second advent. Those who go forth to meet the bridegroom must be prepared. There will be no "T.E." on the timecard of life to excuse our carelessness. We must keep our lamps burning brightly as we see the day of our Lord approaching. The thoughtless approach of not being ready for that moment will bring about the mortifying words of our Lord, "I do not know you!"

Thought to ponder: "Of the 10 virgins, 5 were wise and 5 were otherwise."

November 23

"Nay, in all these things we are more than conquerors through him that loved us." Romans 8:37 (KJV)

Being the sports fanatic I am, seasons of the year are defined by the respective sport. When fall comes around, it's all about football, especially the college kind. The summer means that baseball will be around from April to the World Series. As winter and spring make their appearance on the calendar, it's basketball time, and if you are a diehard hockey fan, the games are on. It's a continual roller coaster as my teams win or lose. The ultimate fan lives in one of two worlds: "My teams is the best; or there's always next year." I rise or I fall as my favorite team has victory or defeat. My seasons are filled with the "thrill of victory or the agony of defeat!"

Can you image what it would be like to experience lasting victory in life? That may sound like a sales pitch to sign you up for a thrilling ride; but it's not, because the Bible teaches us that we are more than conquering saints; we are over comers. When the sudden setbacks come along

November 23

whispering gloom and doom, we are assured that we have victory through the Lord Jesus Christ. As we depend upon Him, He not only provides the needed strength to face trying circumstances, but also gives us proper perspective to overcome the heated trials of life. We can live from moment to moment in the assurance that we are in the loving hands of a caring Father. Our faith in the finished work of Christ on the cross assures us that we can face whatever the world may hurl at us. Each day the Holy Spirit will infuse us with His power to thwart every fiery dart the enemy throws at us. As we pull closer to Him, He will pull closer to us, and as we draw strength from His indwelling, victory is lasting.

Thought to ponder: The victory that has overcome the world is even our faith.

November 24

"For his anger endureth but a moment; in his favour is life: weeping may endure for a night, but joy cometh in the morning." Psalms 30:5 (KJV)

A few years ago our insurance agent wanted us to list all of the valuables in our house. His instructions were to start with the most valuable and work our way back to the smaller, less expensive items. Along the way we discovered that we had some out-of-sight treasures hidden beneath some boxes. We were pleasantly surprised when we uncovered those long lost-treasures. They were there all the while, but we had misplaced them and over time had forgotten them. This situation caused me to wonder how much more buried treasure we may have in our house and not know it.

As Christians, we have been given the joy of the Lord. It's the kind of delight the world knows nothing about, can't give us, and thereby can't take away. Joy is one of those qualities God included in His gift of salvation. The agony and the pain of the cross on which our Lord suffered gave to us this enduring gift of joy unspeakable and full of glory. Out

NOVEMBER 24

of His sorrow came our gladness. From His suffering came our bliss. Joy is a precious endowment that keeps on giving, even in the midst of sadness.

There are times when we mislay this precious gift and allow the joy robbers to seize the moment and wreak havoc in our daily walk. We may be totally unaware that our joy is hidden beneath the daily grind of material things. Our life may be dragging the bottom of the barrel of sorrow and the moment may catch us unprepared to raise up our banner of gladness. The enemy can't take our joy unless we allow him to do so. We must always be on our guard when he comes to do his conniving work. The thief's chief purpose is to steal and kill and destroy. He is bent on doing whatever he can to steal our joy. The fiend of our soul is determined to kill our testimony any way he can, and the adversary will use everything within his arsenal to destroy all we stand for.

Thought to ponder: "Joy is the oil of life in the gears of everyday living."

November 25

"Lest Satan should get an advantage of us: for we are not ignorant of his devices." 2 Corinthians 2:11 (KJV)

I was watching a college football game between the Mississippi Rebels and the Florida State Seminoles. It was the first game of the season for both teams. Sideline shots showed the players and coaches getting together to mentally prepare themselves for the upcoming battle. The coaches were thumbing through their playbooks, hoping to give the players the right plays. The players went through their exercises to help them get their timing down. Some of the "Ole Miss" players displayed tee shirts which read, "No Days Off!" The team had sold themselves out for the season and were committed to make every day count.

Our arch enemy doesn't take a day off. He is on the job "24-7." From the rising of the sun to the going down of the same, and all time in between, the devil is on the prowl. There are no days off for him. The plans he has hatched are directed at each one of us. His intention is to destroy everything and everyone who has anything to do with God. He

NOVEMBER 25

will attack us with some of the most insidious measures. When God opens the windows of heaven to bless us, the rival of our souls will open up the doors of hell to blast us so our intended response will be to take, "No Days Off!"

Our undertaking should be to match the enemy's assault by being on our guard every waking minute and not taking one day off. We are no match for the enemy in our flesh or spirit unless we yield ourselves to God and follow His plan of defeating the adversary. The Heavenly Father has an organized design to defeat Satan at every turn. He has given us a playbook, called the Bible, which will instruct each one of us how we can utilize the weapons made available. Our pledge to the Father should be to acquaint ourselves with these "Weapons Of Mass Destruction." There is no need for us to ask Him for this weaponry, for they are at our disposal. We are not ignorant of his devices; therefore we can be victorious at every turn.

Thought to ponder: "May we be found standing on His promises and not setting on our premises."

November 26

"O give thanks unto the LORD, for he is good: for his mercy endureth for ever." Psalms 107:1 (KJV)

I received an email from a pastor friend of mine who had recently moved to a new pastorate. He outlined for me what God had led him to do and how things seem to be falling into place. He further stated that he was excited to see where God was at work and join Him to be on mission. Even his wife and children were infected with his enthusiasm. He promised to keep me up to date with the Lord's activity in and around his calling. Toward the end of the email he said, "I want to wish you and your family a merry Thanksgiving and a happy Christmas." I thought that he had gotten his seasonal greetings turned around, so I responded by saying, "Shouldn't you have said, 'I want to wish you and your family a happy Thanksgiving?'" His response was, "No! This year I am going to have a new perspective on Thanksgiving. I plan to eat, drink, and be merry!"

My friend's good will is on target. This year at Thanksgiving, I plan to eat the good which God has blessed

NOVEMBER 26

me with. The menu will consist of ham and turkey along with sweet potato soufflé. My plans are also to drink my annual eggnog, hot apple cider, and add a pumpkin smoothie to my list of drinks this year. Aside from the eating and the drinking, which is all a part of the celebration, I want to take my pastor friend's perspective of having a merry Thanksgiving, and that's going to take some discretionary decisions. I enjoy the festivities of the season, but there is more to Thanksgiving than the physical and material aspect. There is a spiritual undertone that I want to tap into this year.

I intend to be thankful for God's provisions. After all, that's what Thanksgiving is all about. Since last year at this time, I have been blessed beyond measure. The Lord has met all of my needs and has even given me some of my desires. I also plan to be grateful for God's patience. I have not been the poster child for the kingdom. I have fallen along the way, but God, through His patience, has picked me up and put me back on right way. I will be humble for God's protection. He has been there with me every step of the way to guide my every footstep, and He will be with me till the end of my earthly sojourn.

Thought to ponder: "Our thanksgiving is the spiritual food we give back to God through praise."

November 27

"For who hath known the mind of the Lord, that he may instruct him? But we have the mind of Christ."

1 Corinthians 2:16 (KJV)

"Relax, we have your head in our hands," are the words of a local business who specializes in cutting, trimming, and grooming hair. If this had been my first visit to this salon, I would have been reluctant to believe their claim. Over the years, and after many satisfying visits, I am confident that this establishment can keep their promise of taking care of all my hair-styling needs. Now this doesn't mean that every person who comes in will always have their hair cut the way they desire. With me, when my name is called, I confidently take my seat and drift off into a temporary shutdown and the hairstylist begins her work of art.

We are challenged in the scriptures to have such intimacy with Christ that we will go above and beyond a shallow commitment of our life. The Bible assures us that when we take on the mind of Christ, our very being takes on new meaning. Life as it was in the past dims as a dying star, and the new

November 27

life that comes through the Spirit of Truth takes on a radiant light beam that shines brightly. The Holy Spirit is the agent by which we have the Father and the Son's perception. The initiative of pursuing this life-changing event rests upon our shoulders. Rather than holding onto the choicest parts and giving the leftovers to the Lord, we are to go all the way by giving Him all that we are, and that includes our mind. We are to allow the mind of Christ to guide us in all the avenues we travel.

Having His mind insures that all our decisions and actions will be Christ-honoring. That's reason enough to let the Spirit have full control of our passions. He will guide us into all truth and will reveal the Son in us. That's a part of the ministry of the Spirit of God, for He knows all things, and He searches all things, even the deep things of God. There aren't enough pastors and teachers who could fill our minds with the truths of God. No one can know the things of God but by His Holy Spirit, Who is one with the Father and the Son, and Who makes known the Divine mysteries to the church. That is a clarion call to every believer to relax because the Holy Spirit has our head (mind) in His hands.

Thought to ponder: "When our minds become His mind, we will mind the things of Him."

November 28

"Wherefore gird up the loins of your mind, be sober, and hope to the end for the grace that is to be brought unto you at the revelation of Jesus Christ." 1 Peter 1:13 (KJV)

During the years which followed the second World War, a flood of cheaply made trinkets flowed from Japan to our country. Most of the smaller items cost no more than ten cents. My maternal grandmother collected these small mementos and had a large collection of them. It didn't matter to her what the item was, as long as one was given to her. She was glad to receive more than one of the same kind. When my parents would return from a vacation, Granny knew that she was going to receive a new trinket. She had a curio cabinet full of them, and she treasured each one. After she went home to be with her Lord, my mother told me that Granny looked forward to one of her children, or grandchildren bringing her a "new toy." That little item would make her day, week, and month, all together.

Peter, in his first epistle, reveals to us something the Lord is going to bring with Him as His "revelation." It's a gift that

November 28

we anticipate receiving when we come to the end of this earthly journey. This quality will be brought to every one of God's dear children; no one will be left out. In Peter's own words, he speaks of the "grace" that is to be brought to us at the Lord's return. We are saved by grace; we stand in grace; and one day we will be rewarded with the fullness of grace. The "graceful grace" of which Peter speaks belongs to us, and we will receive its bountifulness when the Lord comes for His Bride. Everything we can think of pertaining to grace, all that we can hope for in grace, and more than we can long for about grace will find its crowning touch when we come face to face with our Master. Today, our minds cannot fully comprehend God's unmerited love and favor, but when eternity is ushered in, we will have the full capacity to receive the awesomeness of "amazing grace!"

Thought to ponder: "It's amazing grace now. It will be fullness of grace then."

November 29

"But as it is written, Eye hath not seen, nor ear heard, neither have entered into the heart of man, the things which God hath prepared for them that love him." 1 Corinthians 2:9 (KJV)

My cousin invited me to take a tour with him of a museum that housed a collection of rare, antique vehicles. He works for a wealthy businessman who has amassed quite a collection of these classics, and my relative wanted to share with me their attractiveness. As we walked from room to room, I didn't think there could be another antique car better looking than the one I just admired. Row after row of these fascinating beauties beckoned for someone to admire them. My heart raced with anticipation as I walked by each car, while rubbing my hand over the slick and smooth paint job each one had. I dreamt of a time when I could own just one of these beauties, but in my mind I heard those sobering words, "Dream on, big dreamer, dream on!" Deep down inside I knew that I couldn't afford one of these rarities.

November 29

As I thought about heaven and all that awaits me there in that beautiful city of God, I realized that it's not a dream but a reality that's just waiting to happen. One day I will walk down streets of gold and see the bright lights of glory. I will stand in awe before gates of pearl and admire the beauty only God could create. A mansion awaits me there, and one day soon, I will move in, never to move out. There will be no separation, no sickness, and no senseless loss in that eternal city of bliss. It will be a gladsome day and nothing on earth can compare to those heavenly delights. Jesus has gone to prepare a place for each one of His blood-bought children, and only He could make such a promise and keep each intricate detail. What we may see down here and desire to have, only to be disappointed, will never happen in heaven. All that we could ever dream of and hope for will be in heaven. There is much more that our eye has not seen, nor our ear heard, nor has it entered our heart those things that await us in that fair city of God.

Thought to ponder: "Heaven is just a short breath away."

November 30

" Come unto me, all ye that labour and are heavy laden, and I will give you rest." Matthew 11:28 (KJV)

A "Welcome Center" along an Interstate highway was undergoing a renovation project that caused it to curtail its activities for several months. Much refurbishing was needed to bring the center up to regulation, and a temporary shutdown was necessary. There had been some vandalism in the area and it forced the Department of Transportation to put a temporary sign on the main thoroughfare that lead by the welcome center. It had these words of warning, "NO TRESPASSING!" The symbolism of the sign contradicted the main function of the center. The two signs seemed to say in unison, "You are welcomed here, but no trespassing!"

There is an underlying truth to the two signs posted together which speak to our hearts about the openness of our church to all peoples, regardless of their standing. The Church of the Lord Jesus is a "Welcome Center" of sorts. The red carpet of welcome should be rolled out every time the

NOVEMBER 30

doors of worship are opened. None should be barred from coming to encounter the God of creation through genuine worship. Men, women, boys and girls, with opened arms, should be posted at the entrance to every church, because that's who we are. At one point we were strangers and outcasts, but through the cross, Jesus opened the way for all to come to Him for forgiveness. Because we were received just as we were, we should in turn welcome all to come to Christ just as they are.

It's one thing to claim to be a welcome center, but an entirely different matter to say to others that they cannot trespass our church. Our light is to shine toward others who live in darkness. The saltiness of our testimony is for those who are without Christ. The beating of our hearts is for those who have lost their way and cannot find the path to God. Our hands, our feet, our lips are all for going, doing, and speaking the wonderful words of the Gospel.

Thought to ponder: "Rest for the weary comes through Jesus; rest for eternity comes from the Father."

December 1

"Behold, I will do a new thing; now it shall spring forth; shall ye not know it? I will even make a way in the wilderness, and rivers in the desert." Isaiah 43:19 (KJV)

I owe a great deal of my spiritual preparedness for life to my parents. They not only raised me in church, they raised me on Christ. I jokingly say that I went to church 9 months before I was born. I say that because my parents were in church at the appointed time. My dad, who was a pastor, taught me the importance of being a part of worship and also the necessity of finding my place in Christ. My mother encouraged me to seek the Lord with all of my heart. She assured me, according to the Scriptures, that the Lord would direct my path, and in all of my years, from childhood to adulthood, those words have been true. I had a steady diet of church activities every week. It was Sunday School in the morning and preaching that followed. Training Union and more preaching came in the evening. Wednesday night was for RA's, and I found my place there. Both of my parents were an inspiration to me as I set out to start a family of my own.

December 1

If you were not brought up in a church environment, you missed some important foundational principles, but it's never too late to build your life on Christ, for He is the only solid rock on which to establish life. Our hope can only be built on Christ the solid Rock, for all other ground is sinking sand. As complex as life issues become, Jesus is the answer to every question in life. When our journey doesn't make sense and the pathway is obscure, He can make a way where there is no way. Though barriers appear to be impenetrable, mountains insurmountable, and paths untraceable, our Guide will lead us through the mazes of life. Only He knows the safe ways to travel, and He makes His way plain. There are no problems so confusing and no passages too tight that our Lord cannot direct our walk. When we come to the end of our rope, He is the knot on which our hand can cling, and His hand has not lost one of the precious children of the Father.

Thought to ponder: "The heavenly highway will always lead us to safety."

December 2

"Honour the LORD with thy substance, and with the first fruits of all thine increase: So shall thy barns be filled with plenty, and thy presses shall burst out with new wine."

Proverbs 3:9, 10 (KJV)

Recently I received an email informing me that I was to be awarded $50,000. A doctor who had recently passed away had no heirs to whom he could bequeath the gift of benefaction. I was told that the only action I needed to take was to mail them 1% of the award in the form of a money order, which would be $500. The funds sent to them would be used to offset any of the expenses covered in the agreement. Furthermore, I was apprised that once I took the initial step, there would be other allotments made of greater amounts of monies. I had to make a choice. I could mail this party the 1%, with an expected return of $50,000 and more to come; or I could delete the message and save myself a lot of heartburn. Well, the decision didn't take long. As a matter of fact, I deleted the email as soon as I read the last

December 2

word. The left click on my computer mouse probably never felt that hard of a push.

In the Bible we are taught the concept of tithing: taking 10% of our earnings and investing it into the work and ministry of the local New Testament church. It is in the Old Testament but has ramifications in the New Testament. All of that which we have been given by way of monies belongs to the Lord, and He asks us to be faithful stewards of those blessings. There are no underlying deceits attached to this request of being managers of God's resources. The Lords tells us to bring the tithe into His storehouse. There is every reason to believe that the Lord has our best interests at heart. When He challenges us to give of our dollars, He promises to open the windows of heaven and pour out blessings upon us which are beyond our imagination. When we faithfully give of our best to the Lord, He is faithful to us to make sure that all of our needs are met. What I give in His tithe and my offering fails miserably when equated to what the Father gives in return.

Thought to ponder: "When we place our best on the altar, the Lord gives us His best in return."

December 3

"Give, and it shall be given unto you; good measure, pressed down, and shaken together, and running over, shall men give into your bosom. For with the same measure that ye mete withal it shall be measured to you again." Luke 6:38 (KJV)

During one of our children's programs at church, my wife asked the children, "What are some things we could give to God?" Some of the innocent answers were: food if He was hungry, water if He was thirsty, and anything He might need. One of the kids spoke up and said in her response to my wife's question this novel way of giving, "We can give God the things we don't need any more." I laughed at her response because she was thinking about those things that weren't needed any more and could be given to someone else for their use.

That got me to thinking about how we oftentimes approach our giving to the Lord and His cause. We are instructed in the scriptures to bring our best gifts to Him and offer them there upon the altar of sacrifice. We are encouraged in song to give of our best to the Master because He

December 3

gave His best for us. What we give to the Lord in the spirit of giving will be given back, pressed down, shaken together, and running over. The promise is that blessings will be poured into our lap. We don't give out of an obligation but rather through a cheerful heart, because God loves a hilarious giver. God will take the little we give to Him and will multiply it back to us. He never disappoints. His bountiful hand will give and keep on giving without end. When we sow into His kingdom enterprise, not only will others be blessed, but we will receive an equal blessing.

Thought to ponder: "The Father does more than add; He multiplies!"

December 4

"Who his own self bare our sins in his own body on the tree, that we, being dead to sins, should live unto righteousness: by whose stripes ye were healed." 1 Peter 2:24 (KJV)

I saw a church sign that caught my attention. It read, "People needed--to hear the GOSPEL!" Those thought-provoking words reminded me of a responsibility I have in sharing the gospel with every individual I met. This church wasn't interested in padding their attendance records. They wanted to attend to the desire of their Lord in bringing the lost to Him. We, as this church, have a debt to every living soul to take the Bible and give them a healthy dose of God's plan of salvation. Sin-sick people need the Lord, and as Christians, we have the cure for their sinful ills. They are separated from God and someone is needed to point them in the right direction. Unless we are willing to shoulder the responsibility of speaking the truth in love, the ministry of soul-winning will not be fulfilled.

The sole purpose for Jesus coming into a sinful world was to give His life a ransom for sinners. His sacrificial death

December 4

on the cross opened the way for the redemption of mankind. Without the shedding of His blood, there would be no remission for sin. We were born in sin and would die in our sin without the precious blood of Christ. He personally carried our sins in his body on the cross so that we can be dead to sin and live for what is right. Jesus loved us so much that He left the portals of heaven, took upon Himself the likeness of sinful man, and went to the cross to die in our stead. His atonement paved the way to a lifetime of fellowship with the Father through the Holy Spirit. Without this sacrifice, there would be no hope for man who had been separated from a holy God by sin. It would be a shameful disgrace on our part for Jesus to go to that extreme, and we not give Him the benefit of sharing His love for men and women.

Thought to ponder: "What Jesus did for me, He did for all, without exception."

December 5

"And who is he that will harm you, if ye be followers of that which is good?" 1 Peter 3:13 (KJV)

A hurricane recently made its way up the coasts of Florida, Georgia, South Carolina, and North Carolina, bringing with it the devastating results of a Category 4 storm. The whistling winds wreaked havoc on houses and trees, while walls of water settled in many houses causing damage which would take months to clean up. The future for many of the citizens would be the months of weariness and worry which would ensue. As I watched the unfolding drama of this fierce storm, I was reminded of the wrath that storms of this magnitude can bring. I watched with horror at the destruction to the properties of some residents. A bright point in the storm came from a first-responder who said, "Sometimes the worst brings out the best in us." He was speaking on behalf of those who responded financially and materially to the needs of the stricken victims of this monstrous storm.

December 5

In our Christian walk we are going to encounter some troublesome times. These epochs, which are to be expected, will oftentimes come unannounced. A morning of bright sunshine will give way to the darkness of night, and yet these experiences can bring out the best in us. I am convinced after reading our scripture verse for the day, that no one and nothing can harm us unless we allow them to do so. It doesn't matter how low we may sink into desperation, and no matter how worn out we may be, God will take what others may throw at us to exasperate our intentions and turn each one of them into good. The hurricanes of life will sweep into our life experiences uninvited. With its foreboding faces of panic and anxiety, we can take courage that God is in full control. These torrents of trouble will be beneficial even if we don't understand them. Even the damaging results can be placed in the Father's hands to become our partner in blessings. The surging storms which stream steadily into our daily walk will try to disrupt our journey. These boisterous eruptions can become our best friends when we allow God to transform them.

Thought to ponder: "God will put a positive spin on the negatives of life."

December 6

"Then he answered and spake unto me, saying, This is the word of the LORD unto Zerubbabel, saying, Not by might, nor by power, but by my spirit, saith the LORD of hosts."
Zechariah 4:6 (KJV)

J. Hudson Taylor, pioneer missionary, was once quoted as saying, "I used to ask God if He would come and help me. Then I asked if I could come and help Him. Finally I ended by asking God to do His own work through me."

Those three statements remind me of a gradual learning process of how to pray and seek God's will. There are times when we come before the Father, in heart-felt prayer, and ask Him to help us out on an enterprise we have felt led to pursue. Perhaps the undertaking sounded good, with great promise, and rich reward, but the end result was one of futility.

There are other times when we commit ourselves to God's purposes by promoting good will among men and promising Him that we can be used to accomplish His will. We present ourselves as workers in the kingdom with the end result in mind of adding members to the body of Christ. Our

December 6

intentions are well-founded upon the call to make disciples of all nations, but again, the order of succession is less than favorable.

Then there is the one time we make the right choice. It is the only quest we have in experiencing the joy of knowing we have done the right thing. That effort is when we allow God to do a work in and through us that only He can do. The energy for this endeavor is provided by the Spirit of God, for it is not by might, not by power, but by the Spirit of God that the work of God can be completed. When we come to the point in our Christian walk to ask God to do His own work through a willing vessel, it is then that the force of God comes to full power.

Thought to ponder: "God's great work is done through empty vessels."

December 7

"For whatsoever is born of God overcometh the world: and this is the victory that overcometh the world, even our faith."
1 John 5:4 (KJV)

It was on this day in 1941 that the Imperial Japanese Navy carried out a surprise attack on the United States Pacific Fleet and its defending Army and Marine air forces at Pearl Harbor, Hawaii. At 7:55 a.m. Hawaii time, a Japanese dive bomber bearing the red symbol of the Rising Sun of Japan on its wings appeared out of the clouds above the island of Oahu. A swarm of 360 Japanese warplanes followed, descending on the U.S. naval base in a ferocious assault. The surprise attack struck a critical blow against the U.S. Pacific fleet and drew the United States irrevocably into World War II.

The day after Pearl Harbor was bombed, President Roosevelt appeared before a joint session of Congress and declared, "Yesterday, December 7, 1941--a date which will live in infamy--the United States of America was suddenly and deliberately attacked by naval and air forces of the

December 7

Empire of Japan." After a brief and forceful speech, he asked Congress to approve a resolution recognizing the state of war between the United States and Japan.

As Christians, war has been declared on us by the enemy of our souls. He has a score to settle, and we are in his crosshairs. He wants to derail, defeat, and ultimately destroy us. He knows that his time is limited and the more harm he can do will bring him limited satisfaction. When Jesus opened the windows of heaven to bless us with the gift of His salvation, Satan then opened the windows of hell to blast us with his most potent of weapons--doubt to the goodness of God. With his dive bombers of fear, he has come against us with his sneer and banter. He has amassed a ground troop of his demonic leathernecks to wage war against our well-being. He assails our soul with the armament of hell. Our stand against him is in the power and might of the Holy Spirit of God, and only through Him, the Spirit, can we emerge victorious.

Thought to ponder: "Victory in Jesus is our marching song as we meet the enemy."

December 8

"I returned, and saw under the sun, that the race is not to the swift, nor the battle to the strong, neither yet bread to the wise, nor yet riches to men of understanding, nor yet favour to men of skill; but time and chance happeneth to them all."
Ecclesiastes 9:11 (KJV)

At a recent soccer game my grandson's team lost their first contest of the year. He was downcast and you could see it on his face and hear it in his voice. His dream season was to go undefeated and lead his team in scoring goals, and now the first half of that vision was shattered. At the time I thought he needed a little encouragement. Trying to be of help I said, "It's not whether you win or lose, but it's how you play the game that matters." Now that's not original with me. It comes from a writer using a cliche' to say, "Reaching a goal is less important than giving our best effort." I wanted my grandson to realize that the most important thing for him at the moment was to do his very best and leave the rest to God.

December 8

We, as Christians, know that we are winners in the end. The great conflict in this world, led by a diabolical enemy, targets us for defeat. There may be some times when we lose a battle here and there, but ultimately we are victorious. Victory has been assured, and we can live daily with the conviction that we are more than conquerors through Christ Who loves us. Since we are winners, the matter of winning or losing is not in the equation, but how we live during our sojourn on earth matters greatly. In these last times we are to walk in love; walk as light; and walk wisely, and in the end we will be known in part by how we lived our life on earth.

It's through the death, burial, and resurrection of our Lord Jesus that we celebrate life. With every step of the way, we are led by the unchanging hand of a loving God. We rest in His trustworthiness and lean upon His loving care. His promise is to carry us safely across the great divide of daily living. With our hand in His hand we are empowered to do what is not in our natural ability. Our submission to His great authority is the key that unlocks the great potential He has for us.

Thought to ponder: "When we say we can't, God says, We can!"

December 9

"But God, who is rich in mercy, for his great love wherewith he loved us, even when we were dead in sins, hath quickened us together with Christ, (by grace ye are saved;)"

Ephesians 2:4,5 (KJV)

The "Miracle on Ice" refers to a medal-round game during the men's ice hockey tournament at the 1980 Winter Olympics in Lake Placid, New York, played between the hosting United States and the defending gold medalists, the Soviet Union. "Do you believe in miracles?! Yes!" described one of the most iconic moments of the Games and in U.S. sports. Al Michaels for ABC television made the famous call of the final seconds of the game. February 22, 1980 was the date that the impossible became the possible.

Do I, as a Christian, believe in miracles? I respond with a resounding, "YES!" I say that because I am a miracle. There was a time in my life when I was dead, not physically but spiritually, in trespasses and sins. My energy was engulfed in darkness. I was at a point in my beleaguered life when I lived as a child of disobedience. I went my way, at my pace,

DECEMBER 9

at my desire. Because of my sinful nature, I followed blindly the dictates of the prince of the power of the air. My allegiance, whether I realized it or not, was to the father of lies. Life for me was dominated by the lustful desires of my flesh and mind. I did everything from the standpoint of doing it my way. The bottom line was that as a child of wrath, I was at enmity with God and a sinner by birth, but then the miracle took place.

"But God" are words which introduce us to a firm belief in the miracle-working ways of Almighty God. If we were to record all the sinful ways which dominated our lives prior to receiving Christ as Savior, they would be instantly canceled with a, "BUT GOD!" The enemy will plant seeds of doubt and our response to him can be, "But God is so rich in mercy, and He loves us so much!" So, when we find ourselves in the slough of despond as Christian did in John Bunyan's "Pilgrim's Progress," God will come and lift us out of the mire of sin and put us on the path to the celestial city.

Thought to ponder: "Do you believe in miracles? ! Yes!"

December 10

"I will praise thee; for I am fearfully and wonderfully made: marvelous are thy works; and that my soul knoweth right well." Psalms 139:34 (KJV)

A gentleman came into the local antique mall where I was working and asked if I knew where some vintage clothing labels and tags may be. I was astonished that someone would be collecting something of that nature. I have learned over the years that people will collect almost anything that has value. This individual was mainly interested in early "Polo" and "Levi Straus" labels. He also had a passion for vintage "Hand Woven Harris Tweed" and "Carhartt Overall" tags, and his collection went on and on as he bragged about his vast treasures. The collection, he stated, had been amassed over a twenty-year period. He claimed to have at least 1,500 different clothing tags and labels. I shook my head in disbelief and wondered why something like that had collectability, and yet the value of items like these labels would be in the eye of the beholder.

December 10

I began to think about a label, or tag, that could be found somewhere on us that was marked with, "Made By God!" Of course you couldn't see the tag, but it's there. His very handprint is upon every created human being. As uniquely made as we are, God created us in His own image and breathed into us the very essence of life itself. If early vintage labels have great value, how much more does this particular label have. As I reasoned how God created each one of us, I realized that we are wonderfully complex in our makeup. God's workmanship is marvelous, and as we dwell upon that knowledge, we know it quite well. Although I don't accurately understand them in all their parts as I wish to do, I know by faith that they are true. The response to discernment of this nature is that of praise and adoration. God's deeds are awesome and amazing, and His knowledge of us is thorough. Our finite minds could not envision such wondrous works as that of our Creator.

Thought to ponder: "Divinely made, and divinely favored are we!"

December 11

"Therefore, my beloved brethren, be ye steadfast, unmovable, always abounding in the work of the Lord, forasmuch as ye know that your labor is not in vain in the Lord."

1 Corinthians 15:58 (KJV)

I heard someone say that there is a definite advantage in a "setback." Nestled in the midst of failure, and a step in the wrong direction, there is room for expansion at a greater speed. Rather than being pushed back, and coupled with a willingness to give in and give up, we can take the amount of space lost to build momentum to press forward. It's like we have more running space provided by the disappointment. We can use that deficiency as a windfall of good fortune. Our path to launch a greater distance can be paved by the scrapes of life. The spread of interruption in the backstep can become our gain if we use it for our improvement.

Some setbacks could be the loss of a job, health, a close friend, family member, or the aging process. We can allow these to bring disappointment and defeat. Our life can be marked by unfulfilled dreams, blighted hopes, and vain

December 11

expectations; or it can be celebrated with a daily walk of victorious faith. Life for the Christian does not have to be an up and down process, but one that is steadfast and sure, unmovable and always abounding in the faith. Therefore, as brothers and sisters in Christ, we are to stand firm and let nothing move us. Our feet are established on an unshakable foundation. We can give ourselves fully to the work of the Lord because we are confident that our labor in the Lord is not empty. Nothing done for the Lord in His name will go unnoticed. May Christ Himself give us faith and increase that faith so that we may not only be safe, but have a joyful and triumphant life. When we come to the end of this earthly life we have a greater reward in heaven.

Thought to ponder: "A setback on our part is a setup from God for greater things."

December 12

"A man that hath friends must shew himself friendly: and there is a friend that sticketh closer than a brother."
Proverbs 18:24 (KJV)

Our Lord was called many names by His enemies. Those who didn't care for Him or His ministry found ways with words to humiliate Him. Jesus was pointed out as being a gluttonous man and a drunkard, a friend of tax collectors and sinners. These slurs and other titles were intended to disgrace Him. Jesus knew what was in the heart of His accusers, and His opposition found ways to foment their disdain for Him. Yet, in the scriptures we read that when He was reviled, He reviled not. Sticks and stones would break His bones, but names would not hurt Him. Some of the labels used against our Lord, though spoken in disgust, would prepare the way for our Lord's earthly ministry.

One of the names our Lord wore gladly, as a badge of honor, was that He was a friend of sinners. At first glance the phrase does exude distaste, but in reality that was the primary reason Jesus came. The apostle Paul would say that

December 12

Christ Jesus came into the world to save sinners, of whom he was chief. Throughout his epistles he would maintain a firm believer that among the sinful he would rate at the top of the list. Paul recognized that Jesus had come into this world to be a, "Friend Of Sinners!"

Jesus, in the Old Testament, was likened to a friend Who would stick closer than a brother. Our Lord is One who will step in when the world steps out and Someone who will stay with their friend through the ups and downs of life. What this world needs now is not merely love, sweet love, but rather friends who will stay as long as needed and will do what is required. A genuine friend is someone who knows all about you and yet will still love you. Those are the kind of friends we need to find, cultivate, and encourage. We must especially be a friend to sinners so that the light of our daily walk may lead them to a loving and forgiving Father.

Thought to ponder: "There can be no greater prize on earth than to have a friend."

December 13

"And said unto them, Why sleep ye? rise and pray, lest ye enter into temptation." Luke 22:46 (KJV)

One of my grandsons recently attended his favorite professional football team's home game. He brought back a tee shirt that had been given away to each attendee and gave it to me for my sports collection. On the front of the shirt were the words, "RISE UP!" It was to be a demonstrative statement of what fans would do for their team. It would show that fans would make as much noise as they could and cheer their team on to victory. I wore this shirt to a devotional service our church has for a local nursing home and assisted living facility. As I walked by several of the residents, someone saw the shirt and asked me what I was going to "RISE UP" for? I don't believe the individual understood that the statement was for a football team, but then, it was a valid question. As a Christian what would I rise up for?

In one way God has extended a call to each one of us to rise up from our lethargy, and pray in such a way that we would not give into temptation. Our Lord suggested

December 13

that an attitude of prayer would help His followers guard against their proneness to sleep. The spirit indeed is willing to intercede on the behalf of others, but the flesh is weak when it comes to responding to the Lord's firm injunction. Our Lord's disciples were well aware that a time would come when they would face their most difficult task, and that engagement was that of remaining faithful to their Master at all times, morning, noon, and night. Now came the hour for them to stand with their Lord, and they would be found asleep at the wheel. At one juncture these diehard followers had vowed to die with their Master, but now these were only words spoken rashly with very little action taken. There are many things we can rise up for, but only one, and that is prayer, that will set the tone for daily victorious living.

Thought to ponder: "Wake up! Stand up! Speak up!"

December 14

"He that handleth a matter wisely shall find good: and whoso trusteth in the LORD, happy is he." Proverbs 16:20 (KJV)

Someone has made the claim that it takes 37 muscles to frown and 22 muscles to smile, and the action to take as a result of these numbers is, "Smile. It conserves your energy!" A smile doesn't cost a penny to give away, and the returns are enormous. Smiles are worth more than a multitude of words. What we may not be able to say to bring cheer into a situation can be conveyed with a simple smile. Smiling can help improve your mood, reduce stress, make you more approachable, and boost your productivity. Why not give a smile a day away; it will have great returns.

Jesus had a happy countenance. He had a sense of joy etched into His facial features. His smile was contagious and most people wanted to be around Him. Children, no doubt, were drawn to Him because they could see the jubilation in His every move. There's something special about an individual, like our Lord Jesus, who celebrated joy in the ordinary things of life. Peals of laughter can take the heaviness

December 14

of life and turn it into times of jubilation. Our Lord wanted to pass many things to His followers, and one of those offerings was a smile.

Those who were healed by our Lord no doubt wore a smile when they opened their eyes for the first time to see the beauty of nature. Many who leapt to their feet and walked for the first time, or flexed muscles which had been inactive for many years, ran away with smiles on their faces. Individuals who were raised from the dead, walked away with gladness engraved on their faces. People who came to know Christ as Savior and Lord wore smiles as they made their way through the daily routine as did the friends and family members of those who had been healed and raised from the dead. They had smiles pressed into their faces when hearing the good news of healing. Why not find someone today and give one of those smiles away. It will improve your day and benefit others.

Thought to ponder: "A smile--you can't give away what you don't have."

December 15

"A word fitly spoken is like apples of gold in pictures of silver."
Proverbs 25:11 (KJV)

During a recent deacon-led ministry, the speaker wore shoes that squeaked each time he took a step. Evidently the noise didn't distract him because he moved about without losing his concentration. He probably had heard the sound so often that he had become oblivious to its cadence. As he talked and began to walk around the platform, the noise from his shoes could be heard. I had been listening intently to the presentation, but now the noise from his shoes became disruptive to me. As the service neared its end, I found myself waiting for the next distraction rather than expecting a word of encouragement. After the devotional time had ended, I wanted to say to my brother in Christ, "I couldn't hear what you were saying because I was watching and listening to the way you were walking."

As Christians we need to make sure that our walk and our talk match. If we are saying one thing and doing another, mixed signals will be sent and confusion will set in. God is

December 15

not the author of confusion. He does not espouse disorder but peace, and as His children, we are not to be the assistants of ambiguity. Our speech must coincide with our steps if we expect to maintain a balance of an effective witness. Just as a word of counsel rightly spoken is especially beautiful, as fine fruit becomes still more beautiful in silver baskets, so can a step fitly taken become the complimentary background to that word. Words and steps taken together can pave the way for meaningful relationships. As we endeavor to be a spokesperson for our Lord, we must be in lockstep with Him and His Word, and our steps must be in line with our speech if we are to have a clarity of conviction. Our words must translate into our walk; otherwise our words will overshadow our walk and drown the sweetness of life.

Thought to ponder: "Don't just talk the talk. Walk it!"

December 16

"Whereas ye know not what shall be on the morrow. For what is your life? It is even a vapour, that appeareth for a little time, and then vanisheth away." James 4:14 (KJV)

A statement appeared in a local magazine that was pregnant with truth. It read, "Don't wait until someday to plan, because there is no someday on the calendar." What a sobering pronouncement that was. It should cause us to stop and consider our daily walk. There are 12 months, 365 days each year, and they have Monday through Sunday stamped upon them, but nowhere do you find a "someday." As hard as you may look to find one; as hard as you may grit your teeth to produce one; there is no "someday" on the calendar. Yesterday has passed and tomorrow hasn't come. The only day we have is the one we posses now so what we do faithfully today will go a long way in shaping our everyday.

The scriptures press upon us the importance of today. It's not the "yesterday" that we are to live in. Whether there be success or failure dotting our path, we are not to maintain

DECEMBER 16

our focus there. The failures of the past will only drag us down, and even the successes of days gone by will oftentimes weaken our dependence on the Lord. It's not the "tomorrow" that we are to cast our hopes upon. We don't know what the morrow may bring. It's as unsure as the waves of the ocean so to project our hopes upon the future will only deceive us into believing that tomorrow will be a better day. That leaves only "today," and we don't know how many of them we have left upon this earth. Our life is as a vapor, and we don't know what tomorrow may bring. Our life is like the morning fog. It's here a little while, and then it's gone. Whatever we may find to do with our hands, we are to do it well, for when we go to the grave, there will be no work or planning or knowledge or wisdom.

Thought to ponder: "When we leave this world, we must leave nothing undone."

December 17

"Come now, and let us reason together, saith the LORD: though your sins be as scarlet, they shall be as white as snow; though they be red like crimson, they shall be as wool."

Isaiah 1:18 (KJV)

In our area of the state, cotton is one of the primary crops farmers plant and harvest. Toward the end of October and the first part of November, it's not uncommon to ride the back roads and see a mass of white covering the land like snow. The cotton seems to stand out against the pale background of the fall colors. As I was riding through an area where there were several acres of this "fluffy" white stuff, I couldn't help but notice that a tall weed of sorts stood erect in the middle of the field. Its position in the field stood out because of the pure whiteness of the cotton. As far as the eye could see there was a blazing color of white, and in the middle of this spectacular sight was this ugly weed. You couldn't miss it because it was so dominating. It was a sight to see for sure.

December 17

We as Christians have been washed from our sins and made whiter than snow in the crimson flowing blood of Christ. From the dingy blackness of sin, which was our master at a point in time, to the purity of cleansing in the precious blood of Jesus, our sins have been forgiven and washed away, never to be remembered against us. As far as the east is from the west, so far has God removed our sins from us. They have been cast into the depths of the sea. Despite our efforts to remain clean in a soiled world, our feet become contaminated with besetting sins. As much as we may try to maintain a constant walk with the Lord in holiness, the enemy will seek to sow wild weeds of disruption. In the midst of our efforts to stay the steady course of "right living," we will discover that the enemy will rear his ugly head, as an ugly weed, to tarnish our walk and induce confusion and terror. He may stand out as a foreboding figure against our attempt to walk the straight and narrow way, but the light of the Lord Jesus shines brighter, and we can walk in that light despite the enemy's behavior.

Thought to ponder: "The blood of Jesus--the only cleansing agent for our sins."

December 18

"But as he which hath called you is holy, so be ye holy in all manner of conversation; Because it is written, Be ye holy; for I am holy." 1 Peter 1:15, 16 (KJV)

In sports, a "time-out" is a halt in the activity of the play. This allows the coaches of either team to communicate with the participants, make adjustments, determine strategy, outline a plan of attack, give the players a breather, and gain a new perspective. Timeouts are awarded to each team and most of the time, they take full advantage of them. Coaches and players know the importance of utilizing what has been given to them for their benefit. Even TV timeouts are called to allow media to air commercial breaks. Teams usually call timeouts at strategically important points in the game, or to avoid the team being called for a delay of game. For teams who have a determination to be perennial winners, it would be foolish to ignore such a time to suspend their activity and take a needed break.

In the game of life, there comes a period when we feel the need for a timeout. It becomes necessary to call for a cessation

December 18

of activity. A brief stop along the highway of experience calls for us to make some observations and adjustments. Life is not one continuously smooth ride where there are no potholes, detours, or obstructions. There comes that moment of introspection when we must stop, regroup, restructure, and reestablish priorities. In the hustle and bustle of life, when our strength begins to wane, the outcome can put a bend in the road and cause us to lose our direction, and suspending activity for a brief moment can give us renewed strength and vigor. Without these breaks, we can slosh through the mundane activities of the day and fail to accomplish our God-given call. Even our Lord, when He walked on earth, understood the need for a span of time when physical activities would cease, and a time of spiritual renewal would rise to the occasion.

Thought to ponder: "It does take time to be holy, and that time will be well spent."

December 19

"Man that is born of a woman is of few days, and full of trouble." Job 14:1 (KJV)

A couple in our church has been going through some trying times. Recently they lost a loved one tragically; their health has been deteriorating over the past several years; and "Father Time" is creeping up on them. They are involved in almost every aspect of our church ministry, but these disturbing circumstances have caused them to stop and take account of their activities. The wife said to one of the ladies in our congregation, "We aren't living the life of Riley; we are going through the life of Job." The phrase, "Life of Riley" is an expression that signifies an easy and pleasant life, where every day is a bed of roses; whereas, the "Life of Job" is a figure of speech that conveys a life filled with struggles.

Our times are in God's hands and the powers of nature act under Him. In Him we live and move and have our very being, and it becomes necessary to pause and reflect seriously on the shortness and uncertainty of human life and the fading nature of all earthly enjoyments. Job understood how

December 19

brief life is and how often troublesome times invade our quietness and undermine our commitment. There is no assurance that life will be trouble free. Jesus said that in this life we would have tribulation, but that we could rejoice because He has overcome the world and its turmoil.

God's ways are always right. His will is always best. His word is forever settled in heaven. We can trust His ways because they are the right ones for us. Just as a physician prescribes what is needed for us, so does our Savior. His will is always best. We are assured that His will carries with it the assurance that we will arrive safe and sound. No need to worry about the bumps in the road for they are what we climb on. His word is forever settled in heaven. We can rest assured on His unchanging and life- changing Word. For heaven and earth will pass away, but His Word will endure forever. Ours may not be the life of Riley, but there is no need to fear for the life of Job is a more productive road.

Thought to ponder: "God's ways, Word, and will are the best sources of encouragement."

December 20

"When they saw the star, they rejoiced with exceeding great joy." Matthew 2:10 (KJV)

When Jesus was born in the little town of Bethlehem on that "star lit" night, the only thing that changed was everything. Nothing would ever be the same following this miraculous birth. The world as they knew it then would be radically transformed into the hope of salvation. No one person, place, or thing could remain the same when this babe of Bethlehem took His first breath. A world of darkness saw a great light shine forth, exposing the ugliness of sin. That light shone in the darkness, yet the darkness did not overcome it. The whole course of nature saw a dramatic conversion when Jesus came forth born of a virgin.

It is said that when the wise men saw the star, they rejoiced with exceeding great joy; they were marvelously glad. They had, no doubt, experienced delight at some point in their life, but this gratification had no measure. If the wise men could still speak today, they would probably remind us of the one event in their life that brought about abounding

December 20

joy--when they caught a glimpse of this "Star of Bethlehem." We like to think of Christmas in that light. When the gladness in our heart overflows with mega-great joy, then we can say that Christmas has the right packaging. If we allow the peripheral issues of Christmas to mask the real meaning, then joy is deflated to just another holiday on the calendar to acknowledge. We will never see another star like that of these wise men, but we can by faith gaze upon the marvelous Light of the World, the Lord Jesus. When we do, we will never be the same.

Thought to ponder: "Star light, star bright, first star I see tonight, I wish I may, I wish I might, have this wish I wish tonight--to see the Star Of Bethlehem."

December 21

"And when they were come into the house, they saw the young child with Mary his mother; and fell down, and worshipped him: and when they had opened their treasures, they presented unto him gifts; gold, and frankincense, and myrrh."
Matthew 2:11 (KJV)

Though there are still many questions about the Magi that may be left unanswered, we can determine that they brought a fourth gift that is often forgotten by many. After they laid their treasures down before Mary and Joseph, they worshipped Jesus. (This is the 4th Gift--the Worship of the King of Kings) These wise men from afar came not just to court favor but to proclaim that they believed Him to be the King of Kings. The greatest gift that we can offer to Jesus this Christmas is our praise and worship.

There may be some of us this Christmas who cannot give a monetary gift of any kind. The money may not be available to give. The budget may be smashed beyond repair; and if the money were available, we would be tempted to spend it on ourselves or our family members. What we can give and must give to the One Who deserves our very best, does not cost us a penny. This fourth gift that we can give can be done throughout the year at any time we choose, and hopefully that will be every day. It is a time when we fall down prostrate before the Lord Jesus and give to Him our regard and honor. Even if we have given monetarily to the needs of others, we can still offer our Savior the one thing He desires--the worship of His child. That is the gift that everyone can give this Christmas.

Thought to ponder: "This Christmas give the most expensive gift of worship."

December 22

"For God so loved the world that he gave his only begotten Son, that whosoever believeth in him should not perish, but have everlasting life." John 3:16 (KJV)

If our greatest need had been information, God would have sent us an educator; if our greatest need had been technology, God would have sent us a scientist; if our greatest need had been money, God would have sent us an economist; if our greatest need had been pleasure, God would have sent us an entertainer; but our greatest need was forgiveness, so God sent us a Savior.

We cannot begin to imagine the Gift that God has given to this world; a Gift that cost Him so much, for in the giving of His Son, He gave Himself. It was a Treasure that would become ours for all eternity. This Present would be One who out gives and out lasts the most expensive gift on earth. God's Bestowal would reach farther than any material reward would give. This Offering will keep on giving, even after the season is over. There can be no human measure of the deepness of this Great Gift God has given.

December 22

Our greatest need this Christmas is still the need for all mankind--the forgiveness of our sins. Our debt is so large that we cannot muster up enough to satisfy the righteous demands of a Holy God. Our sin is so great that no amount of self-effort can offset the cost, for we have all sinned and come short of the glory of God. All we like sheep have gone astray. We have driven a wedge between us and God that can only be removed by Jesus. His precious blood has been shed for the remission of our sins, and we can be the recipients of this great benefaction.

Thought to ponder: "Jesus--God's Present year after year."

December 23

"And she brought forth her firstborn son, and wrapped him in swaddling clothes, and laid him in a manger; because there was no room for them in the inn." Luke 2:7 (KJV)

A television interviewer was walking the streets of Tokyo at Christmas time. Much as in America, Christmas shopping is a big commercial success in Japan. The interviewer stopped one young woman on the sidewalk and asked, "What is the meaning of Christmas?" Laughing, she responded, "I do not know. Is that the day that Jesus died?" There was some truth in her answer.

For the One who is the same yesterday, today, and forever, His birthday seems to change at the juncture of every year. For the One Who was, Who is and Who will be, the events surrounding His birth have seemingly lost their meaning. The freshness of Christmas seems to grow more stale as we allow the most wonderful day of the year to come and go and fail to celebrate its true significance, and the changes have been driven largely by the commercialism of the yuletide season. Christmas for the Christian never changes. Each

December 23

year brings a fresh awareness that the God of this universe stepped out into the human dimension. As someone has stated, "God became a member of the human race."

The glory of Christmas is that God came to dwell among His people, and as His children, we are to welcome the birth year after year with a great expectation of God's love for us. The greatest gift of Christmas came wrapped as a Babe in a manger. May the traditions of our Christmas take a back seat to the One who came to be born of a virgin and give Himself a ransom for us all. God loved us so much that He gave the greatest gift of all, His One and only Son. If we are not careful, Christmas can become the day Jesus died and not the day He was born.

Thought to ponder: "Got your Christmas on?"

December 24

"Now when Jesus was born in Bethlehem of Judea in the days of Herod the king, there came wise men from the east to Jerusalem." Matthew 2:1 (KJV)

As Christmas day approaches, there are a multitude of events already taking place. There are the advertisements and decorations which seem to come earlier every year. There are also family and social gatherings taking place, which oftentimes begin at the first of the month. As the Yule time approaches, there are millions of dollars spent on food items that will be consumed throughout the month. All kinds of delicacies will be made and shared. The church is not far behind in making plans for the celebration of the birth of Christ. Even in the midst of these happenings, there are times when we seem to lose the focus on the real meaning of Christmas. What is the season all about? Is it gifts and foods and other types of merriment? Yes to all of these particulars, but they are not the only things of import.

Here in Matthew 2:1, we see another event taking place when Jesus came into the world in the form of a babe in a

December 24

Bethlehem stable. The text says, that when Jesus was born, there came wise men, seeking Him. This I believe is the true focus of the season. There can be other peripheral celebrations which can point us to the Savior's birth. There can be times of joy and celebration in our advances, but they can never replace the true meaning of the year. The Lord Jesus Christ is at the very heart of our celebrated events. If Jesus is the reason for the season, then wise men and women will come to seek the Savior Who was born on Christmas day. I still believe the statement that has been made, "Wise men still seek Jesus."

Thought to ponder: "We celebrate Christmas because it is the Lord's birthday."

December 25

"And behold, thou shalt conceive in thy womb, and bring forth a son, and thou shalt call his name JESUS."

Luke 1:31 (KJV)

There are many traditional songs of Christmas which we sing every year. Several we have learned by heart and can join anyone who sings them and harmonize with them. These are songs we sing over the years as we celebrate the true meaning of the season, and that is, the birth of our Lord Jesus. I have taken several familiar songs and have changed a word or two in the title to have a more spiritual ring to them. I have taken the secular approach to Christmas music and have put a twist of the heavenly to them.

"Have A Holly, Jolly Christmas" was made famous by Burl Ives. I have changed the song title to read, "Have A Holy, Jolly Christmas." Christmas is meant to be a time of jolliness. From December 1 and counting down to December 25, every day should be filled with merriment. With the anticipation of giving and receiving gifts, the entire season should be that of cheerfulness. At the same time, Christmas should be a time when living a life of holiness is at the top of our list to give to the Lord.

"Have Yourself A Merry Little Christmas" has been made famous by many artists. I have changed the designation to read, "Have Yourself A Mary Little Christmas." Mary, the mother of Jesus, has given us the best approach to Christmas of any biblical character. In her own words, she says to the angel Gabriel, "Behold the handmaid of the Lord; be it unto me according to thy word." There was a willingness on Mary's part to do and to be all that was expected of her.

"I'm Dreaming Of A White Christmas" was made famous by Bing Crosby. I have made this change to the song title, "I'm Dreaming Of A Right Christmas." I want this and every Christmas to be the right kind of celebration, one that recognizes that Jesus is the reason for the season. After all, there would be no "Christmas" if there was no "Christ." Had He not been born, there would be no reason to celebrate the season.

Thought to ponder: "Christmas truly is the most wonderful time of the year."

December 26

"Blessed be the God and Father of our Lord Jesus Christ, who hath blessed us with all spiritual blessings in heavenly places in Christ:" Ephesians 1:3 (KJV)

As my brother-in-law prayed at one of our family get-togethers, he was mindful in his words of the coming new year. With his mind wondering back over the past year, he was looking forward to the upcoming days, and during the course of his petitions, he confidently said, "Father, you have blessed us in the last year; please bless us more in the coming year."

As I listened intently to his intercession, I thought to myself as to how that could happen. God has so richly blessed me beyond measure, and I wondered how He could do any more. I certainly cannot understand how the Lord could keep on benefiting me in the ways He has. His bountiful hand has been pointed in my direction in such a way that I can hardly receive all that He has done. The windfall of boon and fortune has been my lot all these years, and His promise is that these goods and services will not end but increase.

December 26

At every turn in my life, the loving Father surprises me with another harvest of good. It's like the reservoir of His bounteousness never runs dry. His coffers are overflowing with treasures of goodness, and His passionate desire is to pass them along to each one of His children in abundance. Our sufficiency is found in Christ, and Holy Spirit is the Trustee and Accountant of our Father's wealth. It is the Spirit's desire to rain down on us the riches of the Father. Out of the bountifulness of the Lord we have received all we will ever need and more. We have been truly blessed, and we will be wonderfully blessed in the coming year. On this day after Christmas when we have been reminded of the greatest Gift the world has and will ever know, there is more of His bountifulness coming our way.

Thought to ponder: "The Father's resources are the sources of our riches."

December 27

"For our light affliction, which is but for a moment, worketh for us a far more exceeding and eternal weight of glory; While we look not at the things which are seen, but at the things which are not seen: for the things which are seen are temporal; but the things which are not seen are eternal."

2 Corinthians 4:17, 18 (KJV)

When I switch on the ignition in my new vehicle, the instrument panel blazes with a series of lights. Some flash while others make their presence known by shining brightly. There is an ABS warning light, along with the tire pressure warning symbol that catch my attention. There is a low engine oil pressure warning light, and the headlight high beam indicator showing up as well. The low washer fluid warning light plus the maintenance required beam both make their company felt. Several other lights, warning me to be careful, also come into view. Thankfully after a few seconds each one of the flashing/warning lights is extinguished; otherwise, you may think that the vehicle is ready to explode. Those lights, programmed to shine brightly,

December 27

can put a scare in your day that your transportation may not last long enough to get you to your destination.

Afflictions are the common lot of the human race and more especially to the children of God. They come blinking as a kaleidoscope of stars. They frighten even the best of us as we struggle to make sense out of them. It seems strange to think of hardships as appointed unto men and women by a loving heavenly Father. The adverse times and misfortunes are divine privileges we have been assigned. Paul offers some solid encouragement when he speaks of the intolerable situations as being, "light," in respect to the "exceeding and eternal weight of glory." He further informs us that our troubles are "but for a moment." Our faith in an unchanging God looks into the eyes of insufficiency and states unequivocally, "I will rise above these pressures and be victorious."

When the flashing lights of trouble shine brightly in our life, we can be assured that each one will be extinguished when we place our faith in an omnipotent God. Someone has well said, "If trouble comes knocking on your front door, send faith to answer and you will find no one there."

Thought to ponder: "Faith in God gives us courage to wait out the flashing lamps of trouble."

December 28

"Wherefore take unto you the whole armour of God, that ye may be able to withstand in the evil day, and having done all, to stand." Ephesians 6:13 (KJV)

I was a member of a party of 13 who attended a college football game that featured a team from Macon, Georgia, the Mercer Bears. Seven of these ticket-holders were youngsters from the age of 9-12 years. They were your typically energetic boys who wanted to have a good time. For the first three quarters of the contest, these active boys were up and down in their seats, not really paying attention to the game before them. As the sun began to set, the temperature dropped, and the fourth quarter started, these boys became permanent fixtures in their seats. With just a couple of minutes remaining in regulation play, the score was tied, and these guys became more animated than before. The outcome of the game was on the line, and these youngsters, along with myself, wanted to cheer the home team to victory. I've never seen such animation out of a group of kids. At the end of the game, with Mercer being victorious, I asked them

December 28

if it was worth the effort, and they said, "We would do it all over again!"

We are closer to the second coming of our Lord Jesus than we have ever been. He could come at any moment, as in a flash, in the twinkling of an eye, at the last trump. His return has been promised and will be fulfilled. We are not to be worldly minded and seek after other things which are only temporal, and we don't have as much time today as we had yesterday. We are in the fourth quarter of life, with the clock approaching the midnight hour. The first three quarters of the game of life have come and gone. We can't go back and relive the victories or the defeats. The seconds are ticking away as earth's clock winds down. We need to be about the task of being so animated as to bring the lost into the fold of safety. Our responsibility is to be a watchman on the wall and one who will stand in the gap. The home team will win, and that's been guaranteed, but before the victorious team can hoist the flag of conquest, there is a battle to wage and secure. We need to rise from our lethargy and help cheer the saints of God on to victory.

Thought to ponder: "Standing for Jesus will position us for victory."

December 29

"One thing have I desired of the LORD, that will I seek after; that I may dwell in the house of the LORD all the days of my life, to behold the beauty of the LORD, and to inquire in his temple." Psalm 27:4 (KJV)

How long does it take you to get ready for church? Some say about an hour, most say no more than two hours, while others say that it takes up to three hours to prepare themselves for Sunday School and worship. It's not the physical preparedness of which I speak; it's the mental and spiritual aspect of being fit for the Lord's Day. The answer to the above question would be, "six days!" Monday through Saturday are the pivotal days of preparing for a time of spiritual worship. There are no "off days" on the weekly calendar to ready ourselves to enter the presence of the Lord on His appointed day.

The Psalmist said," I was glad when they said unto me, Let us go into the house of the LORD" (Psalm 122:1). There is something unique about our worship that brings gladness to our soul. This God-given gladness reaches its peak when

December 29

we experience the awesome presence of a marvelous and wonderful God. It becomes our blessed privilege to enter the house of worship to honor and reverence the Lord's mighty name. As we enter His presence, our eyes are toward heaven, our hands spread out to Him, and our hearts turned toward Him.

It will take us six days to adequately prepare ourselves for worship. Monday is a day in which we digest what we learned in Sunday School and preaching. Tuesday is a time to build on the truths of scripture we have been taught. Wednesday is a season of refreshment when we attend Bible study and are energized to participate in intercessory prayer. Thursday is exercise time as we build our spiritual muscles through living daily the Word. Faith is believing God's truth, while faithfulness is proving God's Word. Friday becomes a time of introspection. We make sure that our walk is according to what we know to be the truth of God's Word. Saturday is a time of confession. Clearing out the debris and trash the world has deposited at our doorstep becomes the doorway of being ready Sunday morning for a celebration. Once we have prepared ourselves in these six days, then and only then are we ready for worship.

Thought to ponder: "Seven days without worship makes one weak."

December 30

"Neither do men light a candle, and put it under a bushel, but on a candlestick; and it giveth light unto all that are in the house." Matthew 5:15 (KJV)

Of all the lights that will have been shown this Christmas season, in the yards, houses, and stores, they will pale in comparison to the dazzling radiance that will shine from a Christian's daily walk with the Lord. With the time and energy spent to erect these shinning memorials to the Christmas spirit, they must take a back seat to the sunlight of the Lord Jesus sparkling through a child of His. As millions of dollars will be spent to array the yards and businesses of Christmas well-wishers, they cannot match the intensity of a light reflecting Christ. When we allow Him to live His life through us, that light will puncture the darkness of the world and bring hope to a shadowy land. There aren't enough lights radiating today that can overcome this brilliance, and for the Christian, it's all about letting the light of the Lord Jesus shine through them.

December 30

My light may not be very bright, and it may only be one light, but it is a beacon of goodwill that will do much good for a world living in the darkness of sin. This Christmas the best gift I can give to this world is to allow the Lord to shine His light of love through me. Though the times seem to be perilous and uncertain, the light of Christ will brighten the darkest of paths. He is the "Light of the world." As He shines through us, the world cannot help but see our good works, and in turn give glory to the Heavenly Father. As we spend time with the Lord in prayer, meditation, and Bible study, we soak up the Light as a sponge. As a result, the daylight doesn't fade with the waning of the day. On the contrary, it glows much brighter as we spend our time basking in the Heavenly Sunlight. Our light doesn't merely glow during the holiday season but throughout the year. Every day we live and every step we take is because of the glory we share in Christ.

Thought to ponder: "Heavenly sunlight is medicine for the discouraged."

December 31

"When Jesus therefore had received the vinegar, he said, It is finished: and he bowed his head, and gave up the ghost."
John 19:30 (KJV)

On this last day of the year, as I find myself at the end of a life-long pursuit of writing a daily devotional, it's time to bring this "inspirational ship" into harbor. The voyage on the sea of opportunity has been a challenge, and yet at the same time, it's been a tremendous blessing. I started with January 1 in view and have been looking at December 31 all along. As I have counted down the days, I have had a sigh of relief at putting the finishing touch on this work. It has been a daunting task as I set sail for 365 days of inspiration. As I look back on the journey, it seems like it was just yesterday when I embarked on the task.

Jesus, the captain of this ship, has been on board from start to finish, to give direction and encouragement through the perilous waters. The Holy Spirit has been the anchor for the effort, and has also been the animation for every day. The Heavenly Father has been the focus of every word written.

December 31

All of the nouns, verbs, adjectives, and adverbs have been focused on the awesome majesty of the Creator of all things. The Father, Son, and Holy Ghost have had their hand on each day's writing. I trust that you have been blessed as you have read each one. I must confess that I am the one who has been blessed beyond measure.

Navigating through the daily waters of creativity has been worth every effort expended. I'm thankful that when God spoke, I listened to His still small voice and penned the words He laid on my heart. At times the words flowed freely; at other intervals I wondered if this writing had come to an end. God has been faithful to fill my mind with thoughts that could be put into words. My prayer is that the journey you've taken with me each day has caused you to be more determined to have a daily quiet time with the Lord. After all, the entire year has been all about Him.

Thought to ponder: "Tomorrow is the first day of the rest of your life."

CPSIA information can be obtained
at www.ICGtesting.com
Printed in the USA
FFHW010620230919
55106357-60802FF